The Navigators

A Journal of Passage on the Inland Waterways of New York
1793

Philip Lord Jr.

NEW YORK STATE MUSEUM

2003

The Navigators

A Journal of Passage on the Inland Waterways of New York

1793

Philip Lord, Jr.
New York State Museum

NEW YORK STATE MUSEUM
BULLETIN 498
2003

Copyright © The New York State Education Department

Published 2003

Printed in the United States of America

Copies may be ordered from:

Publications Sales
New York State Museum
3140 CEC Albany,NewYork 12230
Phone: (518) 402-5344
FAX: (518) 474-2033
Web address: http://www.nysm.nysed.gov/publications.html

ISSN: 0278-3355
ISBN: 1-55557-142-5

Library of Congress Catalog Card Number: 2002115697

This book printed on acid free paper

Cover Image
This engraving of boats navigating the Mohawk, including a Durham boat passing through one of the WILNC wing dams, was done in 1810 from an eyewitness account from 1807.

"At night I have often hunted for a stone or a stick for a pillow, and in the morning, when I took hold of the oar or setting pole, I had to do it as gently as I could by reason of the soreness of my hands, which were much blistered, &c, in rowing the boat."

Rev. Elijah Woolsey, on the Oswego River, 1794[1]

"This volume commemorates the bicentennial of the completion of the works of the Western Inland Lock Navigation Company in 1803, which opened a continuous waterway westward for large Durham boats and transformed the transportation history of the Nation."

CONTENTS

Preface

On the morning of October 1st, 1793, Simon Desjardins and Pierre Pharoux arrived in Albany on a Hudson River sloop from New York. They were mounting an expedition to view lands in the Black River country of northwestern New York, on which they hoped to establish a new French settlement. Pharoux and Desjardins were agents for the *Compagnie de New York*, a French shareholder company whose mission was to secure lands for the resettlement of French emigrants fleeing uncertain and often dangerous circumstances following the French Revolution. They were immediately joined by Marc Brunel, whom they had met on their Atlantic passage aboard the American ship "Liberty."

The trio had first to go overland to the Mohawk River port of Schenectady, from which they would embark by batteau on a voyage of the inland waterways that crossed New York. This journey would see them fifteen days later on the very brink of the Great Lakes at Oswego, returning once again to the streets of Albany on November 9th. Their journal records a 40 day voyage of discovery along the expanding American frontier.

The year 1793 was a significant one in the history of westward transportation in New York State, and the Nation. The old Mohawk/Oneida navigation corridor connecting the Hudson Valley with the Great Lakes had served throughout the eighteenth century as the only viable route for inland travel. However, as the new nation contemplated opening up vast western territories to settlement, and thereby expanding areas of agricultural production and markets for eastern goods, this network of natural waterways was proving inadequate to the demand.

The year before, The Western Inland Lock Navigation Company, New York's first canal company, had been formed to improve this navigation. By late in 1793, when the French account was written, that company had already undertaken the improvement of Wood Creek west of Fort Stanwix, the most fragile stretch of the transport corridor, and had just begun construction of the Little Falls Canal, the first true canal in New York State, and one of the first in the Nation.

The *Journal of Castorland*, which preserves this account, was rescued from a Paris scrap pile in 1862, and the next year transferred to the collections of the Massachusetts Historical Society. The greater part of the journal, which covered the years 1793 to 1797, dealt with the establishment of Castorland itself, a locale largely restricted to the western Adirondacks. It was, therefore, the noted regional historian Dr. Franklin B. Hough who immediately set about to transform this extraordinary French journal, containing over 700 pages of detailed entries, into an English translation.

The initial entries, limited mostly to 1793 and 1794, document expeditions to and from the Castorland area, before a semipermanent establishment was made there, and so record the transportation route that is the subject of this present work. It is Hough's manuscript translation, now in the New York State Library and previously published only in brief extracts, that has made accessible to us the rich texture, and rare historical insights, of this timely inland adventure.

It is fortunate, indeed, to have a first-person account of travel by water along this route in the Autumn of 1793, capturing images of the works of the Western Inland Lock Navigation Company under construction as no other eyewitness could have. But also to have an account of such comprehensive detail, the record of constant and acute observation of both the cultural and natural environment through which these waterways passed, provides a unique opportunity of which every student of American history should avail themselves.

This absorbing eyewitness account of the journey of Desjardins, Pharoux, and Brunel records the adventure of travel across New York two hundred years ago, and reveals, as no other account has, the unique developments that were taking place along the inland waterways during New York's first era of navigation improvement - nearly a quarter century before a single shovelful of earth was turned for the Erie Canal.

Philip Lord, Jr.

Albany, New York
November 2002

Introduction

Two hundred years ago, a pioneer migrating west, newly arrived in Albany and hungry for land, an Albany merchant anxious to ship merchandise to the expanding western settlements, or a military commander supplying essential provisions to the garrisons along our western frontier, faced an inadequate and severely restricted transportation network.

One first had to hire a wagon in Albany for overland transport across 16 miles of pine barrens to Schenectady, on the Mohawk River. Here, at the old harbor, one would buy or hire a small batteau - the pick-up truck of the 18th century - to navigate up 58 miles of the Mohawk to the portage at Little Falls. This passage would require the boatmen to force their batteau over 57 rapids or "rifts", some of them with only inches of water.

At Little Falls teamsters were paid to cart the cargo, and the boat, a mile overland to the top of the falls, where the craft would be relaunched and loaded to traverse the upper Mohawk to Fort Stanwix at Rome, some 38 miles and 22 rapids further west.

At Stanwix the Mohawk turned north and could no longer serve a westward course. Here boat and baggage would again be lifted from the river and dragged across a two mile portage to be deposited into the almost waterless channel of Wood Creek; a tiny stream running west from Rome, and narrow enough here to jump across. Unable to move their craft, boatmen would walk upstream to negotiate with the miller, who had impounded the waters of Wood Creek in a pond. A release of water from his dam would, with luck, carry the batteau the five miles down to the junction of Canada Creek. From here, with the influx of additional water, one could navigate the remaining 18 miles to Oneida Lake, following a log-choked, shallow stream at times so twisting one could pole a boat a mile by water to advance 30 feet by land. Once in Oneida Lake, small boats could travel by water to Seneca Lake or to the Great Lakes via Oswego with only moderate difficulty.

This tortuous route was the only functional American highway west to the Great Lakes in the late-eighteenth century. And it was the improvement of this water route from Schenectady to Oneida Lake that was the mission of the Western Inland Lock Navigation Company, a private canal enterprise created in 1792.

Just over a decade later, in 1803, this company had realized a considerable measure of success. One could now depart the Schenectady harbor in a Durham Boat, twice the size of a batteau and able to carry 7 times the cargo - the 18-wheeler of the river boat era. Too large and heavy to lift out of the water for portaging, these craft depended on a continuous and relatively deep channel to navigate successfully.

The voyager leaving the harbor at Schenectady in 1803 more easily passed the 57 rapids of the lower Mohawk, some having been deepened by the navigation company with plowed out channels or long V-shaped rock dams. The portage at Little Falls was replaced in 1795 by a mile long canal, equipped with 5 wooden locks; rebuilt with stone in 1803.

A short distance westward, near Herkimer, two rapids that had become troublesome for these larger boats were bypassed in 1798 by a mile long canal, the first to use stone masonry in its locks. And at Rome, the head of Mohawk navigation, a canal was built in 1797 to bypass the two mile portage at Fort Stanwix. After passage through the Rome canal, a Durham boat could smoothly enter Wood Creek where four timber locks, built in 1802 and 1803, raised the normally shallow stream into a series of navigable pools. Passing down the twisting channel of Wood Creek, a Durham boat would take advantage of 13 short canals cut across necks of land in 1793, some of the oldest artificial waterways in North America, which shortened the passage to Oneida Lake by six miles.

These improvements to the inland waterways stand as evidence of the dramatic and unprecedented accomplishments of the Western Inland Lock Navigation Company. Just eleven years after it was chartered, and fifteen years before construction of the Erie Canal was begun, this company had converted an obstructed and interrupted navigation good only for small, portable batteaux, into a continuous, deepwater channel through which large Durham boats could pass unimpeded, and did so at a time when American canal engineering was still experimental. Had these improvements, which included our first canals, not been in place by 1803, our history as a State and Nation might have played very differently.

The 1793 French Journal

The extracts from this manuscript account included in the following narrative, when taken together, are the complete text of the journal from October 2nd to November 9th, except for the ten days spent exploring lands beyond Oswego.

All extracts from this journal, and only those extracts from this journal, are given in bold italics without other citation.

Protocol for Transcription of Primary Text

Many extracts from manuscript eyewitness accounts have been included in this presentation, not the least being the French narrative of 1793 on which it is based. While extremely rich in descriptive information, these primary source texts often contain archaic patterns of spelling and punctuation. Although typical of the style of expression of the late eighteenth and early nineteenth centuries, these idiosyncrasies frequently obscure meaning and distract the reader.

Since it is the information these texts contain that is critical to understanding the past preserved in the observations, a fairly standard editorial method has been applied to this variety of materials to make them as directly readable as they would be had they been written by modern authors undergoing the same experiences. This editing has been carefully undertaken to produce clarity of meaning without otherwise disturbing the original text. Punctuation, capitalization, abbreviation, paragraphing, and spelling have been regularized and corrected without comment.

In most cases the original spelling of place names, the names of people, or other titles and labels used by the authors provides some additional historical insight or regional flavor and has not been changed, even when the correct identification has been known with certainty. Unreadable portions of quoted text have been indicated within brackets. Where materials missing or inadvertently omitted by the manuscript author need to be inserted to provide meaning to the extract, this has been done within brackets in a contrasting type face. Quotation marks and other editorial indicators have been inserted by the author.

Note: Source references following extracts indicate the date of the observation being recorded, not the date of the manuscript or publication.

CHAPTER ONE

The Embarkation

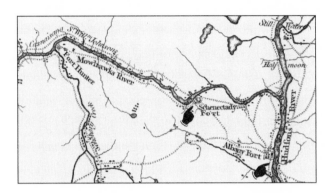

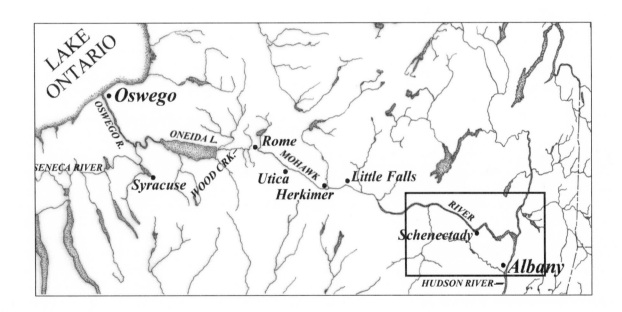

On October 1st, 1793, three French adventurers, newly arrived at the quay in Albany, turned their gaze westward. Simon Desjardins, Pierre Pharoux, and Marc Brunel were about to embark on an inland voyage; a journey of forty days and nights to the eastern margins of Lake Ontario, and back again.

Their expedition would carry them along an ancient water route, followed for decades by explorers, missionaries, merchants, and soldiers; and by Native Americans for centuries before that.

> *October 2nd. Left Albany in the afternoon with M. Brunel in a four wheeled chariot called a wagon, and drawn by two horses. We observed how poorly the woods were cleared. They extract no part of the resin from the trees. We saw that a great part of the forest had been burnt over, from want of caution. Here and there, in spots, there were some few flats of good quality, with springs along the banks, near which were some log houses and all of them with signs! For, to escape the expense of hospitality, every good American puts a tavern sign on his door, if located on the public road; and in these inns we sometimes can find neither bread, nor meat, nor a bed.*

The 16 mile passage through sand dunes and scrub pine vegetation that all westward bound travelers had to endure on leaving Albany was necessitated by the Great Cohoes Falls of the Mohawk, which prevented direct navigation through the Hudson-Mohawk junction above Albany.

One observer, passing along this portage-way through the pine barrens two years earlier, expressed the opinion held by many:

> Traversed a pine barren, sixteen miles, to Schenectady; a considerable town, on the south side of the Mohawk river. Considering Albany as the northern capital of this state, and Schenectady at least the fourth town in rank, as to age and size - and that this road has been the only channel of communication between these two places, for about one hundred and seventy years, its present shameful state is a matter of regret and astonishment; - apparently following the direction of original Indian footpaths, whereas the nature of the ground will admit of a spacious turnpike road...
>
> Elkanah Watson, 1791[2]

The poor quality of the land discouraged farming in the "Pine Bush", but a handful of houses had sprung up along the old "King's Road" by the 1790s. The observation by the French party that many hung out tavern signs to avoid having to provide free hospitality to travelers, which was the custom, is confirmed by another traveler in May of the same year:

> We got into a wagon, and rode sixteen miles to Schenectady, situated near the Mohawk River. We passed about ten houses on the road, each a tavern, the land very poor and covered with pines, the whole of the way.
>
> Jacob Lindley, 1793[3]

By evening, the party drew in sight of Schenectady, having crossed between the Hudson and the Mohawk watersheds. Schenectady's position on the Mohawk, and its natural harbor in the mouth of the Binnekill, had made it a favored embarkation point since before the French and Indian War. Now, in the early 1790s, its role as a major inland port was about to emerge:

> This village is not a very *sightly* place either from a distance or when you are in it. The principal business is boat-building, for which there is a great call by reason of the continual increase of transportation on the Mohawk River for one hundred miles.
>
> Jeremy Belknap, 1796[4]

> "I found this village of much more importance than I expected. It stands on the bank of the Mohawk river, about sixteen miles from the city of Albany. It is approached from high lands, from which you have a pretty view of the town, and a most pleasing one of a fine body of meadows, rich interval. The high lands are but indifferent. The rich meadows, with the advantages of the Indian trade, were the enticements which led people to make an early establishment here. It was originally a Dutch settlement; and the inhabitants are principally descendants from the first settlers, and retain their manners and language, though all of them speak English also. The town, in which are three places of public worship, is prettily laid out. There are three very handsome streets running parallel with the river, and a number of streets crossing those at right angles. There are in the compact part of the town about three hundred dwelling-houses, built mostly after the Dutch form."
>
> Gen. Benjamin Lincoln, 1793[5]

It was here, at the gateway to the inland waterways, that the expedition had come to begin their westward navigation.

> *At night, arrived at Schenectady and lodged at the city tavern in the garret, in beds with dirty sheets; since they only put on clean ones every Sunday. For supper and lodging, the price was nine shillings nine pence for the three. We bought of Mr. Murdock some provisions for the journey as we were not to find our outfit till we reached the Little Falls.*

Although called the "city tavern" in their journal, the inn where the three men lodged was probably John Hudson's *Schenectady Coffee House*, as they identify the proprietor on their return visit as "Mr. Hudson." The association of Schenectady tavern keepers with stage wagon service to and from Albany, begun this very year, is well documented:

> Probably the first regular stage line started by a Schenectadian was run by Moses Beal in May, 1793. It ran from Albany to Schenectady, Johnstown and Canajoharie once a week. The fare was three cents a mile. The success of this enterprise was so great that John Hudson, keeping the Schenectady Coffee House, on the southwest corner of Union and Ferry Streets, now the property of Madison Vedder, Esq., soon afterward established a line of stages to run from Albany to Schenectady three times a week.
>
> Howell & Munsell, 1886[6]

Albany

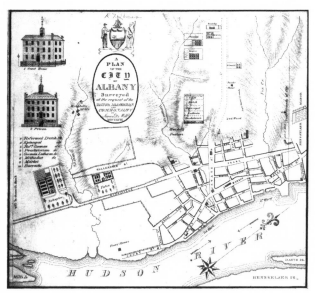

The City of Albany, 1794.

In 1793, the river port of Albany was already almost 150 years old. Established as a center for inland trade, it was the northernmost point on the Hudson River reached by most travelers heading west. Here initial arrangements could be made for an inland navigation that would begin in Schenectady, some sixteen miles to the west:

"I spent the remainder of the day in making some arrangements with General Schuyler respecting boats, boatmen, &c. and in viewing the city of Albany. It is built on the banks of the Hudson. There are three streets running parallel with the river, about half a mile in length; the one called Market is well paved, and thereon are many valuable houses, built on the English mode; but a great proportion of the others are of the ancient Dutch form, with the ends at the street. There are many streets running from the river up and intersect the others nearly at right angles. There are five or six hundred houses in the city, the foundation of which was laid before New York was built. The people were led thus far into the country from the allurements of the Indian trade, which at that day was very important.

"The original settlers were from Holland. They have retained their ancient manners and language, and have so much secluded themselves from the world at large, that their reservedness has the appearance of a want of hospitality. There are four places of public worship, the Dutch church, the Episcopalian, the Presbyterian, and the Methodist. It is a place of considerable business, and I think, by opening the canals and a communication by water with the different parts of the country, it will soon be much more important."

Gen. Benjamin Lincoln, 1793[7]

European travelers frequently expressed mixed feelings about the city they encountered, as they began their tour of the interior. While often dismayed at the accommodations, they were pleasantly impressed with the populace:

"We arrived in Albany, a town already large and well populated, which is situated at the confluence of the Mohawk and the Hudson. Placed as it is 170 miles in the interior it does not have a maritime trade, but it is the commercial center for all the merchandise which comes there from an immense expanse of country, as much by the boats of the Mohawk as by wagons from the Genesee and other regions.

"We stayed at the Tontine Coffee House, an inn setting a good table but with bad service and the house scarcely clean. We found there fourteen people eating at the common table, a great advantage for the traveler, who in short time can thereby acquire information on the locale which he would not otherwise be able to obtain. These gentlemen were polite without affectation, communicative without garrulity. They had that appearance of ease that one finds in Europe only in the upper classes. Here is the fruit of a liberty which they enjoy from infancy and of that spirit of independence which produces hard work and industry; architects of their own fortune they owe nothing to anyone; they believe themselves equal to everybody."

Julian Ursyn Niemcewicz, 1805[8]

The King's Road

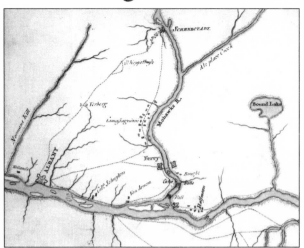

A map showing the King's Road, c.1757.

The "King's Road" followed what may have been an Indian trail through the sixteen miles of pine barrens that separated the Hudson River harbor at Albany from the Mohawk River port in Schenectady. Direct navigation from one to the other was blocked by the "Great Falls" at Cohoes, which presented an insurmountable obstacle even for portaging of light craft.

Although often termed a "highway," this primary land link to the western waterways was little more than a dirt track, which wound its way between sandy dunes and marshes. The climax forests which covered the "Pine Bush" survived conditions that were less than hospitable for agriculture.

It was the use of this thoroughfare for commercial traffic and emigration that supplied a minimal economy along the route, which flourished until a straight-line turnpike was completed between the two villages on an alignment to the north [Route 5].

The "burnt over" condition observed by the French party in 1793 was typical of newly settled areas further west:

> "It is true that in many places steel and fire have already waged mortal combat with these ancient forests. Without doubt the trees must go in order to have cultivated ground but, in getting rid of them one should recover some profit from them. But here it is a sorry sight, to see for mile after mile these enormous skeletons, these gigantic cadavers, shorn of their bark and half-burnt lying about wasted."

Julian Ursyn Niemcewicz, 1805[9]

But these sandy pine barrens west of Albany actually depended on the impact of fire to sustain their peculiar ecology, and the devastation observed here may well have resulted from natural wild fires.

The concept of a Mohawk Valley stage may have more romance attached to it in retrospect than it did to those who actually took advantage of the service:

A typical stage coach of the late 18th Century.

> On leaving Schenectady, the first day's ride warned me of what might be expected on the succeeding ones. The weather was broken, the roads rough and deep, the stage waggon crowded with passengers and luggage, and the party but very moderately agreeable.
>
> The stage waggon which is still used in this part of the country, corresponds exactly with the picture and description which Weld has given. The body is rather long in proportion to its breadth, and contains four seats, each holding three passengers who all sit with their faces towards the horses. From the height of the seats it is open all round, and the roof is supported by slender shafts rising up at the corners and sides; in wet weather a leathern apron is let down at the sides and back, to protect the inmates. The waggon has no door, but the passengers get in by the front, stepping over the seats as they go backward; the driver sits on the front seat with a passenger on either hand. The heavier kinds of boxes and trunks are fastened behind, upon the frame of the carriage, but the smaller articles and the mail bag are huddled under the seats in the inside, to the great annoyance of the passengers, who are frequently forced to sit with their knees up to their mouths, or with their feet insinuated between two trunks, where they are most lovingly compressed whenever the vehicle makes a lurch into a rut. The body of the waggon is suspended upon two stout leathern straps, passing lengthways under it, and secured upon strongly propped horizontal bars before and behind.

John M. Duncan, 1818[10]

In the morning, with final arrangements made, the trio set out from the harbor to begin their voyage up the Mohawk.

October 3rd. Started from Schenectady at half past eleven in the morning, in a bateau which Mr. DeZeng had bought for us for ten dollars. It was fifteen feet long by four wide in the middle, and both ends were pointed. Only

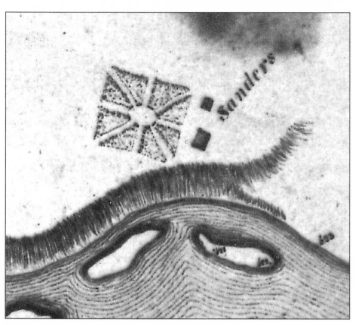

Map showing John Sanders' house in 1803.

two boatmen were needed to take us up to the Little Falls, as we were only half loaded. They labored alternately at the oars, paddles, and setting poles. We embarked only our biscuit, rum, and baggage, as we were to obtain the rest at the house of Mr. DeZeng.

M. Brunel, in true sailor fashion, protested that we had taken on board no fresh water, but we replied that, in case of need, we would supply ourselves from the rivers and the lakes.

Above Schenectady the river forms several islands, which present an agreeable prospect and are very pleasantly overlooked by the mansion of Mr. John Saunderson.

The mansion noted by the travelers was the grand house of John Sanders, which stood on the north bank of the river opposite the harbor.

Schenectady

B y 1793, the harbor in Schenectady already had a significant place in the history of inland navigation. Site of the construction and staging of hundreds of batteaux attached to military expeditions during both the French and Indian War [1755-1761] and the Revolution [1776-1783], this harbor was also the terminal for all commercial transport westward during the eighteenth century.

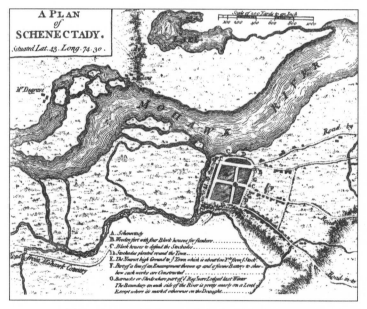

The area around Schenectady in the 18th Century.

Forwarders and merchants, as well as military commanders, forced by the Cohoes Falls to go overland from Albany, found here an ideal harbor. The Binnekill, a branch of the Mohawk River that detached itself a couple miles upriver to the west, ran up alongside the old Stockade section of the city just before reentering the main channel. It was here, in this sluggish, slack-water channel, protected from ice and the force of the main current, that the harbor developed.

Shipping facilities were present here since the first boats ventured westward, and boatbuilding followed as a natural consequence, with boatyards spread along the river bank from the Binnekill to Front Street. But not until 1797, when the efforts of the Western Inland Lock Navigation Company opened up the Mohawk/Oneida route to the larger batteaux and Durham boats, did the port at Schenectady undergo significant growth. Soon after, large warehouses were raised along the margins of the Binnekill, often operated by firms which owned comparable facilities at the other end of the navigation; be it Utica, Rome, or Oswego.

The demand for passenger service increased as well, as settlement expanded to the west after 1800. Larger boats, which depended on the continuous channel created by Gen. Schuyler's navigation company, now entered the system. Their increased carrying capacity required larger warehousing facilities and stimulated wagon transport between the waterfronts at Schenectady and Albany.

CHAPTER TWO

The Lower Mohawk

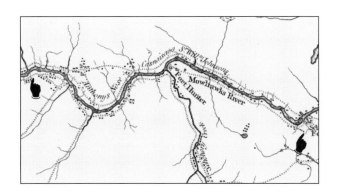

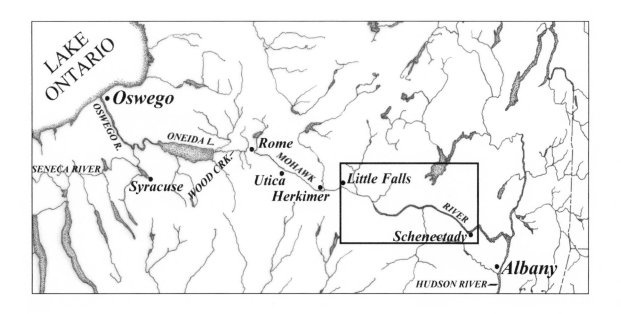

In the early 1790s, virtually everyone who departed the harbor at Schenectady did so in a batteau that they had hired, or purchased, at the waterfront. These flat-bottomed, shallow-draft boats averaged 30 feet in length, six in width, and carried a crew of three, as observed in 1791:

Each boat was manned by three men, two in the bow and one in the stern, to steer. They rowed in still water, setting with short poles at the rapids, with surprising dexterity.

Elkanah Watson, 1791[11]

Such light craft were demanded by the many shallows, or "rifts", in the Mohawk, as well as the several portages that prevented continuous navigation.

We observed that the Mohawk, although of fine breadth, is shallow, and that at this season its usual depth is only three feet, but varying from one foot to five or six in the narrower places. At about one mile we met the first rapid, formed by two currents that meet at the lower point of an island, where it is made apparent by the gravel which bars the river.

As we were getting over this obstacle by means of poles, with spikes at the bottom, to hold against the current, and to advance up through the rapid, we found ourselves upon a plane higher than the rest of the water to the right, the left, and below us. It presented a novel and picturesque spectacle. The pebbles at this rapid were flat and rounded, and their material a brownish quartz streaked with grey and white.

The rapid which so impressed the Frenchmen was undoubtedly the one known locally as the "Knock 'em Stiff" rift. The following year another party had a less enjoyable passage up through this obstacle:

So we tarried a week, and provided ourselves with a boat. Two men had engaged to go with us and work their passage up the Mohawk.... When we came to the first rapids, which by the Dutch people are called "knock 'em stiff," we had our difficulties. I had never used the setting pole in my life, and my colleague was not a very good waterman. When we almost ascended the rapids, the boat turned round and down the stream she went much more rapidly than she went up. We tried again, and when we had almost conquered the difficulty the boat turned again. I then jumped overboard, thinking to save the boat from going down the stream. But the water was over my head. So away went the boat with my companions in it, and I swam to shore.

Rev. Elijah Woolsey, 1794[12]

But the French expedition successfully mounted the rapids and continued on their way.

The banks of the river are adorned with fine farms, upon low and fertile ground called "bottom lands." At a short distance beyond, the surface rises to rocky cliffs cov-

ered with woods. Generally these flats have but little breadth. They have preserved the large trees along the banks, to defend against the ice, the timber, and the rocks, which the Mohawk brings down in its freshets. The lands are very well cultivated.

We continued from this time forward to meet, at almost every mile, little rapids until we came to the farm of Nicholas Filet, who was originally from France. We went ashore to call at his house. At this place we saw a wagon cross the river at one of the rapids, the water being there always shallower than in other places.

As the Mohawk was obstructed by over 90 rifts or rapids between the harbor at Schenectady and the head of navigation at Fort Stanwix [Rome], and since many of these rifts were only a couple of feet deep in the summer, there were numerous places where wagons, horses, and even pedestrians could cross the river with ease.

We observed everywhere along the banks, pebbles of quartz and other ferrugerous rocks, with some of marble and others of gypsum. Not far from this, we observed slated rocks.

At two o'clock we left Filet's house. We noticed that from this place the bottom lands were wider and located alternately upon one and the other side of the river, forming well improved farms. At four o'clock we landed to rest our boatmen, who had within the distance of a mile surmounted six rapids.

At this place, we had an opportunity to observe the excellence of these bottom lands.

The farm buildings where we landed were well built and beautifully located, and near by was a little tannery, proving the industry of its owner. A plow, much resembling that of Normandy, was drawn by three horses and guided by one man. The soil, beautifully sown, was of the richest mould and very deep. Upon the bank, which was adorned with fine trees in excellent preservation, we found some superb Capillaire, already tinted by the autumn frosts. The inhabitants call it <u>Maiden's Hair</u>, and drink an infusion of it in the place of tea.

We observed upon many of the golden rods, an insect gall of very considerable size, as compared with the plant. These galls were as large as pigeon's eggs, and were of a violet color, contrasting beautifully with the delicate green of the plant, and the golden yellow of it's blossoms. So far from injuring its growth, we saw several flowers coming directly out of the galls.

Traveling through the region in Autumn, these French voyagers observed the farmers of the Mohawk Valley in activities that often escaped the observation of others.

At a very fine farm two miles beyond, we saw them boiling cider in large kettles. After reducing it one half in volume over the fire, they mix with it barley, sassafras, spruce boughs and some other ingredients, of which we are not informed. This cider, which we drank in a silver goblet holding at least a pint, was very pleasant. As strangers, they made us pay sixpence a quart, while our boatmen, as Americans, were charged only threepence.

Their cider without this preparation would not keep, as it is made of good eating apples, of the kind we call in France fruit a Couteau. They are not acquainted here with our varieties of sweet-sour apples, of which we make such excellent cider in lower Normandy. The addition of spruce and sassafras corrects the acidity of the apples, of which it is chiefly made, and they might employ a similar method in the provinces of France, where, from want of the proper fruits, they make very poor cider, which quickly sours, and the use of which as a drink is sure to disorder the health instead of proving salutary.

Most of the inhabitants above Schenectady thus far are of Holland origin, and they take great pains to inform you that they are Dutch, and not English.

We re-embarked at half past five, and after having surmounted, but not without difficulty, two other rapids, we stopped twelve miles from Schenectady at the house of Ysayos Swart. It was now eight o'clock in the evening, and we had much difficulty in landing there on account of the gravel which barred the river, and which the darkness did not allow us to observe.

This first day of navigation was the precursor of those to follow, and typical of boating on the Mohawk from the earliest period:

The trade with the Indians along the Great Lakes and the St. Lawrence was carried on by the aid of boats propelled from Schenectada up the Mohawk at great personal labor, in consequence of there being several rifts or rapids in the stream. The first obstruction of the kind was met with six miles above Schenectada, and was called Six Flats' rift; proceeding west came in course similar obstructions known as Fort Hunter rift; Caughnawaga rift; Keator's rift, at Spraker's, the greatest on the river, having a fall of ten feet; Brandywine rift, at Canajoharie, short but rapid; Ehle's rift near Fort Plain; Kneiskern's rift, a small rapid near the upper Indian castle, a little above the river dam; and the Little falls, so named as compared with the Cahoes on the same stream near its mouth.

Jeptha Simms, 1845[13]

Even a decade later, when larger river craft manned by crews of five or six polemen plied these same waters, the river still made progress difficult:

Several boats usually went in company, that the unit-ed strength of many men might aid in the labor before them. Those boats were often half a day in proceeding only a few rods, and not infrequently were they, after remaining nearly stationary on a rapid for an hour, compelled to drop below the rift and get a new start. Twenty hands, at times, were insufficient to propel a single boat over Keator's rift. Black slaves, owned by settlers in the neighborhood of rapids, both male and female, were often seen assisting at the ropes on shore, when loaded boats were ascending the river.

Jeptha Simms, 1882[14]

Also typical of river travel in this period was the extreme variability of hospitality available on shore, even from those houses purported to be taverns.

Fortunately, we had taken care upon leaving Albany to supply ourselves each with a mattress and a pair of blankets. These we spread before the fire in the only room of our tavern. Without this precaution, a traveler runs the risk of sleeping on the bare floor almost every night. As for the rest, these honest descendants of Holland stock, who kept this house, asked us only sixpence a head for the part of our supper and bed which they furnished us.

The second day on the river brought little improvement in their circumstance. But it did provide the opportunity to observe, and record, some of the details of the natural environment that makes this journal so exceptional. This penchant for the examination of a broad spectrum of the reality around them was typically exhibited by gentlemen of the Enlightenment, such as these.

October 4th. Set out at seven o'clock in the morning. After passing several rapids, we were obliged, in order to rest the boatmen, notwithstanding the rain, to go ashore and walk with much difficulty along the beach upon the gravel, about a mile. These pebbles were for the most part granite and marble.

There were also other kinds of rock; one a very fine granite, striped green, white, and grey. These rapids are occasioned by the current in narrow places between the islands of rock and soil, which its channels form in the Mohawk when the snows melt and go off in the spring.

The explorers had never before experienced the mechanics of the Mohawk River. But by the time of their next voyage upstream the following summer, they had correctly ascertained the cause of the very rifts they were contending with:

I observed along our route, that the rapids were all formed at the mouths of creeks, by the stones and gravel, which these streams when swollen and overflowed by the melting of the snows, sweep into the river, where they pile up and form bars. These can not be carried away by the main current of the river, since, as the water subsides, the force of the current is lessened, and soon ceases to move these materials further. The formation of islands is due to the same cause. They begin by rapids, which bring down new deposits of rocks, gravel and sand each year, which gradually heap up to the level of low water, and finally of high water, when plants and aquatic shrubs find root and grow. These form a lodgement for mud and sand, which every freshet brings down, and for these reasons we always find islands at the foot of the rapids of rivers, and below the mouths of creeks. The rapids and islands are always proportioned to the force and volume of the confluent waters.

Simon Desjardins, 1794[15]

Later that morning, the batteau passed by one of the more interesting landmarks on the lower Mohawk, known generally in later years as the "Painted Rocks".

At nine o'clock we observed on the right a long bank of calcareous rock almost perpendicular, like the walls of a fortress, and in large courses perfectly level. Our boatmen insisted, according to their traditions, that some of these walls were built by the Spaniards more than two hundred years ago.

This popular error originated in the striking resemblance of this precipice to a wall of cut stone. Some lime kilns which we saw a little further beyond convinced us still more of the character of this rock.

The lime kilns seen by the travelers appear on a map of the river drawn in 1803 and stood on the western edge of what is now the City of Amsterdam, along the north shore.

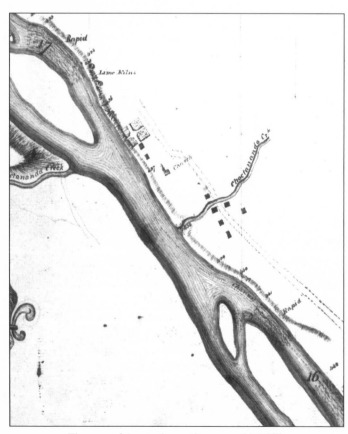

The area of Amsterdam as it appeared in 1803, showing lime kilns west of the settlement.

It was on the same shore, just east of the city, that the limestone escarpment cited in the journal, itself a noteworthy feature

of the riverside terrain, was observed. Although the Frenchmen made no mention of seeing images on these rocks, another, passing by a few months earlier, describes them:

This day we passed a rock projecting out of the bank of the river, whereon was painted, with great ingenuity, in red colours, a canoe with the representation of seven men in it, which is said to be done annually by Indians, coming several hundred miles for that purpose, in order to commemorate the slaughter of seven Indians, who went off from that neighborhood in some former wars, and were all destroyed.

Jacob Lindley, 1793[16]

As late as 1810, when DeWitt Clinton journeyed along this waterway and recorded his observations, the images were still visible:

About sixteen miles from Schenectady, we saw, on the left bank of the river, a curious specimen of Indian painting. On an elevated rock was painted a canoe, with seven warriors in it, to signify that they were proceeding on a war expedition. This was executed with red ochre, and has been there for upwards of half a century.

DeWitt Clinton, 1810[17]

Paintings of this type on rock were no doubt frequently made by Native Americans since prehistoric times, but few could survive more than a few years before they weathered away. Some claimed the figures were "retouched," which prolonged their life. Others suggested a connection between these paintings and the river boat traffic of the 1790s and early 1800s:

The Flat boatmen of the Mohawk held these rocks in such reverence that they at times refreshed the paintings.

LaGrand Strang, 1887[18]

That the images recalled so clearly in the early nineteenth century were the product of various acts of "refreshing" is suggested by the account of a visit to the site in 1796:

Stopped by the way at Miles's (formerly Guy Johnson's house); there met a Dr. Sweet, who fell into conversation, and offered to conduct us to the *painted rock*, which he said was about two miles down the river. Took him up in the carriage and rode with him two miles. Then he and I left the carriage to search for the rock. This ramble took up forty minutes, and I walked about two miles, partly through woods and partly through fields.

The rock is on the north bank of the Mohawk, fifteen miles above Skenectada. It is a perpendicular ledge of limestone, with a pretty smooth surface and about twenty feet high. On the upper part - which is easily accessible, the laminae projecting in various places - appear the remains of some red paint, which has been in the same situation for eighteen or twenty years. Imagination may conceive the paint to resemble almost any thing; but judgement cannot decide without the help of testimony.

The tradition is that it was painted by the Indians in

"Painted Rocks"

Rufus Grider's view of the Painted Rocks, from eyewitness accounts.

The drawings above, created one hundred years ago by Rufus Grider, have preserved for us an image of what the Native American pictograph known as "Painted Rocks" must have looked like to passing boatmen. He based his reconstruction on eyewitness interviews. At that time a number of persons could still recall the site in detail, and related to him their recollections:

"Within the remembrance, possibly of some person still living, there was a large rock on the north shore of the Mohawk, near Amsterdam, to be seen at low watermark, that contained Indian Memorials, such as the figures of men and animals, and supposed by some to have been traced with red chalk, although they may have been in vermilion, which the Whites bartered with the Natives for peltry."

Jeptha Simms, 1882[19]

"The rocks contained 12 or 15 Indians, with two canoes, two Indians in each canoe, one at the bow the other at the stern, going west, other Indians on foot. A duck flying above eastward."

John Winnie, 1887[20]

"I lived all my life in the vicinity of the rocks. I lived on the south bank of the river when the canal was made. Our house was just opposite the rocks and was the first house built [in] the present Port Jackson, and is still standing. There were figures on the rocks, at least 9 in number, they were painted with red colors. My grandfather was a soldier in the Revolutionary Army. He, when passing the rocks in a boat, was shot at by an Indian who lay in ambush and wounded him. It was covered with pines and undergrowth."

David DeForest, 1887[21]

"I was born in Amsterdam in the year 1826 and lived there until I was 21 years old. I remember well the painted rocks. I was very fond of being on the water; and before I was 14 years old I and another boy named Abm. Pulling (now deceased) became owners of a rowboat, and in it passed many hours on the river, and rowed past the painted rocks more times than I can remember. There were two canoes going upstream, as if racing, with two Indians in each canoe. There were 10 or 12 Indians on the bank who were walking westward and apparently watching the canoe race. The work was done in red paint, the figures were about 4 feet high, and could be plainly seen from the opposite side of the river.

"... The pictures at that time had the appearance of being retouched, probably to perpetuate them. I think they are now entirely obliterated. They were on the perpendicular face of the rocks which overlook the river, a little east of the freight house and directly south of the Murphy Bros. warehouse. These tracings were of the plainest and rudest kind."

Moses T. Kehoo, 1887[22]

memory of some canoes of Indians who went thence to war, and never returned; that the painting represented canoes and men in them; and that this painting is frequently *renewed* to preserve the memory of the event. Some add that the renewal is performed in the night, or by some *invisible* hand. The fact is that there is a rock with some appearance of red paint, that the paint has been in some measure defended from the weather by a projection of the rock *over* it, and that the place is easily accessible by similar projections *under* it. This is all that can be said with any certainty.

As to the frequent renewal of the paint, &c., I was assured by Dr. Sweet that he had known it to be in the same condition as we saw it for eighteen years past; and a man whom we took as a pilot, who appeared to be about twenty-five years old, said it always looked just so since his remembrance.

Jeremy Belknap, 1796[23]

Having noted the rock outcrop, the French party passed up to a landing in the mouth of the Chuctanunda Creek [Amsterdam].

At ten o'clock we stopped to breakfast at Isaya's Inn. This place is one for considerable crossing, the river being there fordable at the head of the rapid. There the character of the rock changes, and it becomes slaty, and the bed of the river, instead of pebbles, shows only an immense pavement of slate, which forms as it were large stairways upon the banks. This place is four miles from where we started. The right bank is the most elevated, the soil is here composed of course slate, where the surface is washed, and it is sometimes interrupted by fissures of from two to twelve or fifteen inches wide, and of unknown depth. Out of these fissures spring evergreen trees, and oaks of surprising growth, so that the rock itself and the waste places there appear fertile. These woods were filled with squirrels.

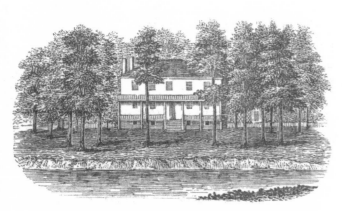

Guy Park.

Reembarked at eleven o'clock and a mile beyond came to the house of Colonel Johnson, a refugee to the Long Saut in Canada. This house was built of stone and is the finest we have seen since leaving Albany. It has been mutilated through the hatred of the populace, as have also the fine orchard and the plantations which he formed. He was forced to abandon them, a fugitive from

the house he had built and the fields he had cleared. The man who took from the Legislature the lease of this house, turned it into a tavern, and lately became its owner when it was sold, with the other confiscated property of the Loyalists.

This house, commonly known as Guy Park, had been the home of Sir William Johnson's son, Guy, until the Revolution. It was one of the most substantial houses in the valley, and is frequently noted in travelers' journals:

...a large, well-finished stone house, which was much damaged and abused during the war.

Jeremy Belknap, 1796[24]

Though damaged, it had fared better than most Loyalist homes in that era. Some that survived the vindictiveness of the "Rebels" were later lost by negligence.

Further on was a very fine house also of stone which belonged to Mr. Claus, which was accidentally burned six months ago. Beyond this there appeared a charming residence built with regularity, with five windows in front and an island and creek adjacent. This property formerly belonged to Sir William Johnson, who also emigrated to Canada, and has been bought of the State by one Mr. Cuyler, a wealthy citizen of Albany. The creek drives a grain mill and saw mill near the dwelling.

Fort Johnson.

"Passed by the first seat of the late Sir William Johnson, consisting of one large stone house and two stone stores and a stone barn, a good garden and orchard. Here Sir William first kept a trading-house and got his estate. He afterward removed further up the river, and four miles from the river, where he built an elegant seat, and lived in the latter part of his life in a very genteel style, and very hospitably, keeping a number of young Indian women about him in quality of concubines, and offering them in that respect to gentlemen who happened to lodge at his house. Many of his children and their descendants are now mixed with the other Indians, and are proud of reckoning their descent from him."

Jeremy Belknap, 1796[25]

Beyond this place to Fort Hunter, where we arrived at four o'clock in the evening, the land is everywhere excellent. The location of the fort is very picturesque. The islands, which the river continues to form, present varied sites and superb points of view. At six o'clock we found the river encumbered with a large quantity of rocks, scattered here and there in its channel, forming three rapids in the course of a mile. Our boatmen had as much as they could do to get up the first of these. This spectacle was imposing to Europeans who had never before navigated in this way, for they always choose the place where the water is swiftest, to leap the fall, for it is there always the deepest. And when they have got above it, you appear suspended upon precipices, and sometimes when almost gaining the top of the rapid, a little failure to push together, in those who use the iron pointed poles between the sunken rocks, will turn the bateau down the torrent, and obliges them to begin again with all their labor lost.

This place of difficult passage, through the gravel bars and shoals formed by the outwash of the Schoharie Creek, was substantially improved in the following years by Philip Schuyler's Western Inland Lock Navigation Company, which built "wing dams" here as part of an array of attempts to increase the navigability of the natural channel.

> In the riffs a channel was made by throwing out boulders which were in the way. In time the line of deepest water became defined and all the riffs came to be named and were land marks in the itineraries of travelers. The efforts of the boatmen during a century were furthered by the "Inland Lock and Navigation Company," which built a series of wing dams on all the riffs. They were usually crude affairs and intended only to serve their office in low water. These wing dams - collections of stone which were dragged from the channel and arranged in the shape of a V, the wings stretching over the shallow from the shore to the center, where there was a narrow outlet. The effect of this was to throw what water there was into the center of the stream and float the boat. Then by dint of wind and muscle - sail and poles, and men towing at a long line, the boat was hauled over the rapid into stiller water again and so pursued her journey.

Jonathan Pearson, 1883[26]

As innovative as these works may have seemed when completed here in 1799, they drew criticism from those who knew the power of the river to frustrate the efforts of boatmen:

> The Canal Company have endeavored, by dams and other expedients, to deepen the river and improve the navigation, but they have only encountered unnecessary expense; the next freshet or rise of the river has either swept away their erections or changed the current.

DeWitt Clinton, 1810[27]

Having surmounted these rapids without the aid of wing dams, and in spite of the seasonally low water they must have encountered here, the boatmen pushed on to a landing at the end of the second day of their voyage.

After this fatiguing passage our boatmen landed us at the house of Mr. Venables, Esquire, a title which most Americans take without ceremony, notwithstanding their republicanism. This rank does not prevent him from keeping tavern, like the rest, although he had nothing in the house to eat, not even bread, nor milk, and he had no

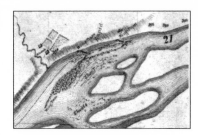

The wing dams near Amsterdam, 1803

Wing Dams

The greatest obstacle to Mohawk River navigation in the 1790s was the shallowness of water at the many "rifts" which existed between Schenectady and Fort Stanwix [Rome]. One method employed by the Western Inland Lock Navigation Company to overcome this problem was the construction of low rock dams to retain and direct the water at the rifts into narrow, and slightly deeper, channels. As many of the rifts were less than two feet deep, workers could easily pile up the rocks while standing in the river. These dams were patterned after Indian eel weirs or fish traps that also existed on the rivers in this period, and for generations before

Perhaps the best eyewitness description of Mohawk River wing dams was recorded by Christian Schultz:

"The Mohawk is by no means dangerous to ascend, on account of the slowness of the boat's progress; but, as it is full of rocks, stones and shallows, there is some risk in descending it of staving the boat; and, at this season, is so low as to require it to be dragged by hand over many places. The channel in some instances is not more than eight feet in width, which will barely permit a boat to pass by rubbing on both sides.

"This is sometimes caused by natural or accidental obstructions of rocks in the channel; but oftener by artificial means. This, which at first view would appear to be an inconvenience, is produced by two lines or ridges of stone, generally constructed on sandy, gravelly, or stony shallows, in such a manner as to form an acute angle were they to meet, the extremities of which widen as they extend up the river; whilst at the lower end there is just space enough left to admit the passage of a boat.

"The water being thus collected at the widest part of these ridges, and continually pent up within narrower limits as it descends, causes a rise at the passage; so that where the depth was no more than eight inches before, a contrivance of this kind will raise it to twelve; and, strange as it may appear, a boat drawing fifteen inches will pass through it with safety and ease. The cause is simply this; the boat, being somewhat below the passage, is brought forward with considerable velocity, and the moment it dashes into the passage, its resistance to the current is such as to cause a swell of four or five inches more, which affords it an easy passage over the shoal."

Christian Schultz, 1807[28]

beds for us to sleep on. We had recourse to our own provisions and mattresses. The house, although so poorly furnished, was full of guests, among whom was a handsome American woman who was very successfully making a journey on horseback from Cooperstown, and had still eighty miles to travel, of which sixty were through the woods.

There was also a good hearted German named Christopher Lange, a tailor by trade, and a resident of Fort Plain. He had a strong liking to the French, and remembered having been well treated in Canada, where he had learned to mangle some phrases in our language. The impulses of this brave man, a little exalted by the grog (a beverage composed of rum and water) which he had taken, induced him to offer us his house and all that he possessed, in return for which he supposed himself entitled to partake of whatever we had. Upon retiring to bed he accordingly edged up near us, to share little by little the mattress of his friend Pharoux, until he crowded him off upon the floor.

The following year, in spite of this encounter, Desjardins and Pharoux renewed this friendship:

...I improved this interval in enquiring after Christopher Lange, the German tailor, our officious friend whom we had met at Squire Venable's. I saw him a little afterwards, but he had no longer on his Sunday clothes, and was carrying a sack of corn to plant his little field, which he appeared to hold only by a lease. He complained of the high price of the lands, which he hired at twenty shillings an acre... He asked of me for a place in Castorland, which I promised him with pleasure when our survey should have been completed, but which could not occur during the coming year. In short we parted well pleased with one another.

Simon Desjardins, 1794[29]

The team ended their day recalling some visual impressions, including those of a bird that was unfamiliar to them.:

Throughout its whole course, the Mohawk presents along its banks lands of the greatest fertility. The more distant hills are covered with wood, with places cleared, and the beginnings of clearings.

We killed some birds with red throats, larger than a lark, with a short beak, and mixed grey plumage. The feathers were of fiery red under the throat and breast. They fed upon the berries of the Philotarus.

October 5th. In the morning the venerable Esquire demanded of us six shillings. Upon our representing to him that he had furnished us nothing, he gravely replied, "But it is to pay us for the trouble." He deigned, however, although with a scowl, to accept four shillings. His ancient spouse was not of this mind, and with her pipe in a corner of her mouth, shook her head in a manner so expressive that M. Brunel could not keep from sketching on the spot, the caricature which has made us more than once remember these amiable hosts.

Breakfasted at three miles from Venables'. Our host, surprised at seeing us make an onion soup, cried out, "It is then indeed true that all Frenchmen are cooks!" He furnished us tea, roast pork, eggs and maple sugar, and charged us a shilling a head.

From Venables' the river is free from obstruction for six miles, 'till we come to a gorge in the mountain which is named "Anthony's Nose". But this mountain does not so much resemble a nose as the Anthony's Nose on the North River. The soil is quite fertile, and the plains extend up into the recesses of the mountains.

We landed at the foot of Anthony's Nose, where the stage road has only just width enough to pass, and went on foot to Spraker's Ferry and Tavern, a mile beyond.

This passage through "The Noses" was as picturesque as any on the inland waterways, and rarely missed mention:

A short distance below De Wandalaer's, you pass a remarkable rock called the Nose. The mountains here are high, and are like the Highlands of the Hudson on a small scale. The river must have burst a passage for itself. The opening of the mountains exhibits sublime scenery.

DeWitt Clinton, 1810[30]

The steepness of the mountains, and the narrowness of the gap through which the river flowed, made land travel precarious:

Passed by a projection of the rocky mountain, which is called "Anthony's Nose." Here the road is very narrow between the rock and the river, and goes partly over a wharf built with timber. The water here is said to be very deep.

Jeremy Belknap, 1796[31]

But navigation through this passage was also full of risk, as here existed the infamous "Keator's Rift", recalled by DeWitt Clinton in 1810:

...in order to facilitate the passage of our batteaux over Kater's Rapid, which extends a mile from this place, and which is among the worst in the river, we walked to the head of it.

DeWitt Clinton, 1810[32]

Keator's Rift

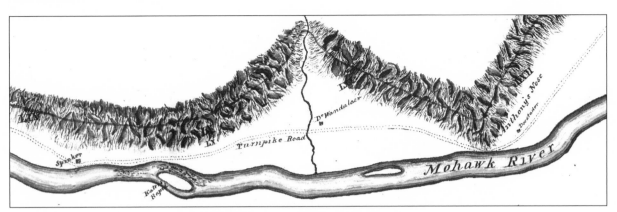

A map of the area by Benjamin Wright, 1811.

Just west of The Noses, outwash from the mouth of Flat Creek [Sprakers] since prehistoric times had created a low island and shoal in the Mohawk River. The force of water passing through the constricted space and over these shallows had produced, by the eighteenth century, the most difficult, and dangerous, passage on the Mohawk navigation, as described by Gen. Philip Schuyler during his initial survey of the river in 1792:

> "On nine miles, in perfectly good water, current gentle, to the rapid commonly called Kettar's Rapid, great velocity of water, sufficiently deep, obstructed by large rocks, the rapid extends about one quarter of a mile."
>
> Philip Schuyler, 1792[33]

Keator's Rift witnessed its share of boating disasters, including one which has been preserved in some detail:

> "[We]..came on to what is called Caty's rift... At this unfortunate place commenced my ill fortune. I at first hired only two bateaumen, but previous to my leaving Schenectady I hired a third, hoping by this I had put it out of the power of any accident to happen. The boat, being manned by three professed bateaumen and one good hand (though not a boatman), ascended this rift to within a boat's length of being over, when she took a shear and fell back, and soon acquired such velocity that the resistance of the boatmen became quite inadequate to stopping her. The consequence was, she fell crosswise of the current, and when she had descended the rapids about half way she brought up broadside upon a rock (which lays in the middle of the stream), and sunk almost instantly about four or five inches under.
>
> "In this situation she lay about two hours before I could procure assistance to get her unloaded; the delay of getting to her, together with the difficulty of coming at her cargo, made us three hours before we could relieve the boat, during which time we expected to see her go to pieces, which would undoubtedly have happened had she not been a new boat, and well built. It was particularly unfortunate that it was on board this boat that I had almost all my dry goods, which got most thoroughly wet. Upon getting the boat off I found she had two of her knees broke, and one of her planks split, and leaky in several places.
>
> "I immediately had one-half the cargo reloaded, and set forward up the rapid, at the head of which lives Mr. Spraker. Here I unloaded, and sent the boat back for the residue. Upon her arrival I set about opening the goods, all of which were soaking wet. The casks I had the goods in would have turned water for a short time, but the length of time the boat was under gave an opportunity for all the casks to fill. The three boxes of tea were all soaked through. The difficulty of getting this article dry was heightened by the very showery weather we had Tuesday and Wednesday; but by paying the greatest attention we were enabled to get it all dry by Wednesday evening. The goods I had all dried and repacked; the boat I had taken out of the water and repaired; almost everything was now ready for setting out in the morning."
>
> Nathan Ford, 1796[34]

At the head of the rift, where the Mohawk divided around the small island, the Western Inland Lock Navigation Company erected a low rock dam in the late 1790s to deflect water onto the rift, thus extending, somewhat, the season of low-water navigation.

Such inconvenience, at the very least, produced delay, as the expedition discovered.

As our boat encountered a head wind, which blew strongly through the gorge of the mountains, we were obliged to wait a long time. Besides this, the great depth of water in passing the place compelled them to use the oars alone, and, after coming through the passage, there were three strong rapids, a little above, that must be overcome before reaching the ferry. We amused ourselves, in the meantime, in carving on a face of the limestone rock and marble, at the foot of which Spraker's house is built. We found there some rock crystals and enjoyed a view between the trees of the river the plains and the mountains upon the opposite bank. At the water's edge at the rapids, we observed many stones sprinkled with large flakes of gold and silver colored spangles.

Many roadside taverns, such as Spraker's, served a dual function if near enough to the river:

Spraker's Tavern

An early view of Spraker's Tavern.

Spraker's Tavern commanded one of the premier locations along the inland transportation route to the West. It stood at the head of Keator's Rift, where the King's Highway [State Route 5] came to within a few yards of the north bank of the Mohawk. At this spot a rope ferry had been established, connecting land traffic on both sides of the river.

According to one nineteenth century writer, it was here, as Spraker's Tavern, that the concept of canal navigation in New York passed its first test:

"The navigation of the interior waters of the state had engaged the attention of General Schuyler at a very early period. This intimate knowledge of its hydrography revealed to him the practicability of a system of state improvements, which should connect the lakes with the Atlantic. He even then perceived that New York commanded the outlet to the ocean for the produce of the west and long before Dewitt Clinton embarked his fortunes in the Erie Canal, General Schuyler had projected a more feasible plan for attaining its proposed object. His scheme consisted of slack water navigation up the Mohawk to Wood Creek, thence to Oneida Lake, and so through the Oswego River to Lake Ontario. But to complete this chain, a system of locks would be necessary to overcome the descent in the Mohawk at Little Falls.

"The success of his project depending very much upon the favour with which it should meet from the Dutch settlers on the Mohawk, he proceeded to possess them with his views. They assembled by prearrangement at Spraker's Tavern. There the General met them and opened to them his plans. They perceived the advantage, and were pleased with the prospect of the Mohawk's bearing the commerce of the state past their doors; but they could not understand how boats could ascend the Little Falls. The General explained that they would be carried up by locks; but to no purpose. They liked the General and would take his word for anything, but he couldn't make them believe that water would run up hill. At this, they parted in the night - the Dutch men to their beds, and the General, worrying over his failure, to his.

"At a thought, however, he arose, and lighting his candle, took his knife and a few shingles, and going into the yard, dug a miniature canal of two different levels, which he connected by a lock of shingles - Then providing himself with a pail of water, he summoned the Dutchmen from their beds, and pouring the water into the ditch, locked a chip through from the lower to the upper level. "Vell, Vell! General," the Dutchmen cried, "we now understands and we all goes mit you and de canal" - The canal was dug and the locks were built - They can be seen at Little Falls to this day - Such was the policy which afterwards shaped the Erie Canal, and such its origins with General Schuyler."

John Cochrane, nd[35]

Whether apocryphal, or anecdotal, there could have been no more appropriate place at which to speak to the problems of surmounting the river rapids of the inland navigation with canals than here, at Spraker's Tavern above Keator's Rift.

Along the river road near some of the rapids there were public houses, a share of whose custom came from boatmen. Near those inns, as possible, boats often tied up for the night, a lot of Mohawk sailors having their own jolly times. The late Jost Spraker's tavern, near Keator's rift, was one of this class, having, among its many patrons, not a few who came by water.

Jeptha Simms, 1882[36]

There was perhaps no more strategically placed tavern in the Mohawk Valley, situated as it was at the head of the most dangerous rapid on the river. Here boatmen bound downriver could fortify themselves for the run, and those lucky enough to make it up through Keator's Rift, could celebrate their success, or perhaps recover from disaster.

The following year, Desjardins and Pharoux twice again passed through The Noses. Their journal entries underscore the strategic location of Spraker's Tavern:

...at half past nine, arrived at Spraker's Ferry, beyond the rapids of Anthony's Nose, which we passed very easily, considering that it was dark. Our men united in passing up one batteau after another. This Spraker who keeps the tavern and ferry, made us pay four shillings for a piece of bread, some butter and a dozen eggs. I had to pay eight pence a quart for milk, which I found indispensable after the fatigue of the day.

...arrived at Spraker's tavern. For three hours the snow had been falling so abundantly that there was now more than two feet on shore, and it was not without difficulty that we able to get to the house, as we were moreover benumbed with cold. We found a good fire, and what is more rare, a good supper. This tavern is opposite Anthony's Nose.

Simon Desjardins, 1794[37]

Their 1793 journal continues, as they once again reach deep water above Keator's Rift.

We re-entered the boat at half past one. After stopping at various places to rest our boatmen, we landed at half past six at a farm house, where we could find only cider and milk. They had neither meat nor beds. Before the door was a spring, which the owner had leveled, and which discharged at three feet from the ground by a spout. From this house we got a view of Fort Plain and Canajoharie, one of the most pleasant and fertile sections of the Mohawk. Here the Schenectady Stage stops, and they take another for Whitestown. It is called forty miles by land from Canajoharie to Schenectady. We made twelve miles by water this day.

October 6th. Left at half past six in the morning. Paid for cider, milk and shelter a shilling a head. At three miles we breakfasted at the house of a young German, upon milk-soup, tea, eggs, and roast meat.

It being from this place only nine miles, (three long leagues) to the Little Falls, M. M. Pharoux and Brunel resolved to travel this distance on foot, on the left bank as we go up. They told them to follow the main road.

For the first six miles that they traveled, they saw nothing but fertile lands entirely cleared. The road then ascended into the woods, where they saw some clearings made, and others begun, interspersed with pieces of land still covered with woods. They then came to the finest timber they had yet seen, (such as oak, elm and ash) the most of which was straight and very tall.

In a very steep hill which the road passed over, they observed some layers of very shally slate, much broken and cut out in forming the road.

CHAPTER THREE

The Little Falls

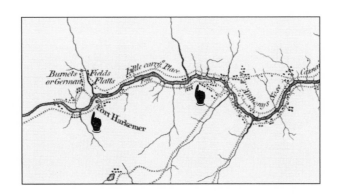

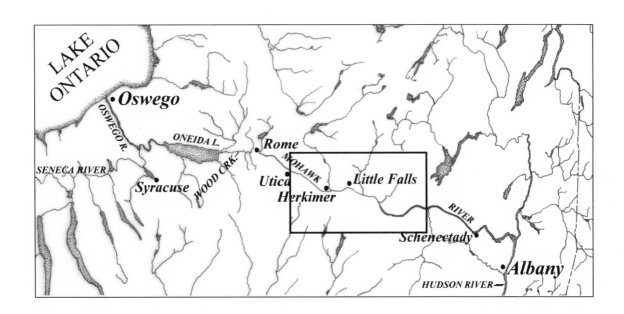

Passing along the high road west toward Little Falls, so named as being the smaller version of the Great Falls at Cohoes, Pharoux and Brunel temporarily lost their way.

They passed over two streams over which bridges had been thrown. The first was rustic, and built of trunks of trees, and the other was built of carpentry work.

Not being acquainted with the Little Falls road, they followed the stage route, but after going about three miles, they found out their mistake. They went down towards the Mohawk, by a road through the woods made of brush in swampy places. It led between natural rocks, and they had upon their right a granite rock exceedingly steep, crowned with fir trees. One of these firs, overturned by the wind, had continued to grow upon a crag of the rock so that its roots were flattened perpendicular to the trunk.

They met an Indian family. The father was laden with a pack on his shoulders and was clad in a kind of grey waistcoat with a belt and some pieces of red stuff that covered his legs. His two children had bows and arrows, and his wife, who was clothed in a short frock, carried a basket full of skins and furs.

A little beyond, M. M. Brunel and Pharoux crossed over the bridge at the Little Falls and arrived at the house of Major DeZeng, who, as inspector of the works on the Canal, is lodged by the company.

In their approach to Little Falls, Pharoux and Brunel had crossed the three most typical methods of bridging water in the late eighteenth century frontier. The simplest was the causeway, or "causey", used in marshy places and seepages. It is described in a contemporary treatise on roads:

... swampy places should be covered to a good depth with well-bound faggots or fascines placed close together, and that upon these a range of saplins should be laid, touching each other, and the whole covered with earth. The water will subside through the interstices of the wooden materials and leave the road dry, while the floor of saplins will prevent any depth of ruts or possibility of stalling.

Anonymous, 1787[38]

The road "made of brush in swampy places" noted by the travelers was made on this design.
But Pharoux and Brunel also crossed two small bridges, both

no doubt thrown up by the local residents to carry the road across narrow streams. The one described as "rustic" was probably little more than trunks felled across the channel, while the one "built of carpentry work" was made of squared timbers joined with pegs, perhaps of the "King Post Truss" design.

M. Desjardins, who had remained with the boat for security of their effects, continued the route by water. At three miles, they stopped at Hudson's tavern - a place well located, and the house well kept.

It is unfortunate, indeed, that all three journalists did not take advantage of the opportunity to visit Hudson's Tavern, as it was one of the most interesting places, and more popular, along the Mohawk navigation.

The following year, they did have an opportunity to revisit the place, with the following favorable comment:

We stopped to lodge at Hudson's Tavern six miles from the Little Falls. It is the best on the route, and the first place where they did not make us pay for our fire wood.

Simon Desjardins, 1794[39]

Those remaining in the batteau continued their approach upriver from below the Falls.

From thence, six miles to the Little Falls, there were still some rapids near Schuyler's Island, and the aspect of the country was delightful, with a labyrinth of canals cut by the river, which winds among islands blooming with flowers and diversified by shade. The meadows are quite broad and the soil is excellent.

Within three miles of the Little Falls, the plain begins to narrow, until we arrive within a mile of the

The Little Falls Gorge.

Hudson's Tavern

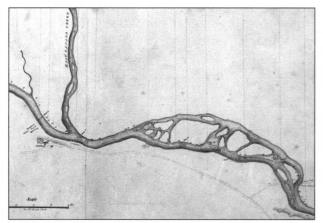

The ford at Hudson's Tavern in 1803.

H udson's Tavern was as well situated as it was well thought of by early travelers. It stood on an elevation above the river along the south bank, with a commanding view of the mouth of the great East Canada Creek opposite to the north. But it also stood on most historic ground; the site of the Mohawk's Upper Castle in the era of the French and Indian War [c. 1755]. The first mention of it can be found in General Schuyler's accounts of expenses on his 1792 expedition to survey the Mohawk for the Western Inland Lock Navigation Company. However no mention of its accommodations is given.

The first descriptive citation of Hudson's is found in Vanderkemp's journal in the same year:

"After dinner I crossed the Mohawk, three miles above Palatine-Town, & did see Canojohari ... After a ride of seven miles farther, I tarried at a ci-devant Indian castle, now a very recommendable inn, kept by Mr. Hudzon, to drink a dish of superior good tea."

Adrian Vanderkemp, 1792[40]

But it was not until three years later that we have the full historical significance of the location presented to us:

"Breakfasted at Hudson's, at the mouth of East Canada creek, - a good tavern, seated on the same ground where Hendrick lived, the Mohawk sachem who was killed in Johnson's battle, 1755, near Lake George.
"It is a beautiful eminence, commanding a pleasant prospect, and here are many apple-trees of at least fifty years old, called Hendrick's orchard. We had some of the cider, and it was excellent. Here was a fort, built by the British troops in 1756, called 'Fort Hendrick', the rampart, ditch, and glacis of which are visible; and here was found, about four years ago, a golden medal, which it is supposed was the property of some Indian chief. It was worth about seven dollars' had an Indian on one side and emblematic figure on the other. It was sold at Albany to a Mr. Lansing. This place I take to have been the lower Mohawk castle, as marked on Holland's map of New York, though I believe that near Fort Hunter was called the lower castle seventy or eighty years ago."

Jeremy Belknap, 1796[41]

It was here, in the time of the French and Indian War, that the Mohawk's had established their "Upper Castle." And it was on this spot, in 1755, that the British constructed their fort, described in 1757 by a French spy passing down the valley:

"It is a square of four bastions, of upright pickets, joined together with lintels. They are fifteen feet high, about one foot square, with port holes inserted from distance to distance, with a stage all round to fire from. This fort is one hundred paces on each side. It is not surrounded by a ditch. There are some small pieces of cannon at each of its bastions, and a house at each curtain to serve as a store and barrack. Five or six families of Mohawk Indians reside outside the fort."

Anonymous, 1757[42]

The stone quarry indicated on Benjamin Wright's 1803 map of the area (below) no doubt drew as much interest in that time as did any historical association with the Mohawks, for good building stone was in great demand as Schuyler's engineers contemplated the reconstruction of the wooden locks at Little Falls. Years earlier the value of laminated shale and limestone outcrops such as this was stressed in a W.I.L.N.C. report:

"The dam, guard, and river locks may be built with stone, to be obtained on the south side of the Mohawk, at the little falls - the land carriage will not exceed one mile, and it may then be conveyed in boats to the desired spot - the quality is well adapted for these or other works, where strength and duration are required - the stones rising in lamina, of different thickness - the beds perfectly parallel, and the dimensions as large as may be required..."

William Weston, 1795[43]

falls, when their vicinity is indicated by the banks becoming suddenly steep. In entering this strait in the mountains, you find yourself at once in the shadows between two banks of perpendicular rocks, overgrown by evergreen trees.

This scene, perhaps the most dramatic on the voyage, never failed to impress the traveler:

> On the approach to the Falls the scenery of the country experiences a sudden and picturesque change; the river becomes contracted to about one-third its usual breadth; on each side the mountains rise to a towering height, the sides of which, although inaccessible, are covered with lofty trees, which fasten their roots in the fissures and crevices of the rocks, and firmly maintain their station in spite of storms and tempests; while, as you advance, the river seems lost in a wilderness of rocks and precipices.
>
> Christian Schultz, 1807[44]

The extraordinary terrain presented here by the gorge of the river clearly made an impression on the journalists.

A little further the rocks appear broken and torn in a thousand forms, and two little islets of rock occur in the middle of the channel. Finally you land at the foot of the fall, at the mouth of the projected canal. This spot presents a scene at once grand, wild, and romantic, and it might well nourish melancholy thoughts of ruin, chaos, and desolation.

The water is tranquil up to the foot of the fall, which is a succession of different rapids so that the noise is as great as that of cascades in sheets, although you do not hear them so far unless the wind is favorable.

"The Mohawk, after winding through a fine plain of twenty or thirty miles extent above the falls, is all at once stopped by a vast ridge of rocks, probably 300 feet above the level of the river below, through which, with violent force, he breaks his way, foaming, dashing, and roaring, from one descent to another, until finally having gained the bottom, he glides through an immense chasm, seemingly cut out of the solid rock by art..."

Joshua Marsden, 1816[45]

M. Desjardins caused the effects to be carried by the boatmen to the house of Mr. DeZeng, which is half a mile from the landing. This house, as well as most of the others at this place, was built at canal company's expense.

Mr. DeZeng had been waiting for us two days. Mr. Desjardins was quite uneasy at not finding his fellow travelers, who had not yet arrived, and was sitting down at the table as they came in. After resting, we caused the bateau to be carried above the falls, by the portage which was made on the other side.

The wagon was made with two pairs of wheels, and wooden reach of the length of the bateau, and was drawn by four oxen.

Our boatmen were not willing to undertake the voyage of Lake Ontario, and we accordingly paid them five shillings a day for coming and returning.

We also paid Mr. DeZeng one hundred dollars on account of expenses of the journey. Supped and slept in our conductor's house.

"The people are principally English, and they seldom have preaching. The place abounds in vice, especially profanity. Since my arrival on the river I have heard more cursing and swearing, horrid oaths and imprecations, then in ten years past. They fell chiefly from the lips of boatmen. In some taverns were English and Dutch farmers drinking and swearing, and the English appeared to be the most abandoned."

Rev. Caleb Alexander, 1801[46]

October 7th. The Little Falls derive their name from cascades formed by the Mohawk at this place. They are quite small in comparison with the fine fall at Cohoes, down which the river plunges a height of sixty six feet, almost vertically, at a place twelve miles from Albany, and six from where it joins the North river.

The Mohawk is here compressed between two rocky mountains, through which it makes its passage, in some places with violence, and in others broken by the rocks, which are mostly smoothed, turned, and undermined by the wearing of the water. These several falls and rapids, in a length of a hundred toises, descend little by little about forty or forty five feet.

They have thrown over these falls a framed bridge, which is very fine and neatly built. It is made in a single span, with bents and railing, and is supported above the current upon rocks, which are covered by the swollen waters of the spring floods.

They are now digging a canal, to facilitate the navigation of the Mohawk and lessen the expenses of portage, which are now half a dollar a wagon-load which do not average more than a thousand pounds weight. The canal is undertaken by an incorporated company, whereof General Schuyler is the president, and who has given the plan of the works. Major DeZeng being Inspector and Storekeeper, the office is kept in his house.

This was the first of several encounters the Frenchmen would have with the works of General Schuyler's canal company under construction. Perhaps in no other location would the potential for improvement be better seen then here at the Little Falls, as described in the report of the Western Inland Lock Navigation Company:

The falls, previous to the improvements above stated, being impassable, even for empty water craft, these with all their cargoes, were transported by land, over a road as rough, rocky and as bad as the imagination can conceive; of necessity, therefore, the boats were of such construction as might be transported on a wheel carriage, consequently of little burthen, seldom exceeding a ton and a half; each boat, was navigated by three men; and a voyage from Schenectady to fort Schuyler, a distance of one hundred and twelve miles, and back to the former place, was seldom made in less than nine days.

Philip Schuyler, 1798[47]

The opening of this canal would, when completed, further stimulate the growth of Little Falls as a commercial center, and the operations of the canal certainly figured highly in the development of the village during the coming years.

Yet the community was already a viable hub for inland transportation, deriving wealth from water-powered industry and status from its position at the river portage.

Mr. Porteus, to whom we had letters of recommendation, is at the head of the Company of proprietors of the grant. He has built here a very fine flour mill with four run of stones, a saw mill with two saws for making plank, and a fulling mill, besides a store of well assorted merchandise. He carries on an extensive trade in flour, etc. An English house, Ellis of Montreal, is of the number of the associates.

The Little Falls Portage

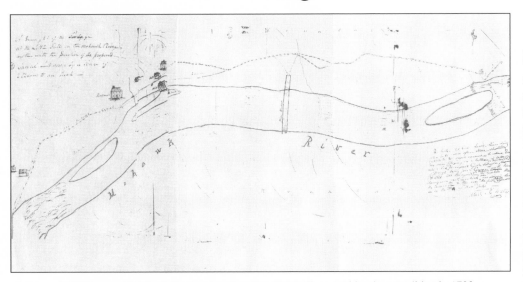

A 1792 map of Little Falls showing the "New Bridge" crossed by the expedition in 1793.

At the Little Falls, named in contradistinction to the "Great Falls" at Cohoes, the Mohawk River dropped 40 feet in less than a mile. This rocky passage was not navigable, even by canoe. Thus at a very early date, Palatine Germans established a carrying service here, assisting boatmen in transporting boat and baggage along a narrow haul road that skirted the falls on the north bank.

By the time the French expedition of Pharoux and Desjardins passed through Little Falls, an embryonic community had begun to form at this most strategic location. This settlement was catalyzed by the impending completion of the first of Philip Schuyler's inland canals, designed to circumvent these rapids. In fact, construction of that unprecedented artificial channel had already begun in the summer of 1793, although completion would be much delayed.

It was a year earlier, in August of 1792, that Schuyler's expedition to survey the Mohawk by batteau for the Western Inland Lock Navigation Company, passed this very spot, describing the work cut out for them:

"From the landing at the foot, to the landing at the head of the Falls, is about three quarters of a mile, the height thirty-nine feet two inches, the ground stony, rocky and rough..."

Philip Schuyler, 1792[48]

The map above is the earliest detailed image we have of the portage, before construction of the canal here changed the landscape significantly. It was drawn during Schuyler's 1792 expedition by Moses DeWitt, a surveyor who fell in with the survey party at Schenectady on his way home to Onondaga [Syracuse]. He was the nephew of Simeon DeWitt, the Surveyor General of New York, who the Frenchmen would meet later on their journey. On this map one can see the portage road, alongside which is drawn the line of the proposed canal, and, arranged along that road, the several buildings that existed then, the core of what would become the Village of Little Falls.

A notation in the margin by Elkanah Watson, one of the survey committee accompanying Schuyler in 1792, suggests the blasting of a dangerous rock at the lower end of the falls was the first actual work of the newly formed canal company, although rocks in this spot continued to plague boatmen exiting the Little Falls Canal long after it was completed in 1795.

As this establishment was burnt by the Indians in the Revolution, the English associates obtained from Parliament an indemnity so generous that they have erected their works ten fold better than before. Mr. Porteus, in his circumscribed sphere, following the English maxims of monopolizing trade, will sell no land but on the expressed conditions that there shall be built no stores.

It is only ten months since they began to clear off and build the canal, and they have made great progress for so short a time. Mr. DeZeng assured us that the locks and all the fixtures would be finished by the end of September 1794, and we hope he will not be disappointed.

In fact, this estimate proved optimistic, as the canal did not open to traffic until November of 1795, over two years after this visit and a year later then DeZeng had predicted.

Frederick Augustus, Baron de Zeng, who served informally as the agent for this expedition, and who would accompany it westward as guide, first came to New York in 1780 with the "Hessian" mercenary troops aiding the British during the Revolution. Discharged in 1783, he remained in the United States, became a citizen and was commissioned a Major in the Ulster County militia in 1792.

Frederick DeZeng.

Having surveyed the inland route from Albany to the Genesee country, Major DeZeng was chosen by Schuyler to supervise the construction of the Little Falls Canal in 1793. His knowledge of the inland waterways, and his position with the canal company, coupled with his station at Little Falls, recommended him to guide this, or any, expedition to establish western settlement.

Mr. DeZeng had hired for us as chief boatman a German named Simon, at five shillings a day, and for oarsmen, two Yankees (New Englanders) at four shillings a day each. Our visit being made to Mr. Porteus, and our goods put aboard, we set out at noon, and at two miles beyond found other rapids. We had a very agreeable view. This fertile country is called the German Flatts.

At five miles we observed the village, church, and Court House, at a considerable distance. At this place the Mohawk forms a bend and has very strong rapids, which are difficult to pass on account of the shallow water, as the river is here quite wide and flat. These rapids are occasioned by the rocks and gravel which the Great Canada Creek discharges by its two mouths into the Mohawk. We were obliged to land and walk a mile on foot to Fort Herkimer. Our boatmen got into the water, and by main strength dragged the bateau over the rocks and gravel.

The Fort Herkimer Church.

Their passage through the region known as the German Flatts, which may have seemed uneventful to the passengers of this small batteau, brought them through a stretch of river channel that would later see one of the most significant undertakings of the Western Inland Lock Navigation Company; the building of the 1798 German Flatts Canal.

The gravel bars, islands, and shoals that lay in the river at Fort Herkimer had been created over eons by the outwash of West Canada Creek, often just called the "Canada Creek" and referred to by the Frenchmen as the "Great Canada Creek".

Such accretions in the channel produced major rifts that obstructed passage. A measure of the need for improvement here is the reference in the journal of having to disembark the passengers and crew of the batteau to lighten it. Even then, the boatmen, standing in the river, had to drag it over the gravel of what was without doubt, "Wolf Rift".

Considering the difficulty of passing even this small batteau over these rifts, it is not surprising that with the advent of larger boats in the latter half of the 1790s, when the portages at Little Falls and Rome had been by-passed with canals, a canal here became indispensable.

But clearly these travelers, perhaps spurred on by their newly acquired guide, Major DeZeng, were drawn to the settlement itself, not the navigation. On foot, and relieved of the labors of moving the batteau, the quartet enjoyed a reconnaissance of the local historic sites, and then proceeded.

The German Flatts Canal

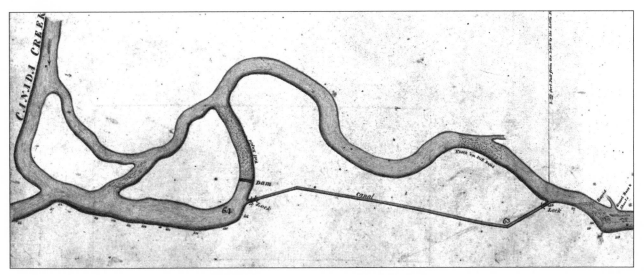

The German Flatts Canal as it appeared in 1803.

As early as 1791, the rifts at German Flatts were recognized as a serious hazard in need of improvement:

"From the Little Falls, thus far, the river is nearly competent to inland navigation, with the exception of a serious rapid, and a great bend at the Germanflats, called wolf-riff, - which must be subdued, either by a cut across the neck of land, upwards, one mile, or by removing the obstructions."

Elkanah Watson, 1791[52]

A year later, General Schuyler seconded this concern during his batteau survey of the Mohawk:

"...a strong rapid, formerly called Orendorff's rift, falls a foot in about eighty yards, two feet water, a fine gravel bottom ... then arrived at the Wolf rift, extending about one half mile, bottom fine gravel, shallow, and the channel crooked, occassioned by banks of gravel in the river..."

Philip Schuyler, 1792[53]

Schuyler went on to suggest the solution, which was to become the German Flatts Canal:

"From the falls [Little Falls] to Fort Schuyler [Rome] the only impediments of any amount are occassioned by the two rapids called Orendorf's and Wolf's rapids, these are sharp and extended, and the river here forms a circuit, which lengthens its course beyond a straight line... It is believed that merely a cut through the chord of this circuit of about a mile, in easy digging and of little depth, would effectually surmount these obstacles."

Philip Schuyler, 1792[54]

In 1795, when Schuyler's English engineer William Weston evaluated this situation, he concurred with this suggestion:

"The best manner of improving this part will be to cut a canal from Fort Herkemer, to the deep water, below Orendorff's rift - the ground is very favourable, being free from rock, and with a gradual and gentle descent... the length will be ninety two chains; and the fall of the lock at the east end ten feet, supposing the fall of the upper gate level with the surface of the water above the Wolf rift. To obtain the requisite depth of water in the Canal, I propose to throw a dam across the river, to raise it three feet - this will save that depth of extra digging the whole length of the canal, and will also improve the navigation of the two small rapids above Aldridges."

William Weston, 1795[55]

In an historic departure from previous lock construction by the W.I.L.N.C., Weston determined to build with stone, rather than wood or brick, and he cited the value of the laminated rock exposures along the river, similar to those noted at Hudson's Tavern:

"The dam, guard, and river locks may be built with stone, to be obtained on the south side of the Mohawk, at

continued on next page

27

continued from page 23

the Little Falls - the land carriage will not exceed one mile, and it may then be conveyed in boats to the desired spot - the quality is well adapted for these or any other works, where strength and duration are required - the stones rising in lamina, of different thickness - the beds perfectly parallel, and the dimensions as large as may be required."

William Weston, 1795[56]

This plan was adopted and construction was well under way here in October of 1797. During the ensuing winter, stone and other building materials were dragged to the site on sleds, and just a year later the canal was in operation. Although of limited scale, it was more than sufficient for even the large Durham boats of that period. The stone locks had chambers of about 12 by 70 feet, just large enough to pass such boats, and the passage along this canal was noted by some as one of the more pleasant experiences of the inland navigation:

"The canal here is through the Flatts, a delightful body of low lands, which look like the flats of Esopus, and were first settled by the Palatines. The canal is 1 1/4 mile long, 24 feet wide, and 4 feet deep. The land through which it is cut cost the company 120 dollars an acre. It is furnished with a guard lock to prevent too great a flux of water. The embankments afford a delightful walk and the expense of cutting the canal could not exceed that of a good turnpike. A lock here cannot, with economy, be more than 6,000 dollars. The lock was filled in five minutes for our boat to pass. The canal here ought to have been extended further to the east, in order to have avoided another difficult rapid, and this could have been done at a trifling expense."

DeWitt Clinton, 1810[57]

Meanwhile, we went to visit the forts. One was hexagonal and the other square, and they were built of beams laid one upon another. In the former is a twelve pound cannon. On the first floor were embrasures for shooting, on every side, and in the upper story, which projected on all sides, there were loup holes.

The roof was surmounted by a lantern, which served as look-out, and a ditch, half filled up, surrounded it. The second was arranged in the same manner within. These forts were located on an eminence and served to protect the German settlers against the Anglo-Indian rangers in the War of Independence. We found in them, as their sole garrison, a flock of peaceable sheep, who had assembled there to get out of the heat - happy symbol of the peace now enjoyed in this pleasant and fertile country!

Above the mouth of Canada Creek, the river makes several bends and has a number of small rapids. We
stopped to sleep at twelve miles from the Little Falls, at the house of Mr. Dexter.

Dexter's house stood along the north bank of the river, a few miles above the settlement of Fort Herkimer, which the journalists have referred to as "the village of German Flatts." Two hundred years ago the entire area surrounding the mouth of West Canada Creek [Herkimer] was referred to as "German Flatts."

"A few miles further on one finds the fertile plains called the German Flats. It stretches out very far lengthwise but it is narrow. All that is level presents a picture of the greatest fertility and of fine cultivation. It is divided into large regular squares covered with corn, wheat, and all sorts of grain and meadows, through which the river winds."

Julian Ursyn Niemcewicz, 1805[58]

CHAPTER FOUR

The Upper Mohawk

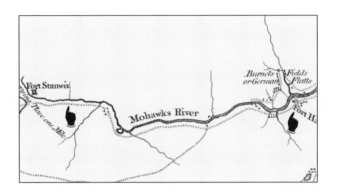

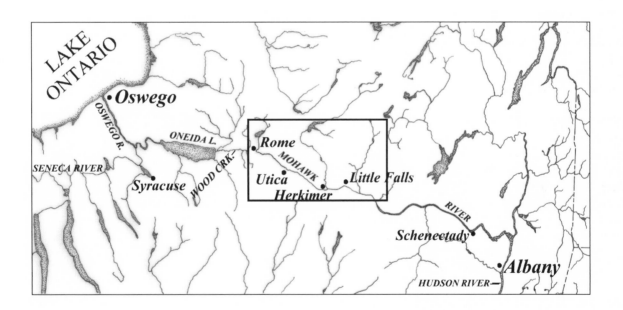

Passage above the gravelly outlet of West Canada Creek generally marked entry into the Upper Mohawk River navigation. The river became noticeably narrower and more meandering, the rapids more forceful and often deeper, and the diminished size of the intersecting streams reduced the volume of rift-creating outwash.

Most travelers' accounts of the period contrast navigation below German Flatts generally with that above, and particularly with that above Old Fort Schuyler [Utica]. The Frenchmen passing here in 1793 were no different:

Tuesday, October 8th. Left at seven o'clock. We found the river more winding, easier to navigate, less embarrassed with rapids and narrower. This country is beginning to be cleared. The further we ascend, the smaller and more tortuous the Mohawk becomes.

The banks are lined with trees which lean over like an arbor, so as to render the navigation shady and very agreeable, and it seems like being in a garden.

The maples, ash, elms, oaks, etc., astonish you by their height, and a European can scarcely conceive of the majesty of these ancient trees - children of nature, which the hand of man has never touched. But the cultivator is little moved by these natural beauties. The fire and the axe will soon destroy these growths of centuries.

Here we find trees girdled all around near the foot, an easy means of destroying them; there they have applied the fire. These immense forests are interspersed with clearings, some finished and sown, while others are begun and exhibiting images of destruction. The trees felled by the axe are made into piles and left until they are sufficiently seasoned, so that they can put in the fire, and convert their ashes into potash.

Cutting and burning girdled trees.

Potash was usually the first product to be shipped downriver from these new settlements; a valuable by-product of the clearing of the forest lands for cultivation:

Having been familiar with clearing up new land from my early childhood, let me describe the process. The ground to be cleared being selected, the first move is to cut all the underbrush and small trees, generally called staddles. The brush are trimmed out and heaped in suitable places, and all such small trees, as can conveniently be handled, are cut and thrown on the heaps, with the old fallen limbs of trees; the small ones being cut near the ground.

You are now ready to cut the large timber; and here great judgement must be used in falling it, so that you can log it to advantage. Trees should be so fallen as to be parallel with each other, and if on hilly land, should be fallen in such a manner that on logging they may be rolled down hill. Those cut up should be in logs, fourteen or fifteen feet long, according to their size. By skillful falling much chopping may be saved, by leaving any large trees to be piled against, on making log heaps.

A good chopper would cut his acre and pile the brush in seven or eight days; I have known it done in less. At the age of twenty-two years I could cut an acre in seven days, but as a general average men would be from seven to ten days; particularly if several worked together. Chopping is hard, but clean work and I was fond of it. A man going into the woods with his axe, soon makes an opening, which being enlarged daily, serves to encourage and stimulate him to vigorous action.

The trees being chopped and brush piled, if done in May or June, should be left through July and August, by which time they become so dry, that the fire frequently runs over the whole ground, burning all the brush, many of the logs, and blackening those that remain. This would be regarded as a good burn, leaving the soil clean of weeds, and herbage. Then follows the logging and burning the log heaps, most dirty, smoky, disagreeable work. The men and a yoke of oxen would log an acre per day, sometimes more, if the timber was light, and well felled and cut. The ashes, worth 6 1/4 cents, must be scraped together, and carried to an ashery, to make black salts, and eventually pearl or potash. All this being done, the land was ready for harrowing and reception of seed, after which fences could be made at pleasure.

Levi Beardsley, c1791[59]

This expedition would frequently see the burning of virgin timber as they pushed westward, where newer settlements were just being cut from the forest. Here, along the upper Mohawk, expanding settlement produced a mixture of land use patterns, often with the margins of the river left in timber.

The greater part of the clearings are not visible from the Mohawk, because they have been made along the great roads, that run some distance into the country. Several masses of trees washed in by freshets, and anchored at the bottom of the water, obstruct the navigation in many places.

At half after two we passed under the bridge of Old Fort Schuyler. This bridge is only a single span of frame work, bent and supported in the middle by posts, but without the necessary braces and stays. It is built in the same style as the one at Little Falls, and the bed of the river is sand and gravel.

The expedition passed by Old Fort Schuyler [Utica] without comment. Re-named in distinction to "Fort Schuyler" of the 1790s, which later became Rome, this community would not gain its regional preeminence for another decade:

Utica is a flourishing village on the south side of the Mohawk; it arrogates to itself being the capital of the Western District. Twenty-two years ago there was but one house; there are now three hundred...

The situation of the place is on low ground, a great part of which is natural meadow. It derives its importance from its situation on the Mohawk, the Seneca turnpike which communicates with the heart of the Western country, and the Mohawk and Schenectady turnpike, which leads to Schenectady on the north side of the Mohawk, independently of a good free road on the south side.

DeWitt Clinton, 1810[60]

In 1793 it was only the new bridge at Old Fort Schuyler, connecting land traffic on the north and south shores of the Mohawk, that was worthy of note in passing, as it had been for another traveler a few months before:

Proceeded forward, and that evening reached Fort Schuyler, where is erected a wooden bridge, whose arch is one hundred and twenty feet wide, without any support from below, the butments are of framed timber without stone in any part of them. The sweep of the arch appeared to be about seven feet.

Jacob Lindley, 1793[61]

This bridge, and the settlement where it stood, would receive a bit more attention on the return trip. But on their passage upriver, perhaps frustrated by the innumerable rifts and delays, the party seemed concerned to push quickly on by.

We breakfasted and dined in the bateau, to economize time, and after having made about twenty four miles on our journey, we resolved, when night came on, to sleep in the midst of the forest. We accordingly landed, and for the first time pitched our tent, built a fire, made our beds, and arranged our packets so as to make convenient seats.

Having made our cooking arrangements for the evening and morning, we partook of a frugal supper and slept from nine till six, as sweetly as on the best beds in Europe.

Where possible, in this period, gentlemen, women, and children lodged at taverns along the river, while camping on the riverbank was left to boatmen and traders. Yet at this early date, public houses were few and far between, and often of extremely poor quality, even for that time:

Shephard's house is thirty-nine miles from Schenectady, on the north side of the river, and close to Canajoharie bridge, which passes over the Mohawk. It is a large handsome house, dirty and un-accommodating, although much frequented. Here is a small village of two or three stores, two taverns, asheries for making pot and pearl ashes, and about eight houses. We relished our breakfast but very indifferently. The swarms of flies, which assailed the food, were very disgusting; and custards which were brought on the table, *mal apropos* exhibited the marks of that insect as a substitute for the grating of nutmeg.

DeWitt Clinton, 1810[62]

This same traveler, when passing up the river west of Old Fort Schuyler, perhaps at the very spot selected by the Frenchmen, opted also to spend his night outdoors:

We pitched our camp on the right bank of the river, in the midst of woods. All hands fell to work, soldierlike; we soon had a roaring fire, and our tents pitched, - open on one side to the fire, and closed at each end with canvass. We found an excellent substitute for feathers, by laying our buffaloes on hemlock twigs; although the ground was extremely moist, yet we were effectually protected from any inconvenience. We enjoyed a pleasant night, with ten times more comfort than we could in the miserable log huts along the margin of the river.

Elkanah Watson, 1791[63]

Having experienced woodland camping for the first time on their journey, the members of the expedition pushed on in the morning.

Wednesday, October 9th. Started at half past six, after loading our baggage. The morning was very foggy. We saw everywhere good land and superb vegetation.

The Frenchman were probably well advised to continue their passage by boat, as the road west was typically poor:

> The road from thence to Whitesborough, continued as bad as possible. Broken bridges, stumps, and my horse at every step knee deep.
>
> Elkanah Watson, 1788[64]

Soon the Frenchmen discovered the cause of some of the timber that had impaired their navigation coming up to Old Fort Schuyler the day before - often called "Wood Riffs" by the boatmen.

> ***We observed that along the clearings they had felled into the river the trees that leaned over it, to get rid of them, which occasioned many obstructions.***

This habit of farmers carelessly felling timber into the river, in apparent disregard for the navigators who depended on the waterway for transportation, was observed in this same spot two years earlier:

In the afternoon we progressed thirteen miles, meeting many obstructions, in consequence of the cruel conduct of the new settlers, (who are wonderfully increased since I was here last,) filling the river with fallen trees, cut on its margin, - narrowing it in many places, producing shoals where the deepest waters had been accustomed to flow, and impeding the progress of our boats.

> Elkanah Watson, 1791[65]

Three years after this passage in 1793, the Western Inland Lock Navigation Company, and its sister company on the northern route to Lake Champlain, cited this same problem in official reports:

> Many of the settlers adjoining the waters on both routes, through which the improvements are intended, and by which the internal navigation, in its present imperfect state, is carried on, have very improvidently fallen the timber from the banks into those waters, to such an extent, as in many places renders it difficult to obtain a passage.
>
> Philip Schuyler, 1796[66]

"The Neck on the Mohock's River"

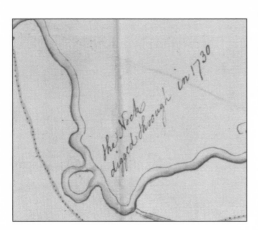

This 1757 map reveals New York State's first artificial waterway.

By navigating up the Mohawk River above Whitestown, the French batteau had passed, without mention or realization, through the first "canal" ever dug in New York State, and one of the first in the world. This cut is not mentioned in any known written records of the period, but it does appear on several manuscript British maps of the mid-eighteenth century, and on several of these it is clearly labeled:

"The Neck Diged through in 1730"

Anonymous, 1756[67]

The narrow neck of land across which this "canal" was cut had been formed in the loop of a meander just west of the mouth of Sauquoit Creek, in Whitestown. The narrowness of the neck, coupled perhaps with the accumulations of sand and driftwood in the loop itself, must have attracted the interest of a batteau load of traders or soldiers who endeavored with simple hand tools to make this first navigation improvement on record in the Northeast.

It was just eight years earlier, in 1722, that a similar neck cut was completed on the Mississippi River above New Orleans, although of a much grander scale:

"The Mississippi has a very winding course, and at every bend there is an eddy in the water... In the year 1722, as a party of Canadians were going down the river, they found at one place such a bend in it, that although the distance across land, from one part of the river to the other, was not more perhaps than two hundred yards, yet by water it was no less than forty miles. The Canadians cut a trench across the land for curiosity. The soil bordering upon the Mississippi is remarkably rich and soft, and the current being strong, the river in a short time forced a new passage for itself, and the Canadians took their boat through it. The place is called Pointe Coupe'e. There are many similar bends in the river at present, but none so great."

Isaac Weld, 1797[68]

With the new trading house at Oswego just completed, in 1727, and traffic to and from that outpost along the inland waterways on the increase, this tiny canal may be the first tentative manifestation of the expanding pressure for navigation improvements soon to follow. Given its situation, and the technology used in its improvement, this cut at "the Neck" was a direct precursor to those to be excavated in the twisting channel of Wood Creek in 1793; over a half century later.

No solution was ever found for this problem, either in educating the rustic population, or in devising techniques for protecting the channel from obstruction. Sunken timber was always a threat to inland navigation, whether created by human negligence or natural forces.

Schuyler's company engaged contractors, late in the 1790s, who attempted to drag timber out of the channel with chains and teams of oxen. Long term solution to the problem of careless homesteaders came only when the riverside timber had all been cut away, usually within a few years of settlement.

Within a couple miles of Old Fort Schuyler, the batteau came in sight of Whitestown, which was the center of commerce and settlement in this period.

At about two miles from where we started, we passed under the bridge at Whitestown, which is finished. This bridge is a framed structure with railing and braces above, and vertical supports. Two bridges which serve for farm purposes were also framed with solidity and elevated above the highest floods.

The country on the left bank, from Fort Schuyler, is called Whitestown, from a Mr. White who first came to establish himself in these woods, some eight years ago. There are now actually built some six hundred houses.

The settlement at Whitestown eclipsed Old Fort Schuyler [Utica] until after 1800, when the completion of the Seneca Turnpike [State Route 5] drew traffic, and commerce, to that more easterly Mohawk landing.

"I remained one day, recruiting, at Judge White's log-house, the founder of this settlement, and slept in his log-barn, with horses and other animals, some on four legs, some on two. Whitesborough is a promising new settlement, situated on the south side of the Mohawk river, in the heart of a fine tract of land, and just dawning from a state of nature into civilization. The settlement commenced only three years since. It is astonishing what efforts are making to subdue the musky forest. Log-houses are already thickly scattered in the midst of stumps, half burnt logs, girdled trees, and confusion.

"I observe, however, with pleasure, their log-barns are well filled. A few years past, these lands might have been bought for a trifle; at present, the lands bordering the river, have risen to three dollars an acre, and few miles back, to one dollar. Settlers are continually pouring in from the Connecticut hive, which throws off its annual swarms of intelligent, industrious, and enterprising settlers, the best qualified of any men in the world, to subdue, and civilize the wilderness."

Elkanah Watson, 1788[69]

In spite of its size, and evidence of rapid growth, this community drew little notice from the passing batteau, which pushed on by.

We rested, after going about eleven miles and a half, at the mouth of Oriskany Creek, a fine little river, where two bateaux were lying; one bearing a New England family on their way to settle at Niagara, on English territory, where, according to them, there are already some four thousand families located; and the other occupied by a New Jersey family on their way to Kingston, formerly Fort Frontenac, at the entrance of the St. Lawrence, where there are, as they assured us, still larger settlements.

The sight of Americans emigrating to English territory appeared to us very strange. We were not less surprised to learn that, this very year, six hundred families, each with its bateau, had taken the same route. Their ostensible reason is that there are not enough places in their own country, that land is there very scarce, and that the new lands are too dear, while in Canada they are given away grattis. Thus the very people who have, for seven years, maintained a Civil War to escape the yoke of England, leave their own happy and flourishing country, to beg land at the hands of those whom they have rejected with horror, -and put themselves voluntarily under their sway. This is a fit subject for reflection, to the preceptors of Mankind!

Our Major DeZeng, who is not given to Philosophy, sought to quarrel with the Jersey people, and in a menacing tone, after some words, raised his axe over them. But seeing that he scared nobody in the least, he returned it quietly to its place.

The emigration which travelers observed along the inland waterways during this period was in part inspired by the creation of Upper Canada [Ontario] in 1791. Established initially as a refuge for Loyalists from the United States, many of which had lived in the Mohawk Valley, these vacant and inexpensive lands drew the disillusioned from their exhausted New England farms. With lands along the waterways within New York already taken up, or priced too dear, families stepping into their batteaux at Schenectady intended only on passing through to Lake Ontario.

This was a preview of the great westward migrations of the next century, where hopes and dreams traveled in covered wagons along the rutted trails of the Great Plains. This present migration, of necessity, was forced into small boats on the inland waterways by the lack of adequate roads for heavily loaded wagons and carts, even a decade later:

We set off on our western tour, through roads as bad as deep ruts, broken bridges, and rapid torrents could make them ... a foot deep in mud, full of stumps of trees, intersected with streams, and these sometimes covered with rotten poles, and others not covered at all, with now and then holes, gaps, and excavations, sufficiently large to swallow up a horse and cart; indeed, most of the American roads are a libel upon common sense... We had, it is true, the delightful Mohawk River on our left hand, whose banks are covered with finely cultivated plantations, affording some beautifully romantic landscapes.

Joshua Marsden, 1816[70]

The emigrants of the 1790s were very familiar with the water route to Canada, via Oswego, and much of the early settlement of Ontario was rooted in these crowded batteaux, navigating the upper Mohawk westward, as observed in the preceding decade:

We met numerous bateaux coming up the river, freighted with whole families, emigrating to the "Land of Promise." I was surprised at the dexterity with which they manage the boats, poling up the river against a current at a speed of three miles an hour.

Elkanah Watson, 1788[71]

The Frontier Homestead

A homestead of log structures in the late 18th century.

The image of the frontier homestead, consisting of a crude log cabin and a few acres of cleared land, is deeply ingrained in the stereotype of eighteenth century New York. It is important to recognize, however, that regardless of the level of architecture first constructed, each settler constantly strove to upgrade that structure, making it larger or replacing it with one more sophisticated or comfortable.

It was not uncommon to find a series of houses built in succession on a homestead:

"Hitherto he has lived in a log-hut; in which he has entertained most of the persons traveling in this road during the last eight years. In my journey of 1803 I found Rosebrook in possession of a large, well-built farmer's house."

Timothy Dwight, 1803[72]

These cycles of replacement were repeated as each new area was opened to settlement, and sometimes as new settlers first entered areas already occupied by others. This frequently revealed a mixed pattern of architecture, with a preponderance of the earlier log cabin styles as one went further west:

"Their dwelling-houses are principally of logs; but they are beginning to form better, and will soon be lodged very comfortably."

Timothy Dwight, 1803[73]

As soon as one could, the original log cabin, often small and uncomfortable, was replaced with a log house made of squared timbers, framed windows and doors, and a functioning fireplace and chimney:

"A log cabin... was a temporary structure built of round, unhewn logs, caulked with moss, straw or mud, having no windows, and a hole in the roof in lieu of a chimney. A log house... was a dwelling built of hewn logs, the interstices stopped with stones and neatly plastered, having glass windows, a chimney, and a shingled roof."

Thaddeus Mason Harris, 1803[74]

Chronology was less critical than geography in determining the predominant type of house one would encounter, and often communities to the west exhibited mostly log cabins, while those in the east had long since converted to log frame houses:

"...the wooden house at which we stopped had reached the second stage of civilization for it was a frame house, that is to say, a house with glazed windows."

Madame du Pin, Massachusetts in 1794[75]

"... a miserable log hut is the only symptom of man's residence."

Basil Hall, Western New York in 1827[76]

The migration of families to the west in batteaux was frequently preceded the year before by individual exploratory expeditions by land; often with an air of desperation:

...we met daily with groups of five or six men on horse back, in search of land, with intention, if succeeding, to move on with their families the next winter or following spring, while every day one or other accosted us to purchase lands, of which we did not own one single inch.

Adrian Vanderkemp, 1792[77]

Had the French party ventured up the Oriskany Creek to the terrace above, they might have seen remnants of the Iroquois settlement that had existed there throughout the eighteenth century. Even as late as 1788, significant Native American activity was noted here:

At Oriskany creek, I passed a small tribe of two hundred Indians, the remnant of the once formidable Mohawk nation, the terror and dread of the New-England frontiers.

Elkanah Watson, 1788[78]

But the French party contented itself to remain in the mouth of the creek to enjoy their breakfast.

We breakfasted on the bank with a good appetite, upon the pork and peas cooked last evening. After reembarking we found the river more and more obstructed by drift wood. Fortunately the two bateaux left before us, and made themselves a way, axe in hand, from which we profited on our passage.

We were at length obliged to land to rest the boatmen, but the bank was still more difficult than the river. We all went into the water, and M. M. Brunel and DeZeng assisted the boatmen in drawing the bateau over the rapids, while Pharoux and Desjardins regained the bank. But the route in the woods was very difficult, on account of the trees that had fallen across it, some of them half consumed by time, and into which they sank in trying to get over them. There were a great many plants and tall herbs, which fettered the legs, and springs and swamps, into which they sank very easily. But the most disagreeable obstacle that they met was the abatis of the new clearings. The trees fallen and pressed together, their branches interlaced, and trunks piled one on another, presented a front that it was almost impossible to scale, and these tangled masses were sometimes one or two hundred toises wide.

To crown the whole, it was found necessary to cross a creek. It appeared to have but little water, but M. Pharoux, in attempting to pass it, at once sank waist deep into the mud. If he had not luckily seized a branch of a tree, by which he was enabled to crawl out, he would have remained stuck in the mire, and would have sunk deeper into the pool, before assistance could have been rendered. M. Desjardins, who witnessed this passage, did not think proper to follow his tracks, and called to the bateau, which, after receiving M. Pharoux, took him up at the mouth of the creek, not without great difficulty, but radically cured of his curiosity for traveling in the woods without road or paths.

Having endured the monumental exertions of navigating the upper Mohawk channel in low water, and having witnessed first-hand the near impossibility of traveling overland, Pharoux and Desjardins took refuge that evening in their riverside encampment.

At sunset we landed on the right bank, in the woods, on a spot a little elevated, where we cooked and supped in the most rural style. After getting dried, cleaned off and well warmed, we retired to rest.

CHAPTER FIVE

The Great Carrying Place

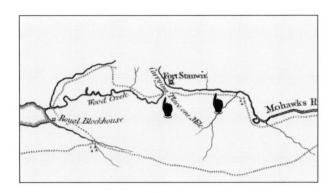

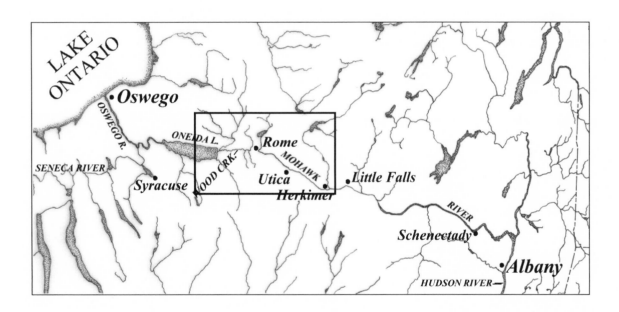

Thursday, October 10th. Embarked at six o'clock. After going a mile, M. M. Pharoux and Brunel got off to relieve the boatmen. Mr. DeZeng assured them that the ground was better, and gave them the directions so perfectly that after walking a mile they found the Fort Stanwix road, and arrived there soon after. M. Desjardins remained with the boat. The river became more and more winding, and constantly diminished in breadth and depth.

Between the lower and upper landings of Fort Stanwix, it is only half a mile by land, while the distance is two miles by water. In many places the boatmen were obliged to cut their way with the axe, where trees had fallen across and were floating or embedded. Finally, at ten o'clock, we met at Fort Stanwix.

The difficulty of approaching the head of Mohawk River navigation, near Fort Stanwix [Rome], varied with the season. In the typically dry weeks of September and October, water levels were at their lowest. Normally boats in this season were taken out at the Lower Landing and portaged overland.

But it was to the high water landing opposite Fort Stanwix that the boatmen on this expedition were determined to go. The conditions they encountered, almost blocking navigation, indicate a significant period of dis-use, suggesting that the Upper Landing had been generally abandoned by 1793.

It is likely that the road discovered by Pharoux and Brunel on their way to the Upper Landing was in fact the haul road from the Lower Landing to Fort Stanwix.

It was in the clearing surrounding the Upper Landing, and in the shadows of the ruins of Fort Stanwix, that the pair waited.

Meanwhile, the two bateaux for Canada, which had preceded us, were drawn out of the water by oxen and then loaded upon a double wagon, upon a beam adapted to the size of the bateau. They were borne upon this simple vehicle to the banks of Wood Creek. In waiting for the return of the wagons, we took breakfast on the grass at the place of landing.

The Fort Stanwix portage as it would have looked in the 1790s.

The portage between the Mohawk and Wood Creek is a mile and a quarter in length. It is to be observed that the waters of Wood Creek, which flows through Oneida into Lake Ontario and the St. Lawrence, and those of the Mohawk, which are tributary to the North river, have between them only a narrow space of ground, almost level with Wood Creek, and not more than two feet higher. A canal has been therefore projected to join these two rivers, or rather brooks. It is the same company as that of the Little Falls, under the name of the "Western Inland Navigation Company".

The expense of portage is the same as at the Little Falls. The vehicles having returned, our bateau was loaded upon a truck, and our goods upon a wagon, while we followed on foot. The road is very smooth.

Fort Stanwix, c. 1790.

"The site of Fort Stanwix or Fort Schuyler is in this village. It contains about two acres, and is a regular fortification, with four bastions and a deep ditch. The position is important in protecting the passage between the lakes and the Mohawk river. It is now in ruins, and partly demolished by Lynch, its proprietor. Since the Revolutionary War a block-house was erected here by the State, and is now demolished. About half a mile below the Fort, on the meadows, are the remains of an old fort, called Fort William; and about a mile west of Rome, near where Wood Creek enters the Canal, there was a regular fort, called Fort Newport. Wood Creek is here so narrow that you can step over it."

DeWitt Clinton, 1810[79]

We left to the right Fort Stanwix, which cost the English £60,000 Sterling to build, as a barrier against the French in Canada. The Americans seized it in the War of Independence. The English allied with the Indians came to besiege it, but a panic made them raise the siege, believing that General Schuyler was coming to fall upon them, although he was no nearer than Albany. Mr. Gansworth of Albany, an American General, defended this post, then in good condition, but now quite in ruins. This place is nevertheless one of the best located for building an arsenal and depot for Congress. The elevation of the fort is altogether of made land, which rendered its expense so enormous as compared with its small size.

Although standing at the division between the eastern and western watersheds, and in spite of having been a place of intense military activity for the bulk of the eighteenth century, this locale had not exhibited any significant growth by the early 1790s:

The situation at Fort Stanwix appears destined to

The Oneida Carry

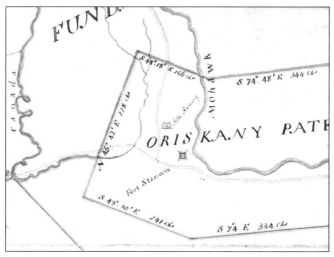
The Oneida Carrying Place in 1792.

Navigation westward from Old Fort Schuyler [Utica] did not present so great an obstacle as one might have suspected, for although the channel was narrow, it lacked, for the most part, the troublesome rifts of the channel below:

> "At noon, we reached Fort Stanwix, to which place with the aid of some art, the River continues adapted to inland navigation to boats of five ton burden."
>
> Elkanah Watson, 1791[80]

However, the traveler arriving at the head of Mohawk River navigation in the 1790s encountered a barrier to their westward voyage consisting of a mile or more of rugged lowland separating the Mohawk, which now ran in a north-south direction, from Wood Creek to the west. Here a portage had existed from the earliest days of travel, as no one could continue westward by any other means except Wood Creek. And it was here that the several British forts had been built in the mid-eighteenth century to guard this portage - the gateway to the Mohawk Valley and the fertile heartland of the region to the east for hostile forces descending from the west.

Although only a piece of low ground, with the waterways on either side of it differing less then two feet in elevation, the Oneida Carry was the summit of the entire inland route. It separated the eastward flowing Mohawk/Hudson watershed, with its outlet to the Atlantic at Manhattan, from the network of westward flowing waterways which eventually entered the St. Lawrence via Lake Ontario. These west flowing waterways began here with tiny Wood Creek.

In the season of high water, batteaux could come up the narrow Mohawk channel to a point nearly opposite Fort Stanwix, termed the "Upper Landing." From here boats were portaged along a crude road to the ruins of Fort Newport, on the banks of Wood Creek, about a mile to the west. There they could be reloaded and float downstream on the surge of water from Lynch's millpond. Such was the experience of General Lincoln's treaty expedition, which passed here in May of 1793:

> "Our boats and stores being all in Wood Creek, which at the head is little more than the width of a boat, and very little water running in it, being ponded above, for the use of mills, - when we were ready to go down, the gates were hoisted, and the creek was soon so full of water as to float the boats. We went down with the current, which would have been very agreeable, had not the creek been very full of timber, which had from time to time fallen into it. There are considerable lands on each side this river which are interval, and are often, in the spring, overflowed."
>
> Gen. Benjamin Lincoln, 1793[81]

The French party, passing this same place five months later, faced a frustrating lack of water on both sides of the carrying place that was more typical of the conditions encountered by travelers. On the Mohawk they could only come up as far as the "Lower Landing", nearly a mile downriver. Although their batteau was brought over to the same departure point on Wood Creek, near Fort Newport, it was forced to go down empty as far as Canada Creek, while its cargo went the same distance overland. This was often the case during the later summer months:

> "From the Mohawk, at fort Schuyler, to wood creek, there is a carrying place of one mile. In the spring there is generally a sufficiency of water to enable the batteaus to descend with their cargoes on board; but in summer season, it is necessary to convey the lading further by land, to Canada creek; and then there is some difficulty to float the empty boat down, though aided by a flush of water, collected in the mill dam, during the preceding night."
>
> William Weston, 1795[82]

become a great city. It lies in an open plain, - healthy, and exactly between the eastern and western waters. There is a large clearing round the old fort, and two or three scattering houses. No progress has, however, been made since I attended the treaty here in 1788, although the plan of a city is now contemplated.

Elkanah Watson, 1791[83]

It was the completion of the Rome Canal, in 1797, which transformed the embryonic settlement of Fort Schuyler into the village of Rome:

> Rome was laid out into a town, after the Canal was made or contemplated. It derives its principal advantages from this communication.

DeWitt Clinton, 1810[84]

Significant as this catalyst to local development was in 1797, a decade later a traveler through that canal saw little evidence of prosperity:

> Rome, formerly known as Fort Stanwix, is delightfully situated in an elevated and level country, commanding an extensive view for about ten miles around. This village consists at present of about eighty houses; but it seems quite destitute of every kind of trade, and rather upon the decline. The only spirit which I perceived stirring among them was that of *money digging*; and the old fort betrayed evident signs of the prevalence of this mania, as it had literally been turned inside out for the purpose of discovering concealed treasure.

Christian Schultz, 1807[85]

In 1793 the area surrounding the batteau landing on Wood Creek, the embarkation point for all traffic into the western waterways, was still in the most rudimentary stages of settlement, as revealed by the French journal.

> *We pitched our tent at the Wood Creek landing, as the stream was then almost dry. We could not go at once, but must wait for the waters of a mill, a quarter of a mile above, which the millers only let off when his pond was full, to the great detriment of travelers. This mill ought to be suppressed, when the plans in contemplation are executed.*
>
> *They had made some clearings at the place where we were encamped. After having pealed the bark the preceding year, to allow them to dry on the spot, or to make fences, all the underbrush and branches of the large trees are piled and burned. The trunks are cut into logs fourteen feet long, either for making fences around their clearings, or for sawing into plank, or for use in building log houses. All the unsound trees, as well as those that are dry or useless, are drawn together to be burned. They carefully gather their ashes, which they sell at from sixpence to a shilling a bushel, according to quality. An acre of well grown wood will yield three or four dollars worth of ashes, and actually costs eight dollars to make the clearing.*

> "The trees were chopped down, cut into convenient lengths, hauled together, and rolled into piles along with the limbs and brush and then the whole heap was burned. As soon as the fire had died, the ashes were gathered and leached and the resultant lye boiled in big potash kettles shaped like a half eggshell. The bottom of the kettle was cast thick so as to endure the strain of evaporating the lye down to a solid mass. The resultant cake was known as "black salts" and was dark in color through carbon and other impurities. This black salts was the form in which potash was sold by the farmer.
>
> "The usual price was about three dollars per hundred pounds...and this was sometimes the only cash money the pioneer saw. At this same period butter was fourteen cents a pound, but this was 'in trade' as the phrase was and not in cash. Sometimes after the burning of a huge log pile which represented a week of hard work, a sudden heavy shower would leach the ashes before they could be gathered, thus entailing a total loss.
>
> "The asheries which purchased the black salts from the producers were establishments thickly scattered over some parts of the state. At these asheries were brick kilns in which these crude salts were burned at a high temperature, consuming the carbon and fusing the mass into a bluish white and much purer product, then known as 'pearl ash'.
>
> "Not all farmers did even their own leaching and boiling. Some asheries maintained teams which went around the countryside collecting the ashes and paying eight cents a bushel for them, an actually surprising price in that day when a dollar seemed a very considerable sum of money."

Jared van Wagonen, 1953[86]

A typical rural ashery.

The production of potash was the first commercial venture for newly arrived settlers in the West, and would remain a major segment of agricultural production along the moving frontier for decades to come.

Batteaux carried thousands of barrels of potash and pearl ash down to Schenectady, to be forwarded on to European markets where the demand, in this time, was extremely high.

The company of three French explorers, three Yankee boatmen, and their German guide, were eyewitnesses, as they camped on the western fringes of the Mohawk Valley, to a scenario repeated innumerable times as settlers pushed the frontier into virgin forest.

Using fire as a tool, woodland was being rapidly converted into crop land:

The Rome Canal

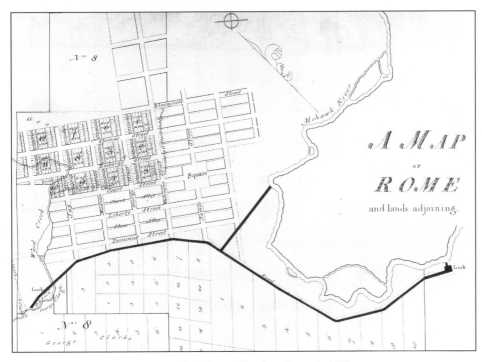

The route of the Rome Canal as shown in 1809.

Perhaps the most ambitious of the unprecedented navigation improvements of the Western Inland Lock Navigation Company, and without doubt the most strategically located, was the Rome Canal completed in 1797. This nearly two-mile long canal surmounted once and for all the Great Carrying Place that had, since prehistoric times, separated the eastward and westward flowing waterways that made up the inland transport route.

Although the route of this canal, which roughly followed the old portage road from the Mohawk "Lower Landing" to the Wood Creek landing near Fort Newport, crossed nearly level ground, excavation of the artificial channel had to be forced through virgin timber and swamps. Being built at the summit separating two major watersheds, the westerly of which was very poorly supplied with water, the Rome Canal had to be served by a long feeder, cut to it from a dam on the upper Mohawk, above Fort Stanwix.

Two locks, of a ten foot lift and an eight foot lift, allowed boats to pass into and out of the canal, with the lock on the Mohawk being served by an ample turning basin for boats waiting to pass into the river. In contrast to the wooden locks built at Little Falls a couple years earlier, and the stone locks to be built the next year at German Flatts, the locks of the Rome Canal were constructed of oversized bricks, made at a temporary brickyard built in Rome for the purpose.

In October of 1797 the first boats passed through the canal, enjoying an easy passage of just 40 minutes where a laborious portage of hours duration had existed previously. The following year General Schuyler reported on this, the most triumphant of his navigation improvements:

> "The length of the canal from the Mohawk to Wood Creek is two miles and three chains, one-third of which distance is cut through a gravelly hill from twelve to eighteen feet in depth. The width is thirty-seven and a half feet, and boats drawing three and a half feet of water may pass freely along it.
>
> A lateral branch is cut from the canal to the Mohawk River, upwards of five hundred yards in length, and from ten to twelve feet deep; by means of this feeder any quantity of water can be taken into the canal and discharged into Wood Creek or the Mohawk, as circumstances may require... There is a lock at each extremity of the canal, the one of ten feet lift, and the other of eight feet. Five handsome and substantial bridges are constructed over the canal and feeder."

Philip Schuyler, 1798[87]

The completion of the Rome Canal heralded a qualitative leap forward in inland navigation. Now the size of boats was no longer restricted by the demands of portaging. It was this canal, more than any of Schuyler's other improvements, that catalyzed the introduction of the Durham boat, and transformed the nature of water-borne transport in the region, if not in the nation.

Woodsman heading into the forest.

We witnessed this night a very singular spectacle. Some dry and hollow trees were burning at the top, and appeared like enormous flambeaux. Others formed columns of flame, being on fire the whole length of the trunk, while masses of flaming brush formed the base of the perspective. In the glare of all these fires, five tents belonging to as many bateaux, that were to go in the morning and then lay dry in Wood Creek - the portage wagons - the farm stock - the log buildings - the scattered piles of baggage - the camp fires, around which each party was making their supper, and all illuminated, presented a tableau, as seen from our tent, at once novel and picturesque.

This "spectacle", so often associated with the clearing of new settlements, could still be observed a generation later in the Genesee country:

As a great many settlers had lately fixed themselves in this part of the State, log-cabins were rising in all directions, and the work of clearing was going on rapidly. Each little open spot was covered with masses of burning timber; and the large trees that had been girdled the year before, were in many places in flames even to the tops, producing at night a very extraordinary and splendid effect.

William Newnham Blane, 1822[88]

The destruction of virgin forest appeared less romantically, however, to those who participated in it, as recalled by one who lived in that period:

Those men, with strong arms, hard hands, and iron frame, might daily be seen, wending their way with knapsack on their backs, an axe lashed on the outside, and with gun on their shoulder, seeking a favourite resting place, prepared to grapple with the hardships and privations of frontier life, till the forests could be prostrated, the country improved, and the modes of civilized life and luxurious living, could take the place of unmitigated toil.

Levi Beardsley, c1791[89]

Rather than something to be admired and preserved, the magnificent forests of the western frontier represented a frustrating nuisance to those attempting to establish an agricultural society.

CHAPTER SIX

Upper Wood Creek

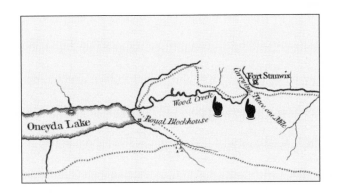

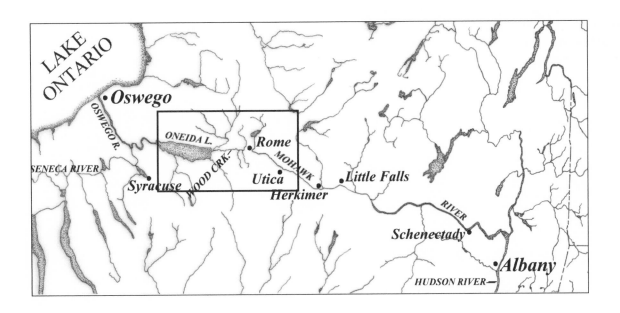

The passage of boats from the eastward flowing headwaters of the Mohawk navigation, at Fort Stanwix, to the westward flowing waters of Wood Creek brought navigators to a point in the stream just below Dominick Lynch's millpond, near the site of old Fort Newport.

Even in periods of good water, help from the millpond was desirable, as the stream at the landing was almost unimaginably tiny:

> ...this day got our batteaux &c. over to Wood Creek - Wood Creek at this place being no more than a shallow Brook of about 10 or 12 feet wide.
>
> William Hartshorne, 1793[90]

In the dry season, the miller's assistance was essential. But even with this added surge of water, passage down the upper section of Wood Creek was difficult:

> Although aided by the sluice, we progressed with infinite difficulty. In many places the windings are so sudden, and so short, that while the bow of the boat was ploughing in the bank on one side, her stern was rubbing hard against the opposite shore. In some places our men were obliged to drag the boats by main strength; and in others, the boughs and limbs were so closely interwoven, and so low, as to arch the creek completely over, and oblige all hands to lie flat. These obstacles, together with sunken logs and trees, rendered our progress extremely difficult, - often almost impracticable.
>
> Elkanah Watson, 1791[91]

Boatmen looked forward to reaching the junction with Canada Creek, several miles to the west, where some relief was to be found in the added water. But reaching Canada Creek was not always easy:

> On their arrival at the landing-place, the boat was unladen, hauled out of the water, and conveyed, together with the cargo, on wagons across the carrying-place, to Wood creek, where, if it happened that there was a sufficiency of water, the cargo was taken on board again, and the boat, aided by a flush from a mill-dam, descended the creek to the Oneida Lake; but if the water was low (which was generally the case from the beginning of June to October), the lading was conveyed five miles further to Canada Creek, along a road scarcely passable. The delay and consequent expense at this season was very great...
>
> Philip Schuyler, 1798[92]

So it was with the French expedition.

Friday, October 11th. The flotilla of bateaux was unable to move until about nine o'clock. The miller having detained the waters, the men, who were there in numbers, made him open the sluices. Notwithstanding this momentary relief, it was still so low that M. M. Pharoux and Desjardins undertook to go by land to the mouth of Little Canada Creek, where the bateau would find some water to float in, from the junction of the two streams.

It was seven miles from the portage to Captain Reynis' tavern, built at the junction of the two creeks. We crossed on the bridge in front of the mill, which had so much delayed our movement, and found the road very bad. Although causewayed in marshy places, it was built of trunks of trees bedded in the ground, crosswise and side by side. These causeways had been neither repaired nor kept up, and the road was so cut up in many places, that it was often very difficult to get along even upon foot.

Travel along this westward extension of the portage road at Rome was necessitated by periods of low water, as the journalists experienced in mid-October of 1793. Batteaux were sent down empty from the landing below Lynch's millpond to the Canada Creek junction, while passengers, often encumbered with baggage, struggled over the land route. Another party, passing this way in the Spring of this same year, made note of the situation:

> It took up this day to get the boats and baggage across the carrying place, one mile, to Wood Creek, a small stream about ten yards wide, and very shoal. Five of our company, on the morning of the 17th, took wagon, and proceeded down Wood Creek by land. But such a ride I never had before. Pole bridges, slotches of mud and water, and short nob hills, sometimes one side, then another, like to overset. And the wagon, very shackling, made the tour very disagreeable. However, in about three hours, we arrived at Captain Ranney's, at the junction of Canada Creek, the whole of the eight miles, a dreary hemlock and beech wilderness, without inhabitant that I saw, except musquetoes in thousands. It appears well adapted for their existence.
>
> Jacob Lindley, 1793[93]

It was to this same tavern that the three Frenchmen walked during the morning of October 11th.

We arrived at noon at Captain Reynis' tavern. It was a very good one, and we found there a great many travelers.

Here they awaited the arrival of the batteau they had left at the landing in Rome, and here, again, they were able to examine the nature of the stream that would carry them west.

The Wood Creek derives its name from the quantity of wood with which it was encumbered. The canal company has cleared it out as far as to this junction, yet, notwithstanding these repairs, our bateau did not rejoin us until half past four o'clock in the evening, and our people were so fatigued that we could not think of going any further. We pitched our tent at the mouth of the Little Canada Creek, which forms the boundary of the Rosevelt Patent and extends from thence to Lake Ontario, and to the Constable purchase.

During the next ten years, this isolated outpost of civilization would grow to include two taverns and a small warehouse for goods awaiting forwarding, all standing along the north shore of Wood Creek. Almost forgotten on a low ridge opposite, were the remains of an even more isolated outpost, constructed by the British in the 1750s:

Canada Creek Junction

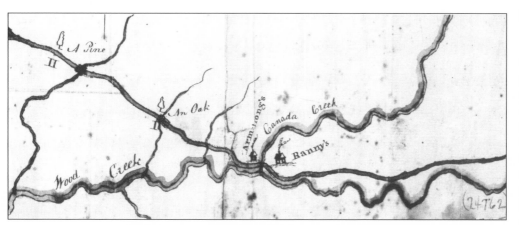

A map of the road passing the junction at Canada Creek, c. 1795.

The junction of Canada Creek with Wood Creek was a stopping place of some import, since prehistoric times. Aside from incidental clearings associated with the innumerable boatmen's and soldier's camps pitched around this intersection in the eighteenth century, no improvements were made here much before the 1790s.

The tiny fort that was the only occupation of any substance before then, Fort Rickey, stood on the south bank of the stream and had long since rotted away. But by 1792, the family of Archibald Armstrong had staked its claim to the spot:

> "At the junction of Canada Creek and Wood Creek is a good farm; possessed by the Widow Armstrong. She has about twenty acres cleared and it is a good situation for business, it being always a halting place for batteaux."
>
> James Cockburn, 1792[94]

In this time, a woods road ran through the area along the north bank, westward toward Oswego, and a primitive bridge no doubt carried land travelers across Canada Creek to the opposite bank. Ten years earlier, however, one was left to devise their own crossing:

> "On arriving at Canada Creek, a tributary of Wood Creek, two trees were fallen to bridge the stream."
>
> Capt. Alexander Thompson, 1783[95]

The widow Armstrong's home served as a public house in the 1790s, and her hospitality was cited by at least one grateful traveler:

> "There came up a great rain storm, with thunder and lightning; we proceeded rapidly, and discovered after a few minutes a light in a small cottage. It was that of Widow Armstrong on the corner of Wood and Canada creeks, 7 miles from Fort Stanwix... we are now engaged in drying our clothes by a good fire and Mrs. Armstrong is preparing our supper and couches. On Sunday we bid adieu to the good widow Armstrong, who left nothing undone which was in her power to render her homely cottage comfortable to us."
>
> Adrian Vanderkemp, 1792[96]

Eventually, however, another house, perhaps built specifically as a tavern, was erected on the opposite side of Canada Creek. It is without doubt that it was Seth Ranney's ["Reynis'"] tavern at which the Frenchmen waited for their batteau to catch up to them in October of 1793. Ranney had come to the area around 1786 and had initially settled near Fort Stanwix. There he built the first two story frame house in Rome, later used as a tavern in 1792 and a storehouse in 1793.

He apparently operated the tavern at the Canada Creek junction in 1793, which later became "Gilbert's", a place much noted in journals of the early 1800s:

> "Gilbert's house is a decent comfortable house, considering the little resort of travelers. The grounds around it are overflown by the creek, and the situation unhealthy."
>
> DeWitt Clinton, 1810[97]

The Gilbert and Ranney families were related by marriage, and it was Thomas Gilbert with whom General Schuyler lodged in 1802 as he supervised the construction of the first of the four wooden locks built in Wood Creek by the Western Inland Lock Navigation Company. A number of his reports from the field were written from "Mr. Gilbert's house near Canada Creek..." Gilbert had a storehouse near the bank of Wood Creek in which he held goods waiting to be forwarded by wagon or batteau. The tiny commercial complex which grew up here, isolated in the forest, was an oasis on the margin of an otherwise dismal navigation down Wood Creek to Oneida Lake.

Just after passing the store-house, which is situated below the last lock, a considerable rapid stream, called Canada Creek, unites with Wood Creek from the right. This is nearly as large as the former, but not navigable. Immediately opposite their junction are the remains of Fort Rickey, a fortress of some consequence during the old Indian wars; but at present employed to a better purpose, being covered with a good orchard.

Christian Schultz, 1807[98]

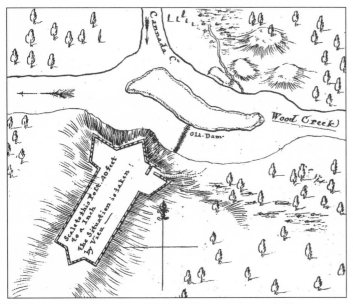

Fort Rickey, at the Canada Creek junction, c. 1758.

The lock mentioned in the 1807 account was one of the four wooden locks built in this stretch of Wood Creek in 1802 and 1803 to provide a deep water navigation for the larger boats of that period, including the huge Durham boats.

It was particularly these larger craft that were frustrated by the lack of water above Canada Creek, but even the smaller batteaux found navigation very tenuous:

I have heretofore remarked that the mode adopted to render Wood Creek navigable was to collect the water by means of a mill dam, thus creating a sudden flood to carry boats down. Some times boats did not succeed in getting through to deep water on one flood and were consequently obliged to await a second one. As we were coursing down the creek during the voyage on our first flood we overtook a boat which had grounded after the previous one, the navigators of which were in the water ready to push her off as soon as the coming tide should reach them.

Augustus Porter, 1790[99]

The bottleneck which this section of poor navigation produced for shipping, particularly that coming in from the west, threatened the success of the Rome Canal [1797] and the viability of the navigation company. It was this threat that prompted Schuyler to complete the improvement of the upper section of Wood Creek:

Above Gilbert's the Company have erected four wooden locks, which are absolutely necessary, at a small expense, when compared with their stone locks at the Little Falls...

DeWitt Clinton, 1810[100]

The lock near what was then Gilbert's Tavern, at Canada Creek, was completed in 1802. It was the most westerly of the locked canal improvements of Schuyler's company, and enhanced the minimal commercial development here, represented in 1793 by just one, isolated tavern.

We dined and supped in the tavern, which is surrounded by the woods, although a part has been newly cleared. M. M. Pharoux and Brunel visited the woods in the afternoon to hunt, but they found no game. On every hand it was a fearful solitude. You are stopped sometimes by impassable swamps, and at other times by heaps of trees that have fallen from age, or have been overturned by storms, and among which an infinite number of insects and many squirrels find a retreat. On every hand we see the skeletons of trees overgrown with moss, and in every stage of decay. The Capillain and other plants and shrubs spring out of these decaying trunks, presenting, at once, the images of life and of death.

"We went this day as far as Gilbert's Tavern on the north side of the creek, six and a-half miles by water, and four and a-half miles by land, from Rome.

"We saw a bright red-bird about the size of a blue-bird. Its wings were tipped with black, and the bird uncommonly beautiful. It appeared to have no song, and no one present seemed to know its name. I saw but three besides in the whole course of my tour, one on the Ridge Road west of the Genesee River. It is, therefore, a rara avis.

"On the banks of the creek were plenty of boneset, the Canada shrub, said to be useful in medicine, and a great variety of beautiful flowering plants. Wild gooseberry bushes, wild currants, and wild hops were also to be seen. The gooseberries were not good; the hops are said to be as good as the domestic ones. In the long weeds and thick underwood we were at first apprehensive of rattlesnakes, of which we were told there are three kinds - the large and the small, and the dark rattlesnake. But neither here nor in any part of our tour did we see this venomous reptile. The only animals we saw on this stream were the black squirrel and the hare, as it is called in Albany, a creature white in winter, of the rabbit kind, although much larger."

DeWitt Clinton, 1810[101]

An eyewitness image of the Canada Creek junction in 1815, revealing the covered lock of the WILNC (center, background).

CHAPTER SEVEN

Lower Wood Creek

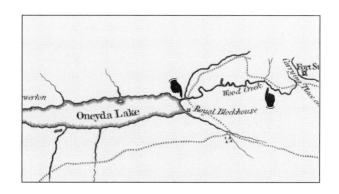

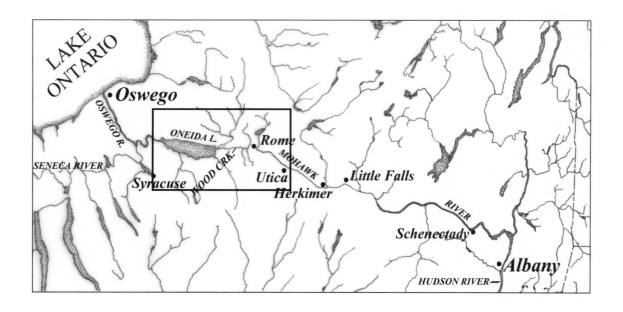

O f all the inland navigation from Schenectady to Oswego, on the Great Lakes, there was no more fragile passage than that down Wood Creek. So noted James Cockburn during field surveys in the region in 1792:

Wood Creek at present is so crooked and so full of timber that is with difficulty a common batteau can pass.

James Cockburn, 1792[102]

The removal of the obstructions to transportation which this tiny stream presented was so critical, in a region through which no roads worthy of the name as yet passed, that General Schuyler made it his first priority on assuming the presidency of the Western Inland Lock Navigation Company in 1792. In July of the following year he announced his plans:

The western Wood Creek is comprised to extend from the landing at Fort Stanwix to the Oneida Lake, between 24 & twenty eight miles, and such were the obstructions from sunken & other trees when the water was low that a boat could not descend in less than two days, altho passages had been cut through the heaps of timber which extend from the bottom to far above the surface of the water, hence the impediments to be removed there are probably greater than between Fort Ann & Lake Champlain and yet a Mr. Richardson ... has undertaken to clear the Western Wood Creek,... and is to cut thro 4 or five necks of land, and to clear the banks, the whole for £900...

Philip Schuyler, 1793[103]

It is not surprising, therefore, that the Frenchmen observed evidence of these activities as they passed down Wood Creek in their batteau. It is perhaps fortuitous that they availed themselves of the batteau, and the company, of one of Schuyler's contractors in their passage below Canada Creek, as they undoubtedly received the benefit of his running commentary on the work underway.

Saturday, October 12th. Left at half past seven in the morning. We discharged a part of our baggage into an empty boat belonging to a contractor for clearing Wood Creek, who was endeavoring to go down to rejoin his workmen. The beginning of our route was still difficult, on account of the very little depth of water and the trees that had fallen in. The creek is so small that the branches of the trees on the opposite banks unite over head. There are no clearings either on the right hand or the left. With the exception of some paths made in the woods by the Indians, there are neither tracks nor roads beyond the Canada Creek, whose course is very sinuous and the banks low. Mr. Scriba, one of the proprietors of the Rosevelt patent, has actually marked a road from the Canada Creek to New Rotterdam, an establishment that he has formed upon Oneida Lake.

Along the creek we saw piles of wood made by the workmen engaged on the repairs. They cut large trunks into pieces, eight or ten feet long, and float them to the places where deep water is to be maintained at the entrance of Oneida Lake. They take the rest to the bends of the creek which are to be closed when the cuttings for

straightening the channel have been made. The bottom of the creek is an angular gravel but slightly rounded.

At two miles from where we started, the Black Creek joins its waters, flowing over a gravelly bed, which is washed down in the spring. Mr. DeZeng observed to us that the height of land forming the dividing point of the waters was at Fort Stanwix, in this part of the State of New York, and that on the lakes the east wind brought rain, while on the Mohawk, and thence to the Atlantic Ocean, it was the west wind.

They have cut many of the trees that overhung the stream, which has made it lighter and facilitated the navigation. On our left the lands are reserved by the Oneida Indians, while on the right lies the Rosevelt patent. Beyond Black Creek the bottom is a fine sand, and the low banks present a country very fit for conversion into meadows.

Within a few miles of the start of their journey down the stream, the journalists were to come upon a sequence of truly dramatic and unprecedented waterway projects; thirteen short canals undertaken that summer by Schuyler's contractors. Executed with experimental engineering in the depths of the wilderness, these cuts are some of the earliest artificial waterways in North America.

At four miles from where we started, we came to the first cutting; narrow and very straight and without slope. We are told that in high water the river will soon make a channel here, and of itself finish the work. In the meantime, until Nature, with her all-powerful and most active hand, shall finish the labor thus imperfectly begun by the Americans, we had great difficulty in passing these pretended canals, and not without fear that the banks might cave in and bury our bateau in an instant.

Not far from thence we met the men and oxen of the contractor, busy in removing from the creek some fallen trees. In the part already cleared, there remained a few that were not very troublesome, which had probably been left to be cleared out by some future inundation. If this contractor would use a windlass, or only a cable and pulleys fastened to the trees along the bank, he would do thrice the amount of work in half the time; but no mechanical appliances were used, and everything was done by the sheer force of men and animals. They appeared not even to know the use of a ladder, much less of a crane, or of the simplest labor saving power. This first cutting shortens the distance half a mile.

At eight miles beyond is another cutting worked in the same way, which shortens the creek three quarters of a mile. A little before reaching it there occurs on the left side a place called the <u>White Oak Orchard</u>.

Although one of the most historic sites along Wood Creek in this era, and throughout the eighteenth century, the "Oak Orchard" is given only a passing notice in the journal of the expedition. It may have escaped notice at all, had it not been for the probable commentary of the contractor, accompanying them in the company batteau, or of Major DeZeng.

"Oak Orchard"

T he "Oak Orchard" consisted of a sandy knoll standing in a sharp bend of Wood Creek. Prior to the cutting of a canal across this neck of land by Schuyler's company in 1793, the meander loop provided a convenient batteau landing. The elevated hill, presumably devoid of undergrowth due to the oak grove that had established itself there, provided the camping ground.

As there is no evidence of Native occupation of the site, we may assume the first occupant was La Whiten De Wardenou; a Frenchman who came here in 1796, or early in 1797. There was much romance attributed to this family in nineteenth century histories:

> "In some respects, the truth was stranger than the fiction. De Wardenou and 'Celeste'... were married, and embarked for America... Here misfortune overtook him, and he nearly lost his all, when they emigrated to the vicinity of the Oneida Lake. Even here trouble sought them out. A lovely little child, their first born, sickened and died, in 1797. No coffin could be procured. Its little cradle was substituted. A few years after, when the Western Inland Lock Navigation Company were about erecting a structure at the Oak Orchard, in digging for the foundation, they disinterred a cradle containing the skeleton of a child. This, no doubt, was the remains of the child of De Wardenou, the first deceased from a natural cause, within the limits of Verona."
>
> Pomeroy Jones, 1851[104]

Apparently De Wardenou had abandoned his homestead at Oak Orchard almost immediately after his child's death, as travelers later that year note his absence:

> "At last got up to Oak Orchard... when the men being much fatigued, and the sun almost down, concluded to rest for this night. Here we found several boats which had come down. The crews gave us very discouraging accounts of the scarcity of water above... Slept at Oak Orchard where a man lives who has bought out the Frenchman who formerly lived there."
>
> Alexander Coventry, 1797[105]

The structure cited in the nineteenth century account, being built here in 1802 by Schuyler's contractors, was the lock tender's house for a new timber lock proposed to be built the following year to improve the navigation of the lower part of Wood Creek. Evidence that the rift at Oak Orchard was the first obstacle to eastward navigation encountered by the big boats coming up toward Rome is found in several journals written in the opening years of the nineteenth century. General Schuyler himself confirms this, when he writes in 1802 that once improvements are made in the rivers to the west of Oneida Lake, "...there will be a complete navigation from Oak Orchard to about a mile up the Seneca River beyond Three River Point." On his return trip up Wood Creek from Sylvan Beach, Schuyler chose the relative comfort of the spot to stop, as so many had before him:

> "...ascended Wood Creek. Reached the Oak Orchard, a distance of 8 miles, at 10 o'clock. Breakfasted and proceeded at 12 and reached Canada Creek at half past three."
>
> Philip Schuyler, 1802[106]

continued on next page

continued from page 49

Although the lock at Oak Orchard was never constructed, the locktender's house was finished in October. It was 1 1/2 stories high, with a cellar, brick chimney, and an attic for Company equipment and supplies. The living quarters were to be covered in plaster on lath and well finished, making this one of the grander houses on Wood Creek:

"The house should be 20 feet by 36 feet, with a chimney in the middle. The posts 12 feet long, which will afford a tolerable garret as a store room for the company's effects required in the construction of the lock. The sills of the house should be 2 1/2 feet above the surface of the earth and under one half of it a cellar, the walls of which to be a frame of pitch pine with plank behind the posts to support the earth. If you can procure any person to erect the house, by contract on which you may deem reasonable terms, I wish you to do so - The house should be erected on the south side of the creek as nearly opposite to the lock as circumstances will permit."

Philip Schuyler, 1802[107]

The Company carpenter was brought down from the construction sites of the locks on the upper end of Wood Creek to take care of the house, which apparently was abandoned when the plans for this lock failed to find approval with the Directors of the Company:

"I went to Oak Orchard Monday to examine the house built there & found it completed. & on Wednesday I sent Ambrose Jones (one of our carpenters) with his family to live there & take care of the house. He is to work one month felling timber on the banks of the Creek & have wages as an axman - in case any work is to be done [on the lock] this winter, he will of course be employed. I thought this the best method I could take to secure the house from injury until further orders from the Committee."

George Huntington, 1802[108]

There was concern the following year that the house, now of no use, was at risk:

"If the house at Oak Orchard should be uninhabited I apprehend it may be much injured and perhaps exposed to conflagration, if fire should be left in it, by careless or malignant boatmen."

Philip Schuyler, 1803[109]

Evidence does not permit us to know if this historic structure was eventually burned, or found use at the hands of later settlers.

As recently as May of this same year, General Benjamin Lincoln, en route to a treaty conference in Ohio, had used this site as an encampment for his small flotilla of batteaux:

We encamped at night, for the first time, at what is called the Oak Orchard, from its being a high point of land on which are a few oaks. Oaks are not to be seen in general in this part of the country.

Gen. Benjamin Lincoln, 1793[110]

A Quaker riding in another of General Lincoln's batteaux also cites the location:

...at 6 in the evening encamped by a place called the Oak Orchard, 18 miles by water from Fort Stanwix - here is a high spot on which are a few Oak Trees...

William Hartshorne, 1793[111]

These were only the latest in a long procession of batteaux to stop here, including the monumental fleets of military vessels which plied back and forth through this channel in the French and Indian War and the Revolution.

The dry, sandy hill provided an attractive elevation above the swamps and damp of the rest of the waterway, and apparently supplied the only drinkable water to be had between Canada Creek and Oneida Lake:

In the whole course of our navigation on Wood Creek we saw not one building and found but one spring, called Oak orchard, which was four minutes filling a small glass and the water of which was but of middling quality.

Rochefoucault Liancourt, 1795[112]

With only passing mention of this significant location, the 1793 expedition continued down the narrow channel.

A mile beyond there is a third cutting which shortens half a mile. There is no work done in that part of the stream destined to be filled up. The fourth cutting shortens three quarters of a mile and its bed is already encumbered by the trees and sand that have tumbled in - but all this, they say, will go off in high water.

A fifth cutting also shortens the distance half a mile. The ancient bed of the creek is filled in with wood. The sixth cutting is not yet filled with water and will also shorten half a mile. It is three feet deep in the solid ground and two feet in the sand beneath.

The seventh cutting, filled with water and already

The Wood Creek Cuts

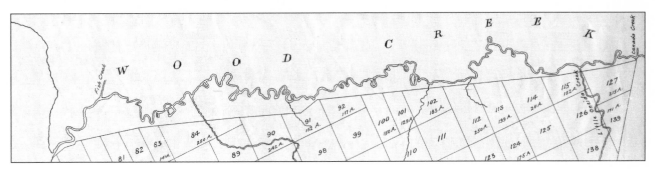

A map showing all thirteen 1793 Wood Creek cuts, c. 1796.

Although extraordinarily shallow and narrow, Wood Creek remained a navigable link between the Mohawk River and Oneida Lake in this period. Running primarily through deposits of sand and clay, its channel was unusually free of rock and gravel, but often cluttered with timber.

The boatmen who navigated this route in the eighteenth century, whether for military or commercial purposes, were forced annually to cut a passage through innumerable fallen trees and sunken logs. But beyond this, the meandering course that Wood Creek followed increasingly frustrated boatmen:

> "We arrived ere long at the singular neck of land, about a mile in length, and so small, that by standing, we discovered the water at the opposite side. This was a tedious circumnavigation indeed. We might have passed it in a few seconds if the passage had been cut."

> Adrian Vanderkemp, 1792[113]

Although this "neck" was the most frustrating of the many meanders, it was characteristic of the problems faced when navigating this 28 miles of narrow stream:

> "In the summer of 1793, the directors caused wood creek to be cleared of the timber which had fallen into it, in such quantity as almost altogether obstructed the navigation; and as the serpentine course of the creek greatly increased the distance, from its source to its mouth, beyond that of a straight line, thirteen Isthmus's were cut, which made a reduction in the distance of more than seven miles. Its banks are, however, so thickly covered with trees of the largest size, and so many of those, either from decay, or by the force of the winds, are annually thrown into the creek, that it will be indispensably necessary to clear the banks of the timber, for the distance of four rods at least, and contracts are proposed to be made for that purpose."

> Philip Schuyler, 1796[114]

This press of virgin forest right to the water's edge not only provided a never ending supply of falling trees to block the passage, but also prevented the use of the banks as a towing path or walkway by which to relieve boats grounded in the shallows. Little improvement in this situation was noted at the beginning of the next century:

> "I could not perceive that the necessary improvement of cutting off the trees on the margin of the river has been much attended to - the consequence is that trees are constantly falling in - & where the cuts have been made at the necks - the stumps are settling into the bed of the channels which are extremely dangerous to descending boats when the water is rapid.

> Elkanah Watson, 1800[115]

The Frenchmen passing down Wood Creek in October of 1793 enjoyed the relative advantages of a newly cleared channel and observed the creation of this unprecedented series of short "canals", just being cut across the thirteen necks of land along the stream's course. From their timely and detailed observations, the only one's known to describe this project underway, we can reconstruct the primitive engineering being applied here in the summer of 1793.

These cuts, among the earliest artificial waterways for navigation in North America, were created by first excavating a ditch, about ten feet deep and half as wide, across each neck, and blocking the natural channel at the upstream end with logs cut off the line of that ditch. The first high water episode to follow, forced to run through the tiny ditch, would quickly carve out a "canal" that was soon indistinguishable from the rest of Wood Creek, and equally as navigable.

encumbered by the same causes, shortens half a mile. The eighth, which has been finished six months, is already much enlarged by the stream. It shortens the distance half a mile, and from the experience here gained, the contractor has not given more attention in excavating the works above.

We passed through a ninth cut, in a sandy soil, which shortens half a mile. The bottom is clay with the remains of trees imbedded. A tenth cut, which is very short, saves a quarter of a mile, [the ground good.] An eleventh cut, [which is very short in sandy soil with a bottom of clay, shortens a fourth of a mile.]

The twelfth cut, which is in a vegetable mold upon sand, is not over five toises long, yet it saves a mile and a quarter. The thirteenth and last cutting, which is already greatly enlarged by nature, in a distance of ten toises shortens a third of a mile.

These tiny canals, finished within a few months, drew almost no mention in the journals of subsequent travelers. In part this may have been due to the fact that once completed, the redirected waters of Wood Creek quickly eroded these cuts to match the rest of the natural channel. Certainly no other account but this one has captured, at precisely the most opportune moment, the details of their construction.

These thirteen cuttings shorten the navigation about seven miles and a half, but it is to be apprehended that the water, when less detained by the bends, will flow more swiftly and not give so much depth as before.

At the outlet of the trenches we came to a very large bateau of frame work belonging to the contractor, which had been built upon the Seneca River. In time of high water he had taken it up thus far, with all his implements and provisions. This gave us an idea of the enterprising spirit of the Americans, who will undertake anything. His bateau has actually arrived, but it must wait till next year until, by the help of high water, it can be moved.

Here, without realizing it, these travelers may have witnessed the first Durham boat to enter the waterways of eastern New York.

The common batteau was 30 feet long and, with a crew of three, carried a ton and a half. The typical Durham boat was 60 feet long, and with a crew of five or six, frequently carried 10 or 11 tons. This type of large river freighter would replace the batteau as Schuyler's canals and other improvements eliminated the portages that had kept boats small and light in the past.

The contractor selected by Schuyler to clear timber from Wood Creek, and for the cutting of the thirteen canals across necks of land, was John Richardson, a merchant of Cayuga, a small village at the upper end of Cayuga Lake. It was only five months earlier, in May of 1793, that he had been recommended to Schuyler for the work along Wood Creek by a letter in which he was connected with the creation of an unusual boat:

John Richardson ... has lately constructed a boat of thirteen tons burden on a plan which has never before been adopted in this State, and he has been so successful that we have no doubt but his improvement will prove extensively useful. He has brought this boat from the upper end of

Cayuga Lake with a freight of six tons without the least inconvenience til about five miles up from the mouth of Wood Creek, & nothing but the obstructions by logs & trees prevented his coming up to Fort Stanwix...

Jonas Platt & Elias Kane, 1793[116]

On November 3rd, 1793, just three weeks after the Frenchmen observed his grounded boat, Richardson wrote from Wood Creek to his friend in Little Falls, John Porteus:

Sir, I am much disappointed respecting the finishing of Wood Creek, which would been completed some time ago if there had been a flood. I do suppose that I could finish in every respect agreeable to contract in one week with the assistance of a flood, but as it is got so late in the season, I conclude to let it lay till Spring. I have a great wish to see you before I go home, but the situation of my matters at home will not admit. It is almost five month since I have seen my family. The nature of my work in Wood Creek was such, when I would be away more than a day at a time the men would get discouraged and be for quiting.

John Richardson, 1793[117]

Durham boats hauling freight.

There can be little doubt that it was Richardson's revolutionary boat that lay stuck in the lower end of Wood Creek. It may have even been Richardson himself that piloted the smaller batteau alongside the Frenchmen, as they descended the stream, explaining his engineering achievements to a captive audience.

Prior to the completion of these extraordinary improvements in the channel of Wood Creek, navigation here, as recorded in 1791, was memorable for its meandering and notable for its rare, but often dramatic accidents:

The innumerable crooks and turns in Wood creek, carried us to every point of the compass. We counted one hundred and eighty-eight distinct points of land, from Canada creek, on both sides. At a place called the Neck, four miles from Oneida lake, we measured seven paces across, and our boat had to go a mile round to meet us on the opposite side.

A ludicrous scene took place this morning, which had nearly proved fatal to one of our men, by the name of Capron, who steered Gen. Van Cortland's boat. This fellow is a confounded glutton; - he devoured at a meal more salt pork than two common men, and was of great bulk. In the act of doubling short round a point of land, propelled by a swift current, immediately after gorging himself with pork,

&c. and half asleep, a sly limb, which hung over the point, struck him across the breast, and capsized him fairly backwards, with a perpendicular plunge, to the bottom of the creek.

As we were directly in the rear of that boat, I distinctly saw this neat exploit. He rose along side of our boat, like a young whale, spouting water from his nostrils and mouth, and splashing the surface with both his hands. We reached him just in time to save him from sinking a second time. He fastened himself on the side of our boat, but as it was impossible to get him in, the other boats came to our aid, - and, between both, we towed him ashore, to the great diversion of our men, who gave him three cheers, as he touched bottom with his feet.

Elkanah Watson, 1791[118]

DeWitt Clinton, soon to be Governor of the State, sustained more insult than injury in a mishap at Oak Orchard in 1810:

We rose early in the morning [at Gilbert's Tavern at the Canada Creek junction], and breakfasted at the Oak-Orchard, six miles from Gilbert's on the south side of the river. The ground was miry, and, in stepping into the boat, my foot slipped, and I was partly immersed in the creek. The captain assisted me in getting out. The dampness of the weather, and the sun being hardly risen, induced me, for greater precaution, to change my clothes. This trifling incident was afterwards magnified by the papers into a serious affair.

DeWitt Clinton, 1810[119]

A couple of years before, Christian Schultz encountered the treachery of the overhanging trees along the lower Wood Creek channel:

The navigation of Wood Creek is not attended with any hazard of drowning, or even staving a boat to pieces; but the sudden turns of the stream, overhung with the trunks and branches of trees, are not without their dangers, as I experienced.

The boat being under considerable way, at a sudden bend of the river, we unexpectedly discovered a tree, which had been overturned by some late storm, stretched across the stream, and supported by its branches in such a manner as not to touch the water. Our captain immediately perceiving that it would be impossible to stop the boat in so short a distance, directed every one to take care of himself, and ran the boat under a part of the tree of sufficient height to admit it; but, as it was much lumbered up a-mid-ships, several of the articles were swept overboard. Amongst these were my traveling trunk and portable desk, containing my money, papers and apparel.

The desk floated along side, but the trunk, being very heavy, sunk to the level of the water and stopped against some of the branches. As it required some time, however, to stop the boat and go up the stream, the trunk, on being taken up, was full of water, to the no little injury of my papers and clothing.

The most laughable circumstance attending this accident was, that on missing my companion, and looking round for him, I discovered him in the top of the tree which we had passed under, whither he had jumped to avoid being crushed, as he had not time to get aft where the boat was less lumbered.

Christian Schultz, 1807[120]

Having avoided any of the misfortune attending the navigation of Wood Creek by others, Pharoux, Desjardins, and Brunel continued westward to an improving situation.

Here we left the contractor and loaded our own bateau. The more we advanced, the more the stream widened and deepened, and about four miles beyond the last cutting we entered Fish Creek, although they are accustomed to call it Wood Creek *to the lake. The Fish Creek is altogether the larger, and should not be robbed of its name by a brook, which is the only term the Wood Creek deserves at the place of junction. We there found the river quite wide and deep, and the lands along the shore very low and wet. The west wind was prevailing, and we heard the noise of the waves on the lake.*

Below its junction with Fish Creek, Wood Creek became so much deeper and wider as to be more navigable than even the Upper Mohawk. The stable mud banks and bottom of the stream eliminated the troublesome rocks that made many smaller streams unnavigable, even for canoes.

Although not part of the inland corridor connecting the Great Lakes with Albany, Fish Creek was a valuable waterway in its own right:

Fish Creek enters Wood Creek, a mile from the lake, on the north side. It is much larger and deeper, and derives its name from the excellent fish with which it abounds, up to the Falls, which are ten miles from its mouth. It is frequented by great numbers of salmon; and we saw Indians with their spears at work after that fish, and met two canoes going on the same business, with their pine knots and apparatus ready for the attack. The Indians have reserved the land on each side of this creek, in order to secure themselves the benefit of fishing.

The confluence of these streams makes a considerable river from this place to the Oneida Lake, deep, wide, and gloomy, and resembling the fabled Avernus. You can see the track of its black and muddy waters a considerable distance in the great basin into which it discharges.

DeWitt Clinton, 1810[121]

Clearly there was some pressure to improve the navigation of the lower end of Fish Creek, for in 1809 a cut was made across the neck of a very large meander, just upstream from the junction. In technique it resembled those made along Wood Creek 15 years before, but in scope it was vastly larger, both in its length and in the size of the meander loop it shortened.

The contrast here must have impressed the boatmen, not only because of the ease of navigation below this point, but because the lands along Wood Creek were so unsuitable for settlement. The spring floods common in this locale had been noted the year before:

I am doubtful whether a settlement could be made along Wood Creek, the good land being so narrow; and I imagine that in high waters it is all overflowed, in which case there is no retreat - the swamp being lower than the land where they must build.

Mr. James Dean the Oneyda Interpreter formerly settled about a mile above Fish Creek, where the vestiges of his improvements are to be seen. I am informed he quit the land on account of its being s much overflowed.

James Cockburn, 1792[122]

The valley of Fish Creek, however, offered a far more favorable environment:

Wood Creek is joined on the right by Fish Creek, which, with more propriety, might be denominated a river, as it is at least five times as large as Wood Creek, but navigable for ten miles only. This stream is much resorted to by the Oneida Indians, on account of the great quantities of salmon and other fish which it affords; as, likewise, from its being favoured with numerous springs of excellent water, which, in this country, is considered as a very great luxury.

Christian Schultz, 1807[123]

Dean's Landing

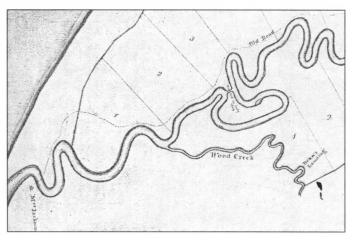

A map of Fish Creek showing Dean's Landing, c. 1809.

James Dean, who had served as an interpreter with the Oneidas during the Revolution, was the first white man to penetrate the wilderness of the Wood Creek flatlands to attempt permanent settlement, nearly a decade before the French expedition passed the remains of his homestead:

"Mr. Dean, ever after the war enjoyed the confidence of the Oneida Tribe. For his services, the Oneidas gave Mr. Dean a tract of land two miles square, the title to be confirmed and ratified by the state. This was probably in 1783. He chose for its location a tract upon the north side of Wood Creek, in the present town of Vienna.

"In the spring of 1784, he left Connecticut with Jedediah Phelps and Andrew Blanchard, in company, to commence the settlement of his land. The day of starting is not known, but they left Schenectady the 3d of May, and arrived at Wood Creek the 13th... After Mr. Dean and his party arrived at Wood Creek, they built a log house and a shop for Mr. Phelps, who was a brass-founder and silver-smith, and intended to work for the Indians. During the summer they made a small clearing, and although now covered with a second growth of timber, it still retains its name of 'Dean's place.'"

Pomeroy Jones, 1851[124]

Apparently the location was selected at least in part to satisfy the commercial interests of Mr. Phelps, placing them on a major navigation route by which to gain access to the western tribes:

"Mr. Phelps was a silversmith and brass founder and he intended to engage in that business, and to manufacture rings and brooches for the Indians and Indian trade. Mr. Dean erected a log house close by Wood Creek, and Mr., Phelps built a log shop near by for his business; they made a small clearing and then and there commenced the first actual settlement of Oneida county, after the Revolution."

Daniel E. Wager, 1896[125]

Their optimism was soon tarnished, however, by the intervention of natural forces:

"In the spring of 1785, the place became inundated to such an extent, that for three weeks they were obliged to live in the garret of their log cabin, and for the purpose of cooking their meals, they descended from their loft into a canoe by a ladder, and then rowing to the shop, used the forge as their only fireplace above the high water mark. On the subsiding of the water, the party were fully satisfied that the selection was an unfortunate one, and unfit for the commencement of a settlement."

Pomeroy Jones, 1851[126]

continued on next page

This prelude to the vast openness of Oneida Lake is often noted in travelers' journals because the passage down Wood Creek had been so confining, by virtue of the lack of clearings and narrowness of the channel:

The lands, on each side of Wood creek, are low, and heavily timbered with beach, maple, oak, elm, lynden, and near the lake, some white pine. Bears are plenty, and deer scarce. Within two miles of the lake, the river suddenly widened; we took to our oars. Within one mile of the lake, Fish creek falls into Wood creek from the north, about one hundred feet wide. Thence to the lake the creek is bold and spacious. We caught a catfish as large as a common sized cod, measuring five inches between the eyes.

Elkanah Watson, 1791[127]

Boatmen reaching the mouth of Wood Creek, and intending to continue west, often were forced to postpone their crossing by the potentially dangerous waters of what must have appeared to them as an inland sea:

About three o'clock, we came to the entrance of Oneida lake, which, though among the number of inferior lakes, makes an awful appearance, and is doubtless a wonderful display of that infinite Wisdom and Power by which the worlds are made. Our course along this little ocean

contuined from page 54

The impact of this situation is recorded in Dean's own words:

"I arrived here [Wood Creek] the 16th instant in a good state of health, but long before my arrival was met by the disagreeable account of the inundation, which like a deluge over-spreads this country, and which I found to be too true. The water has been above two feet deep on my door-sill, and not 'til yesterday were we able to take possession of the lower room. All that I have seen who are acquainted with this country agree in assuring me that the flood was never known to be so high before. However, the present appearance of it, and the possibility of what may happen again, has given me such a distaste to the country as has determined me to quit it as soon as I conveniently can. But as I have already expended a considerable sum of money upon it, besides labor and fatigue, I must endeavor to turn it to some advantage..."

James Dean, 1785[128]

The wide mouth of a small brook, which intersected Wood Creek at Dean's original site, continued to provide a natural mooring for batteaux, and was for many years to come identified as "Dean's Landing."

"Not far from this spot we discovered a clearing, extended towards the fish-creek... known by the name of Capt. Phillips and Dean's improvements. We left our canoe now and then to look at the land; it was low and flat near the borders of the creek, and had the appearance of being annually overflowed."

Adrian Vernderkemp, 1792[129]

The remains of this abortive settlement were still to be noted a quarter century after he abandoned the site:
"We passed James Dean's old house on the right side, about two miles from the lake. He first went among the Oneidas as a silversmith, vending trinkets. He afterwards acted as an interpreter and coaxed them out of large tracts of land. He is now rich, a Judge of Oneida county, has been a member of the Assembly, and is a prominent Federalist."

DeWitt Clinton, 1810[130]

After being flooded out in 1785, Dean decided to renegotiate his grant of land from the Oneidas, and quickly relocated a dozen miles to the southeast, to the vicinity of Westmoreland:

"Mr. Dean stating this to the Indians, they agreed he might change the location to any point upon the west side of the 'line of property' between Brothertown upon the Oriskany and Wood Creek. He selected his land so as to include the falls of the creek, since known as Dean's Creek... Mr. Dean's energies were now directed to clearing a farm, inducing settlers to remove to his patent, and in building mills for their accommodation. Success crowned his efforts, and it was but a few years before every lot offered for sale was 'taken up' by an actual settler."

Pomeroy Jones, 1851[131]

It was in this latter location that the French party would again cross the path of James Dean as they struggled eastward on their return trip toward Utica on an overland route.

A typical frontier homestead in its first year of occupation.

appeared to be a little north of west; and the wind being brisk from that point, we raised our tents, as no habitation appeared.

Jacob Lindley, 1793[132]

So it was also for the seven men arriving there in mid-October of that same year.

> ***Near the mouth, on the left side upon the Indian lands, we noticed the location of Fort Royal, built of logs, which the French had constructed to shut off the English from passing into Oneida Lake, and to hold the Iroquois in check.***
>
> ***We were now about to enter the lake, but the setting sun, and the troubled waves, induced us to return to the Royal Blockhouse, the only place of any elevation in this region, and we encamped there. We observed no other vestiges of the fort than the ditch, which was nearly filled up.***

The members of this expedition were not the first, or the last, to encamp on the site of the Royal Blockhouse. In spite of the strategic location of this place on the transportation corridor that crossed the region, there was neither tavern nor settler here in the early 1790s.

The British, not the French as the journal suggests, built this isolated fortification in 1759 to protect the entrance of Wood Creek; the only military highway open to the French in the region.

The elevation on which the blockhouse had stood remained a cleared and relatively comfortable location for encampment.

The blockhouse itself had already been destroyed by 1768, as observed by a passing Canadian merchant:

> ...the Royal Blockhouse ... has been lately burned by some drunken Indians ... and is situated on the easternmost point of that Lake; Here I slept two nights among the ruins of the Block House, being unable to put out on the Lake, as it was very severe weather. Travelers are here detained sometimes eight days on that account, as in crossing the Lake they are obliged to cut from point to point, at least 10 miles distant; and the landing between these points being very rocky and dangerous, they seldom venture on the Lake, except in moderate weather.

John Lees, 1768[133]

This military structure, which might have served in place of a tavern and as a shelter for travelers had it survived, had been lost in a disastrous fire the year before John Lees encamped there:

> A man arrived at this place (Fort Stanwix) two days ago, who informed me that on the 12th at night, the Royal Blockhouse took fire and was immediately consumed to ashes. The fire (he said) first took in some of the logs near the chimney by its being much worn away - there had been three Senecas, two Oneidas, a Frenchman and three squaws in the house at the time, who had lost all their packs in the flames, by the accident being so unexpected and so furious, even their dogs were burnt.

Lieut. Richard Aylmer, 1767[134]

It may have been its proximity to the breezes of Oneida Lake, or just its elevation above the swampy lowlands of the area, that made this spot a favored campsite. Those unfortunate enough to have to stop along Wood Creek before reaching this spot of refuge, as happened to a party in 1792, faced a more memorable evening:

> The approaching night compelled us to look out for a convenient spot for our encampment, in which we soon succeeded. Our tent was pitched, and a blazing fire prepared by the boys. We spread our carpet, and made our beds ready waiting for our supper. Here thousands of muskitoes welcomed us in their abode, obtruded their company, and exhausted our patience by their treacherous caresses, in which they continued till we had encircled our tents with smoak, and yet we heard their singing... We covered our faces with a veil before we went to sleep.
>
> This was the first time in my life I slept in the woods, and yet my sleep was sound, but short and not very refreshing, as I awoke fatigued, and was not at ease til I drove the sleep from the eyes of all my companions, and had hurried them to the canoe, to pursue our journey.

Adrian Vanderkemp, 1792[135]

It would not be until 1796, three years after the French voyage, that the first, and only, public tavern would be established here, serving to the close of the era.

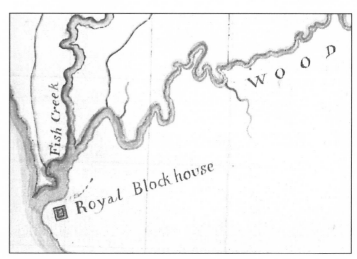

The Royal Blockhouse, c. 1795.

In this earlier time, the locale was entirely the domain of its Native American inhabitants:

> The Oneida Indians, from whom this lake derives its name, are generally settled in this neighborhood. We had, occassionally, met with one or two families of them previously to our arrival at the lake, but here we found a collection of about forty, who were amusing themselves with shooting arrows, pitching quoits, and throwing large stones. We made a stop here for the night, and found them all remarkably civil and well disposed.

Christian Schultz, 1807[136]

Mrs. Jackson's Tavern

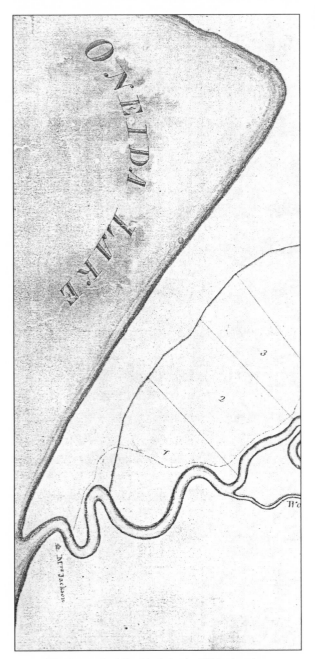

The east end of Oneida Lake in 1809, showing Mrs. Jackson's Tavern at the mouth of Wood Creek.

In 1793, when the French expedition reached the entrance to Oneida Lake [Sylvan Beach], there were no white settlers nor public houses anywhere in the area. It would be three more years before this situation would change.

In May of 1796, Asahel Jackson arrived at the mouth of Wood Creek from Massachusetts and built a house there:

"Very soon after, he opened a public-house for the accommodation of boatmen. Mr. Jackson only lived about ten years after his arrival, and after his death his widow kept the tavern another ten years..."

Samuel Durant, 1878[137]

Before this, travelers had to resort to their own camps, often in the ruins of the Royal Blockhouse near-by. Once the tavern was erected, this oasis of civilization stood out in the minds of many who traversed the desolate wilderness from Gilbert's Tavern on Canada Creek to the cabins at the west end of Oneida Lake:

"There is a tolerably good tavern kept at this place by a Mrs. Jackson... and her sister, a young woman who, you may be assured, displays no ordinary degree of courage in dealing out whiskey to thirty or forty Indians who generally rendezvous at this place, especially as there is no other white settler within sight or call."

Christian Schultz, 1807[138]

Another traveler, passing this spot a few years later, had a less benign opinion of the place:

"Near this tavern there are to be seen the marks of an old fortification, covering about one-eighth of an acre, and called the Royal Block-House. In this place, Col. Porter and the young gentlemen made a tent of the sails and setting poles, and, with the aid of a fire and our mattrasses, had a good night's lodging. The other Commissioners slept in the house; the window panes were out and the doors open. The resort of Indians and the sandy ground had drawn together a crowd of fleas, which, with the musquitoes, annoyed us beyond sufferance the whole night. Some of the family sat up late; the creakings of a crazy old building and the noise of voices, added to our other annoyances, completely deprived us of rest. The house was in other respects a comfortable one. The ice, which we used to correct the badness of the creek water, had a pleasant effect."

DeWitt Clinton, 1810[139]

It was shortly after this last encounter, apparently, that the Widow Jackson took a new husband and abandoned the business for a more peaceful, and perhaps more practical, life.

CHAPTER EIGHT

Oneida Lake

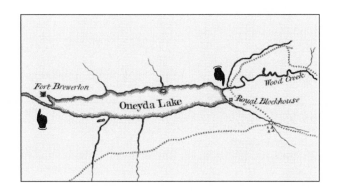

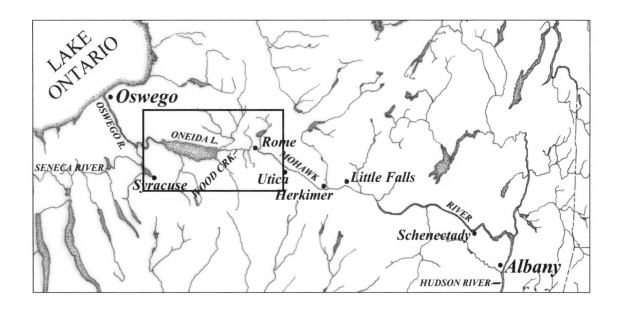

For many navigators, the vista confronting them from the beach at the east end of Oneida Lake was a source of wonder, after so many hours struggling through the overgrown channel of Wood Creek. Here, also, the traveler was often first exposed to the phenomenon of Native Americans in their own domain:

> We arrived at Mrs. Jackson's tavern, at seven o'clock, near the mouth of Wood Creek, which enters Oneida Lake from the north-east. To the west, the eye was lost in the expanse of waters, there being no limits to the horizon. A western wind gently agitated the surface of the waters. A number of canoes darting through the lake after fish in a dark night, with lighted flambeaux of pine knots fixed on elevated iron frames, made a very picturesque and pleasing exhibition.
>
> We walked on the beach, composed of the finest sand, like the shores of the ocean, and covered with a few straggling trees. Here we met with an Indian canoe, filled with eels, salmon, and monstrous cat-fish. In another place we saw the native of the woods cooking his fish and eating his meal on the beach. We could not resist the temptation of the cold bath. On returning to the house, we found an excellent supper prepared; the principal dish was salmon, dressed in various ways.
>
> DeWitt Clinton, 1810[140]

It is here, in Oneida Lake, that the journalists of this period most often note the picturesque spectacle of Native night fishing:

> I made a small excursion along the border of this lake, and, although the shore was low, yet I found a firm, dry, white sandy beach to walk upon; some other parts of it, however, I was informed, were low and swampy.
>
> I was much amused in the evening by a singular illumination upon the lake, which I was at first wholly unable to account for. The water at this part of the lake, it seems, is very shallow for nearly half a mile from the shore, and being perfectly transparent, and the bottom a white sand, the smallest object may by readily distinguished. The Indians have a method of taking salmon and other fish by means of an iron frame fixed in the bow of the canoe, projecting forward three or four feet, and elevated about five; upon this they kindle a bright fire of pine knots, and while one person sits in the stern with a paddle to impel the boat forward, another stands in the bow with a sharp spear ready to strike the fish who play about the light.
>
> Ten or twelve of these canoes moving about irregularly on the lake, on a fine calm evening, with the reflection of their lights, like so many lines of fire, extending from each object to the centre on which you stand, afford the most pleasing prospect, and far exceed, in my opinion, the most brilliant display of artificial fire-works.
>
> Christian Schultz, 1807[141]

"Immediately after breakfast we embarked, - doubled a point of land, and entered the Oneida lake, with our sails filled to a light easterly breeze. The lake opened to our view, like an ocean, spreading before us; - we glided smoothly over its surface, and were delighted with a charming day. On the south is the Oneida reservation, at present inhabited by the Oneida nation of Indians."
Elkanah Watson, 1792[142]

As the batteaumen who came west to this place were far more comfortable in the shallows with a setting pole than on the open water, passage across this lake was usually not on a direct line, but safely by the northern shore:

> This lake is extremely turbulent and dangerous, - a small breeze producing a short bobbing sea, and consequence of shoal water. The batteaumen commonly hug the north shore, as safest, as well as more direct, from point to point; which, on that side, project less into the lake, than on the south side shore.
>
> Elkanah Watson, 1791[143]

As the winds of day sometimes calmed with evening, navigators often rowed all night to cross to Fort Brewerton, at the west end of the lake, before dawn. The batteau of Desjardins and his company did not have that option, and, to the consternation of their crew, initially avoided the relative security of the northern shallows.

> *Sunday, October 13th. At sunrise, the NW wind, which had blown all night, had a little subsided, and although still against us, we resolved to set out, and four other bateaux, which were stopped at the lower point of the mouth of the creek, seeing us pass, resolved to follow.*
>
> *This lake is only nine miles wide by twenty one long, but it appeared like an ocean to our bateau men, and movement of the waves frightened them somewhat. We calmed their apprehensions, and to show our confidence steered boldly out into the lake towards a point called the Nine Mile Point, which shortened the distance fully a third.*

"...the northwest, north & west winds are the most frequent at that lake, and that the boats, immediately when they come out of Wood Creek, make over on the north side of the lake, to the six or the nine mile point, in order to come under that shore, along which by these winds the water is perfectly smooth; and can without any danger or interruption, proceed on their voyage to the outlet on River Onondago. Coming from the outlet 'or Fort Brewenton' the same course is pursued by the navigators over the lake, and commonly go as high up as the nine or six miles points on the north side, and stretch over to Wood Creek. The sand bar at Wood Creek is very dangerous for navigators, and the channel of the creek, in which is four feet water, so narrow and crooked, that it is often missed in going into Wood Creek."
George Scriba, 1804[144]

> *The prospect at the entrance of the lake is charming. Its breadth being only three leagues, we can see both the northern and southern shores, covered with immense*

forests, beyond which towards the west the country rises into high hills, while the eastern shore forming the entrance of the lake is low and sandy.

Near the head of the lake is a sand bar, upon which the lake beats violently when the wind is high. This bar, which is shifting, has only three or four feet of water. As the west and northwest winds are more benevolent on the great lakes, the navigation is easier up than down. The shores are mostly very low, and the slope is so little, that it is quite difficult to make a landing.

The sand bar which partially blocked passage into the lake was mentioned by numerous voyagers in this period, even as late as 1810:

At the entrance of the Wood Creek, and about fifty rods from its mouth, we found a sand-bar forty rods wide. The shallowest part was two feet deep, and the channel between three and four feet wide.

DeWitt Clinton, 1810[145]

Considering that a common batteau, fully loaded, required less than two feet of water to navigate, and even the huge Durham boats could pass on that depth of channel, this bar was more dramatic than it was treacherous.

We entered the lake about eight o'clock in the morning. At about five hundred toises from the north shore, and a little before reaching the second point, is a large sand bank, but the bottom and shores of the lake are usually gravelly.

We were drawn a little out of our course to kill a bear, which Major DeZeng thought that he saw swimming across the lake, but when we came near, we discovered that this bear was only a floating tree, whose black trunk was glistening in the sun on the surface of the water.

At about eleven miles from the entrance, after rowing four hours and a half, we came to three sandy islands, with a few pebbles, in the midst of a great number of aquatic birds, who came thither to lay their eggs, as a place of safety. These islands are beyond Nine Mile Point, and from this point we can see the whole contour of the lake.

The western end of Oneida Lake was characterized by shoals and low bars, providing nesting sites for birds, and dominated by two forested islands, larger than the rest:

There is two islands in the lake, the one about 30 the other about 20 acres. On the westernmost lives a Frenchman with his family... There is likewise three small ridges which is just above water and on each is a single tree - there is no verdure on them. The tree has a pretty effect to the eyes. In June they are frequented for eggs, which the gulls and ducks lay here in abundance, below the high water mark.

James Cockburn, 1792[146]

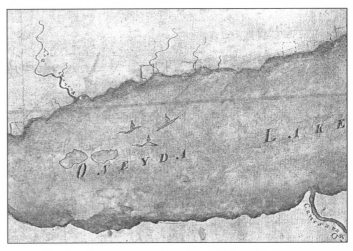

The west end of Oneida Lake in 1792

Here the party saw evidence of the first tentative settlements along the interior of Oneida Lake.

Opposite the first two sandy islands, I noticed the first log house built on the Rosevelt tract, to the right of a point, with some clearings around it, and at about sixteen miles from where we started we came to other clearings begun at the location of Mr. Desvatines, a Frenchman, who, like another Robinson Crusoe, had two years ago come and settled on an island in the middle of the lake with his wife, his children, and his little library. The state having sold these lands to the Rosevelt Company, M. Desvatines was dispossessed, and Mr. Scriba gave him a lot of land in his tract, on the lake shore.

Near this is the future New Rotterdam, now only consisting of three log houses at the mouth of Scriba Creek, which it is difficult to enter. M. Pharoux came near breaking his leg in jumping on a heap of pebbles to relieve the boat. There is also on the creek at this place a saw mill.

"On our passage we had a tolerably fair view of Rotterdam, situated on the right bank of the lake, about six miles above the outlet. The country, generally, around the lake, and particularly in the neighborhood of Rotterdam, has the character of being unhealthy, although the situation of the town appeared to me to be sufficiently elevated. Should the vicinity of these low and swampy grounds be the only cause of this unhealthyness, I am of opinion that a few hundred dollars expended, in opening the channel and removing the bar at the head of the outlet, would lower the lake so far as to drain off the stagnant waters, and thus remove the cause.

"I had an opportunity of examining the whole length of the bar by wading across it, and found it composed of loose stones and gravel, with no more than eighteen inches of water. Unless, therefore, there should prove to be a bed of rocks to impede the undertaking, I am inclined to believe that twenty men, with the necessary implements, might easily accomplish it in the course of a month."

"As the wind would not permit us to stop at Rotterdam, I can only speak of it from information. It is said to contain about thirty houses, but mostly deserted, on account of what they call the lake fever, which, I am told, makes its appearance annually. There is an excellent set of mills built upon a stream called Bruce's Creek, which passes just below the town; and, although the country is extremely fertile, yet, for want of settlers to raise grain, they have but little employment.

Christian Schultz, 1807[147]

Frenchman's Island

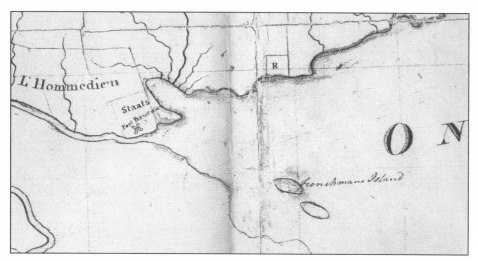

Detail of map showing Frenchman's Island, 1796.

The situation of Desvatines, the man for whom "Frenchman's Island" was named, was recorded in some detail by one who visited him in 1792, the year before he abandoned his island in the middle of Oneida Lake:

"Proceeding on one after another through the stately trees, through which we perceived yet the last glances of the setting sun, we were at once, after a few rods, surprised with an enchanting view, of which it is not in my power to give you an adequate description... We did see here a luxuriant soil in its virgin bloom - we did see industry crowned with blessing - we did see here what great things a frail man can perform if he is willing. ... Our path, gradually increasing in breadth, did lead us to the circumference of a cleared circle, surrounded with lime-trees; at both sides of the path was planted Indian corn, already grown from 4 to 5 feet, while a few plants towards the middle of this patch were six feet long - and this in the middle of June. A small cottage of a few feet square stood nearly in the center of this spot. It had a bark covering and to the left of it a similar one, three-fourth uncovered, and appropriated for a kitchen. Here was the residence of Mr. & Madame de Wattines with their three children.

"They lived there without servants, without neighbors, without a cow; they lived, as it were, separated from the world....Des Wattines sallied forward, and gave us a cordial welcome in his Desmenes. The well educated man was easily recognized through his sloven dress. Ragged as he appeared, without a coat or hat, his manners were those of a Gentleman... A female, from whose remaining beauties might be conjectured, how many had been tarnished by adversity, was sitting in the entrance of his cot. She was dressed in white, in a short gown and petticoat, garnished with the same stuff; her chestnut brown hair, flung back in ringlets over her shoulders, her eyes fixed on her darling Camille - a native of this Isle - at her breast; while two children, standing at each side of her, play'd in her lap. ...Des Wattines introduced us to his spouse. She received us with that easy politeness, which well educated people seldom loose entirely, and urged, with so much grace, to sit down, that we could not refuse it without incivility. This couple was now in the second year on this island, and all the improvements, which we had seen, were the work of Des Wattines' hands exclusively.

"Our refreshment was a dish of tea, or rather their usual beverage from Venus-hair, which she has collected and dried, palatable enough indeed, when sweetened with sugar. It was growing dark before we could be persuaded to leave our new companions, who insisted on our staying with them that night; which we declined reluctantly, but engaged ourselves to return in the morning, and to partake of their break-feast.

"Few trunks, few chairs, an oval table, two neat beds was the principal furniture: a double barreled gun, a pretty collection of books, chiefly modern Literature in the French language, the chief ornaments of the cottage....

"I awoke with day-light, and made the circuit of this fortunate Island...Des Wattines had laid out behind the cottage a pretty garden, divided by a walk in the middle. The two foremost beds, and rabats, against the house

continued on next page

continued from page 62

were covered with a variety of flowers, sweet-williams, Lady-slippers, with a few decaying hyacinths. At the right hand were Bath-beans, large kidney-beans at poles, cabbage, turnips, peas, salade with that strong scented herbage which we call keovel (cheovel)... at the left watermelons, canteloups, cucumbers, persil, string peas with a few of the winter provisions, all in great forwardness, with few or no weeds among them. Behind the garden a small nursery of apple-trees, which was closed with a patch of luxuriant potatoes, and these again were joined from both sides by wheat, describing a semi-circle around it.

"All this was the workmanship of Des Wattines' industry without any assistance, not even of a plow or har-

row, having no other tool but an axe and an hoe. It is true, it was all in miniature, but it required nevertheless an indefatigable industry, to be able to accomplish all this to such a degree of perfection. When I approached the cottage Des Wattines was yet employ'd in dragging pretty heavy wood for fuel towards it, which he chop't and split, in a short time; and in less yet the fire was blazing, when he came with a cat-fish of 16 lb for our break-feast. While he was busily engaged in its preparation Madame appeared, brought him a handful persil, and dressed the table. The table cloth was of neat damask, a few silver spoons and forks, the plates and dishes cream colored, remnants yet of their former affluence, while the contentment legible in her eyes, spread a fresh glow over her countenance, and made a deep impression on our hearts, and, whetted our already keen appetites. ... Salade, roasted and stewed fish, well-baked, warm bread of Indian corn, with good Hyzan tea, which she accepted from us with kindness, soon filled the table. I was seldom better regaled. The fish was delicious: the sprightly conversation gave a fresh relish to every mouthful we tasted, and we might have desired to be Inhabitants of that enchanted spot..."

Adrian Vanderkemp, 1792[148]

We stopped at Rotterdam, where Mr. DeZeng had some business, and slept there, after taking supper with Mr. Scriba's men. At eight in the evening, we were favored by the arrival of Mr. Vanderkemp, a Dutch Minister, one of the leaders in the revolution of 1787 against the Stadtholder; a revolution which, although secretly favored by France, was subsequently abandoned to the Prussian arms, the deplorable state of our finances having made it impossible for the king to undertake a war which would have been a serious one, since England would have joined Prussia in sustaining the Stadtholder.

The leaders of this revolution, after their failure, mostly fled to America, where they have formed a company and bought over a million of acres in the states of New York and Pennsylvania. Mr. Vanderkemp has located his choice on Oneida Lake and has come in a canoe to look for stone to use in the buildings he intends to erect next spring. He speaks a little French, and we gave him a welcome. We failed to see M. Desvatines, our fellow countryman, as he had gone out hunting with the Indians, but we reserved this visit until our return.

At Rotterdam almost all the inhabitants were sick with a fever owing to the shallowness of the lake, and the immense number of fishes which are thrown ashore and which, in low water, decay along the marshy banks, exhaling pestilential and putrid miasms.

By now, Brunel, who had wanted to put kegs of fresh water aboard in Schenectady, might have begun to feel vindicated. In spite of the abundance of water all around them, the travelers were discovering the lack of good drinking water that had been noted by others the year before:

About eight miles from Fort Brewington is a fine spring; which is very uncommon in this country - I having seen no good water since I left Fort Stanwix - even the creeks which run into the lake coming chiefly from swamps are very indifferent water.

James Cockburn, 1792[149]

The settlement of New Rotterdam [Constantia], which the members of the 1793 expedition were observing in its infancy, seems not to have established itself as a viable commercial enterprise during this era, as observed seven years later by DeWitt Clinton:

We dined at Rotterdam, a decayed settlement of George Scriba's, eleven miles from the outlet, containing eight or ten houses, and exhibiting marks of a premature growth. There are mills on a small creek, and while at dinner, our men speared several fish in it..

DeWitt Clinton, 1810[150]

The French party probably enjoyed their stay here overnight, and the opportunity to observe the expanse of water before them after two weeks of tedious river navigation.

Monday, October 14th. At half past six we left Rotterdam with a pleasant sky, and in half an hour came to an island partly cleared by M. Desvatines. There were here two islands, of about thirty and forty acres, of excellent soil, finely timbered, and forming in the lake a charming object of view. It was a very desirable location and our countrymen had made a good choice. The lake is everywhere shallow along the shore, and the banks are lined with grass and rushes wherever the water is not more than two feet deep. Before coming to the Desvatines islands, we noticed one very low, perfectly circular, and with only a single tree in the middle.

"We left Bruce's creek on Friday evening about six, the sky was serene and delightful: - a soft breeze curled the waves, and fringed them with white, while the sun, sinking towards the west, beautified the whole scenery. I did not witness such a grand or majestic sight, since I crossed the Atlantic. It must be seen, before it can be fully appraised... In proportion that we penetrated deeper in the Lake the beauty of this diversified prospect was more and more enhanced - the islands, the shores, the woods, the mountains obtruding themselves to our sight, seemed to vie with other for the preference. At length the slight breeze increased; ere long a brisk wind arose from the west: the increased undulated motion with the white capped waves appalled our raw hands, whose trembling limbs and pale visages too clearly betray'd their fear of a threatening shipwreck. We endeavoured to assuage it, as the wind was steady. If we had any apprehension it arose from their inexpertness, from their unsubdued tenor, from the knowledge, that two or three waves would have been sufficient to sink our deep loaded canoe. We conquered nevertheless, and they rowed on with redoubled alacrity."

Adrian Vanderkemp, 1792[151]

"One Tree Island," noted as a curiosity by the journalists in 1793, remained a landmark for travelers on Oneida Lake:

About four miles from the outlet we passed two islands on our left, sufficiently high for cultivation, and containing about one hundred acres, but destitute of inhabitants.

We also passed a little spot called One Tree Island, which serves the navigators as a land-mark, and, at a distance, has the appearance of a ship under sail.

There are likewise two small sandy islands, generally covered with gulls; the boatmen sometime stop here to look for eggs, which, in the season, are found in considerable plenty.

In passing these islands we ran aground on the top of what appeared to me to be a sunken island, with a very small flat surface; it was an entire rock, not more than seven paces across; and, on every side, we found more than thirty feet water, that being the length of the cord I sounded with.

Christian Schultz, 1807[152]

Rarely did these western islands escape the notice of those navigating this inland route. The sighting of "Frenchman's Island" signaled a successful crossing of Oneida Lake and the approach to its outlet at Fort Brewerton:

Independently of several collections of sand and reeds, which can hardly be termed islands, and of an islet about the middle of the lake, which has a single tree, and looks at a distance like a ship under sail, there are two islands, about two miles from the outlet, half a mile from the south shore of the lake. They are within a short distance from each other. One island contains fourteen acres, and the other, called Frenchman's Island, twenty-seven acres. A person can wade from one to the other; and bears, in swimming the lake, frequently stop here to rest. These islands belong to the State.

DeWitt Clinton, 1810[153]

"I never witnessed a more charming sight: It is indeed exquisitely beautiful: the sun in its full splendour at the western horizon, gilding the enlightened clouds - an extensive sheet of water, in an undulating motion - two Islands towards the south in front, which we were now approaching, a small opening between these, through which we had a view of the southern coast, one single, covered with grass, and with one tree adorned rock, behind which in perspective appeared the country of the Oneydas with the Canoserago Hills."

Adrian Vanderkemp, 1792[154]

The French party noted, to the south, the stream that bounded the Oneida lands.

On the shore of the lake, opposite, is the mouth of the Canaseraga Creek, a stream of considerable size that separates the Oneida Reservation from the lands they have released to the State. The shore is here more elevated, and the soil is excellent.

During this period the stream opposite Rotterdam was often called "Canaseraga", even though later termed the Chittenango Creek.

The crossing of this vast inland lake was nearing an end.

From the Desvatines islands we can see the outlet of the lake and the site of Fort Brewington, which the English built to guard this pass. At this place the west winds meeting the waters of the lake have formed a large bar, which only allows bateaux to pass close to the site of the fort. This pass is about eight miles from New Rotterdam, and, as the water was very low, we found it quite difficult to get out of the lake into the Onondaga River. The bar is formed of pebbles.

CHAPTER NINE

The Oneida River

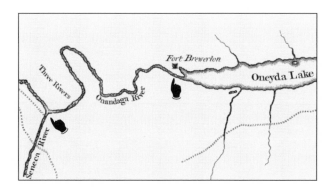

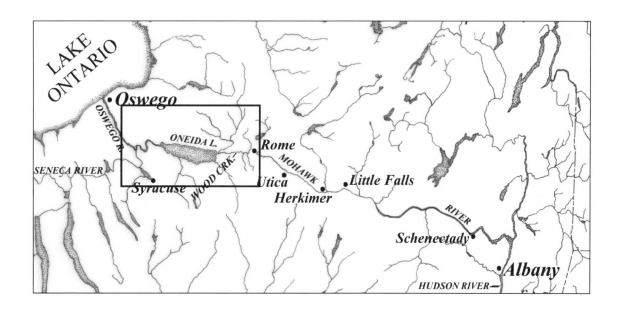

Just as the Royal Blockhouse at Wood Creek served as the focal point for early activity at the inlet to Oneida Lake, so did the fortification of Fort Brewerton for the outlet into the Oneida River. Established also in 1759, this small military outpost, coupled with a more favorable situation, catalyzed settlement at an early date.

The first white resident of Oswego County was Oliver Stevens, who located at Fort Brewerton in 1789, began trading with the Indians, and kept a rude tavern for the accommodation of boatmen. In 1791, Major Ryal Bingham settled in the vicinity of the fort, on land leased of a Mr. Kaats, who had procured the title. He, however, remained but two years, while Stevens became a permanent resident.

Crisfield Johnson, 1877[155]

Voyagers stopping here on their way west were often surprised at the quality of hospitality provided, particularly at a location so far beyond the frontier:

We arrived at fort Brewerton about noon, situated on the North-western corner of the Lake. ... I was highly gratified with excellent bread and butter, feasted on milk for my beverage, and purchased two pints of it, which we carried to our Bateau. The situation alone renders this spot of considerable consequence; and its importance must be heightened as soon the backlands are settled, and the navigation of the western waters shall be carried to that summit, to which it eventually must ascend. The soil is clay, of which a large quantity of brick was made

Adrian Vanderkemp, 1792[156]

While the French party stopped here and availed themselves of breakfast, they offer no comment as to the quality of the experience, except to note in some detail the methods used by these settlers to procure and store their produce.

A log house occupies the site of the fort, and its occupant has piled up stones and gravel in a triangular form, almost entirely across the river, and at the point is a opening where there is fastened a willow basket called an eel weier. These structures almost entirely destroy the navigation, and although forbidden, yet in these wilds there are none to see that the laws are carried into effect.

We landed at this log house, and after breakfast went to see a mill built after the Indian fashion. It was the trunk of a tree hollowed out like a mortar, with the pestle hung from a pole as a counterpoise, and with this simple machine one could grind maize with very little fatigue.

The shelters for their corn and pumpkins (a kind of Indian gourd) are not less simple. They are long cribs, made of poles as large as the arm, laid one on another two or three feet high, with short poles notched at the ends, and about an inch space open between them. Into these they throw their corn or pumpkins, and then cover them with wide pieces of bark, while the snow completes the winter covering. Thus their grain, open to the air, does not heat, and is no more exposed to the squirrels, etc, than it would be in granaries. But as for these they have none.

An early form of samp mortar.

> "Indian corn... was their all, and it was dried as they best could, in the sun when it shone and at other times by their fires. Thus prepared, it was pounded in a *samp-mortar*, of which almost every settler had a specimen, formed by burning out the end of a log."
>
> Pomeroy Jones, 1851[157]

The obstruction noted in this journal at the outlet of the lake consisted of an extensive gravel bar, compounded by one or two eel weirs. Motivated by a desire to improve the value of his lands at Rotterdam, which were being offered for sale to potential settlers, George Scriba appealed to Schuyler's company in 1803 to add the removal of this bar to their efforts to improve Wood Creek:

By removing this bar or natural dam across the outlet at Fort Bruenton will be the means to lower the lake from five to six feet; consequently it would give a greater current in Wood Creek, and be the means by which the sand bars constantly forming therein would be removed, for want of current to carry it through into deeper water, or into the lake; and there is no doubt this experiment would prove a great relief to the navigators in Wood Creek.

The sand bars which are therein formed by the swelling of the lake in the spring & autumn: there comes by the different streams of water which empty themselves into that lake, six times the quantity of water into the lake than can go out at the time of these freshets, particularly when the snow goes off in the spring.

The swelling of the lake backens the water from 8 to 10 miles up that creek, and makes it a perfect <u>still dead water</u>, in which no current can be observed, and overflows at the same time an immense tract of land on both sides of Wood Creek. By a mark at the Lake Oneida, the lake was <u>eight feet higher</u> for several weeks in the month of April during the freshets when the snow went off, then it was in August & September: the sand banks thus are formed at the time of these freshets, there being no current to move the sand, and the outlet of the lake, being dammed by a natural dam or bar, requires long time in dry weather, by which the water coming into the lake diminishes, and before the lake can come to its level, & the very slow falling of the water in that lake, thus leaves all the sand carried downwards in Wood Creek in it, and obstructs the navigation in the season, when the water has diminished therein.

George Scriba, 1804[158]

Fort Brewerton Landing

This 1798 map of the landing at the mouth of the Oneida River shows the ruins of the fort and the house of Oliver Stevens.

Oliver Stevens, the first white settler in the area of the Oneida Lake outlet, established himself at the site of the abandoned British fort in 1789; his homestead being observed a few years later:

"We stopped at Fort Brompton [Brewerton] at the entrance of the lake. This structure also is surrounded with pallisadoes, erected last year; it stands at the foot of an ancient entrenchment, constructed by the English during the American war, on an advantageous ground, commanding the entrance of the lake. The work was thrown up in a zigzag figure; but from the remains no distinct idea can be formed, how the cannon could be pointed to advantage. All the antiquities of this country consist in the remains of forts, built in the wars of 1776 or 1756. Fancy must live in future ages, to find occupation in this infant country; past ages can exist here only for generations not yet born."

"The proprietor of the house had gone to Rotterdam three days before. A girl of fourteen was left behind to take care of the house, and of a little brother, who was sick, and whom she actually nursed with a solicitude truly affecting. The girl, poor thing, did all she could for our accommodation, but nothing was to be procured. We should have been obliged to content ourselves with a few small potatoes, which we pulled up in the fields, if the Indians, who were encamped on the opposite bank of the river, had not brought us a large pike, which they had caught in the morning with a harpoon."

Duke de la Rochefoucault Liancourt, 1795[159]

Almost twenty years after its initial settlement, the situation at this place had changed very little:

"This night we slept at Steven's, at the outlet of the lake, nine miles by land and eleven by water from Rotterdam. Here commences Onondaga or Oneida River, the only outlet of the lake, about as large as the mouth of Wood Creek. The bars at the outlet are rocky, wide, difficult to remove, and so shallow that a horse can easily pass over them. There are two eel weirs here, in which many are caught. Stevens has lived in this place, which is in the town of Constantia, eighteen years; has rented it for seventeen years, at $75 a year. He has no neighbors within four miles on this side of the river. On the other side is the town of Cicero, in which there are several settlements. This is a clean house, in which we were as well accommodated as the situation of the country would admit...Steven's house is one quarter of a mile from the mouth of the lake. Deer come close up to it. We saw an adder and another snake sunning themselves on the ramparts of Fort Brewser, in the rear of the house. This was erected in the French War, was a regular work, ditch and bastions, all covering about an acre. This must have been an important pass to defend, and would now be an excellent site for a town."

DeWitt Clinton, 1810[160]

The natural gravel bar that had accumulated here over the centuries created a shoal which virtually blocked the outlet of the lake. George Scriba, concerned with the state of navigation in the opening years of the nineteenth century, suggested its removal:

"I would advise to take away the bar at the outlet of the Lake Oneida, which place must be improved on account of the difficulty the boats meet with there to get over it: this bar is about half a quarter of a mile in length; this natural dam or bar consists of loose stones of which the people make in every direction eel wares."

George Scriba, 1804[161]

However, the very stone weirs which Scriba complained about suggested to Elkanah Watson a solution to the problem. He recommended "... enlarging the scale of the eel ware at the west entrance of the said lake..." which would raise the water over this shoal. In fact, from this particular case he extrapolated a solution for all the problems of shoal water navigation along the lower Mohawk:

"Should the rapid be not very extensive, some contrivance like the eel ware at the west end of the Oneida would probably answer the purpose. This raises a head of water sufficient to enable loaded boats to pass out and into the lake, which is effected by the simple and cheap expedient of throwing up loose stone obliquely from each shore in the bed of the river. At each of the terminations a sufficient passage is left open where the water rushes through forming a channel way..."

Elkanah Watson, 1800[162]

The settlers here, however, might have argued against the removal of this gravel bar and its associated fish trap – a potential source of food and income. The shoal water created by this bar, coupled with its location at the outlet of a lake, produced the ideal situation in which to build a stone weir:

> Eels are found here in the greatest abundance, and are the finest and largest that ever I saw. They have an invention for taking them similar to our eel-pots, but made very large, and requiring no bait. These are always set in a strong current, either at the inlet or outlet of a lake, or on some swift part of the stream upon the rivers. Two ridges of stones are piled up in the manner before described on the Mohawk river, at the lower end of which the pot or basket is set. I was present when one of the baskets, which had been set over night, was taken up; it filled two barrels, and the greater part of the eels weighed from two to three pounds each.
>
> Christian Schultz, 1807[163]

Such structures, although of ancient native origin, were still common on the inland waterways in the 1790s, often maintained, as here, by the newly arrived homesteaders. These fisheries provided an immediate level of subsistence, specialized though it was, that was usually unrivaled for ease of harvest and richness of diet:

> Fort Brewerton, which we reached at four in the afternoon, was to us a delightful sight. Capt. Bingham was from home on the salmon fishery; and Capt. (Stevens) with the women was on a visit to the island. His eldest daughter, nevertheless, a smart young girl, prepared us a good supper - a bass of two pounds; a dish with stewed eels; with fresh bread and butter. Our breakfast was congenial, having secured two capital eels, with a pot of milk and rice...
>
> Adrian Vanderkemp, 1792[164]

A native cabin recorded in 1791 of the type in evidence west of Oneida Lake.

> "The eel of the Oneyda Lake is equal to the best of the Holland market, and far surpasses every kind which I have ever tasted here, in size, in fatness, in tenderness of the fish."
>
> Adrian Vanderkemp, 1792[165]

As one moved west, one encountered more of these fisheries being managed seasonally by the Native American inhabitants, who came to sections of the rivers where no white settlers had yet established a foothold. Such a place, perhaps the most concentrated Native American fishing station on the inland route to Oswego, was passed on the morning of October 14th by the French batteau, floating down the "Onondaga" (Oneida) River:

> *The Onondaga River is about as wide as the Seine in Paris, but is no deeper than the Mohawk, and its navigation obstructed by bars. In some places we meet rapids quite difficult to pass, especially at a dyke of gravel made by the Indians for an eel trap. Here on the right bank are the cabins which they occupy in the fishing season. They are built of poles supported by crotched posts, covered and sided with bark.*

This complex of weirs stood in the crook of the Oneida River at Caughdenoy, and apparently had been well established by the mid-eighteenth century. This location eventually became part of the fisheries of the white settlement that grew up there. Some of the eel weirs that had served continuously in this spot for generations may have stood on the ruins of ones built here in prehistoric times.

In passing down the Oneida the year before, Vanderkemp noted the rift at Caughdenoy. He used, as was common in that time, the name "Onondago" to apply to the linked Oneida and Oswego rivers:

> We arrived in the Onondago river, which even as the fish-creek, has generally very steep banks - more so however on the west-side. We passed sometimes, through our inexpertness, large rifts with difficulty. It was said here was an ancient Indian eel-wear - by which this natural obstruction in the bed of the river had been increased. The stream was otherwise very placid, and our progress of course, easy.
>
> Adrian Vanderkemp, 1792[166]

Traveling late in the season, the French party was exposed to bouts of severe weather, which they noted without further comment.

> *We encountered quite a storm of sleet from eleven o'clock till noon. The lands on the right, belonging to Rosevelt, are low and swampy, the timber poor, and the soil fit only for pasturage. Those on*

American Museum of Natural History

the left, belonging to the military tract, are about of the same quality.

The bottom of the channel is covered with broken and angular pebbles, and the river is full of fish. The shores that are higher are sandy and covered only with pines and other evergreens, which indicate a poor soil.

At sunset, we landed on the right bank, near a little hill, where some trees had been formerly burned, to select a place for our tent, and cleared away the underbrush that had already sprung up.

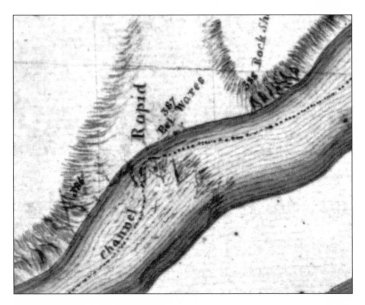

Mohawk River eel weirs typical of the late 18th century, mapped in 1803.

Given the heavily forested banks of the inland waterways this far west of the frontier, travelers had to rely on their own camping gear for their lodging. Often old Indian clearings provided a convenient spot. But the continuous selection of favorable spots by boatmen ended up creating inviting riverside rest areas, noted as early as 1768:

...I slept that night... at a camping place, as it is called, or a spot cleared in the woods by the side of the river; such places travelers have made in the course of time, and are to be met with at every 10 miles distance.

John Lees, 1768[167]

Inviting as these camping sites might be, one was advised to stay close by the river:

A sudden shower compelled us to land about three miles below fort Brewerton, where we encamped that night - being resolved if the rain might abate, to take a view of the land.

The soil is rich, with a great variety of luxuriant trees, a black loom with a mixture of fine sand of the same color, many inches deep, then clay - the timber majestic, spreading its branches and foliage, beach, oak, maple, black ash, with here and there a pine and hemlock.

I had ventured, rather imprudently perhaps, a few miles in the woods: the beauty of the stop had lured me

deeper and deeper, till at last I knew not from where I came, or wither I went: the sun being set, I had lost this unerring guide - my only refuge was now my pocket-compass, by which I again discovered the course, which I had to steer towards the river. This nevertheless would have brought me two miles below my encampment, had not DeZeng, apprehensive of this issue, sent out the boys to hunt the straggler.

Adrian Vanderkemp, 1792[168]

Although tempted to look into the forest beyond the edges of their camp, the members of the expedition had the good sense to remain close to the river, which also provided for their sumptuous dinner.

Behind the hill, at the foot of which we were encamped, is a little valley and other hills. Our men caught some catfish, thus named from the long barbs on their heads like the whiskers of a cat's face. Its fins are armed with a spine, which they raise or relax at will. This fish, named <u>le Mal</u> in ichthyology of the Encyclopedia, grow to a great size in the lakes, but is here of moderate size, weighing from three to four pounds. Its flesh is delicate, fat, and flavored like that of the carp and the eel. We also caught some tench, perch, and suckers, a kind of carp. We caught eight fish in two hours, with only two lines, and finished by making an excellent supper at the river's expense.

"These waters abound in catfish, salmon, bass, eel, and corperals, all very fine, and fat. They are caught in eel weires, formed by Indians thus: - Two walls of loose stones are thrown up, obliquely descending across the river, to a point, - where they are taken, at a small opening, in baskets, or eel pots. Salmon are caught at the Oswego falls in the night, by spearing them as they vault up the falls, by the aid of torch light."
Elkanah Watson, 1791[169]

Tuesday, October 15th. Left at seven o'clock. The river is often rapid and its bottom gravelly, its banks lined with rushes and aquatic plants - valerian, Golden-sheaf, and the cardinal flower - whose blossoms had a very pleasant effect. The shores, although low, soon rise into banks beyond.

Passing this way a few years later, Christian Schultz warned of being too much distracted from the demands of navigation by the beauty of the passage:

In descending the Onondaga River from the outlet, the land is low on both sides for about five miles; the right shore then begins gradually to rise and improve in appearance, while the left still continues low for a considerable distance further. This is a pleasant, and, in some places, a rapid stream, increasing to the breadth of one hundred and twenty-five yards; its length, according to its meanders from the Oneida Lake, to its junction with the Seneca and Oswego Rivers at Three River Point, is twenty miles.

Overland Travel

Heading due north earlier that summer [1793] to attend a Town meeting about 20 miles away [Pulaski], Oliver Stevens left the security of his home at Fort Brewerton to attempt an overland journey:

"He started off early in the morning, with his gun in hand, and a knapsack of provisions on his back. There was no road nor scarcely a path; he relied mainly on his skill as a woodsman, and his knowledge of the wanderings of the sun to guide him safely through his journey. He traveled on, unconscious of harm, till near the middle of the afternoon, when he found himself in the vicinity of a pack of hungry wolves. By their howling, he was aroused not only to a sense of his danger, but to the fact that he had lost his way, and that he had no means of recovering it. He set forward with vigor, in hope of coming out at a 'clearing' in the vicinity of the place of his destination, but all to no purpose; the more he exerted himself, the more he became convinced of the peril of his situation. The wolves drew nearer and nearer, and seemed by their boldness, to be meditating an attack. At length, one bolder than his companions, a large black one, advanced to within a few paces of him, upon which he fired and killed him dead. The scent of the blood of the dead wolf seemed to increase the voracity of the survivors, and for a time he thought he should in turn be slain.

"Nothing daunted, he stood at bay looking them firmly in the eye, and after a while, they retired to a respectful distance, sitting around on their haunches as if holding a council of war. During this cessation of hostilities, Mr. Steven's struck a fire and kindled it, reloaded his gun, and sallied forth, dragging the dead wolf by the heels to his fiery fortress. At this stage of the war, it seemed as if the fury of the wolves was ungovernable; they came very near, growling and snapping their teeth, in the greatest anger. He cast burning brands among them, and finally they dispersed. Upon this, he added more fuel to the fire, got up a bright light, and began to feel somewhat secure.

"His next business was to secure the skin of his fallen foe, which was soon effected. By this time it became quite dark. A quantity of fuel was gathered. Here the solitary wanderer stood all night, not daring to refresh himself with sleep, amid the din and howlings of the hungry wolves. Towards morning he was relieved from his anxiety by the retreat of the wolves, who left, and disturbed him no more.

"He now prepared a hasty meal at the fire, partook of it, and concluded to retrace his steps. Packing his wolf skin, he proceeded homeward. The sun rose to meridian, and still he traveled on; night came, and for ought he could tell, he was no nearer home than when he started in the morning. Being weary with his day's journey, he again kindled a fire, laid himself down to rest, and slept soundly till morning. At early dawn he again set forth in quest of home, and about ten o'clock in the morning, to his indescribable surprise and joy, discovered the British flag flying from the fort at Oswego.

"The officers of the garrison, to whom he related his adventure, treated him with great kindness. With them he spent the remainder of the day, and next morning set out with a light heart for home. The day following, being the fifth from his departure, he safely returned to the bosom of his family, who had already become somewhat alarmed for his safety.

"The bounty then paid by the State for a full grown wolf, was forty dollars, which he in due time received. This in some degree proved a balm for his sufferings; but for which, he would not again encounter the danger he had so greatly risked."

Joshua Clark, 1849[170]

It was the mortal risk of land travel in these western regions, as well as the extreme inconvenience, that conspired to keep travelers within their boats and on the waterways. Even as late as 1810, overland travel through this region was discouraged. In describing the route west from Fort Brewerton to Three Rivers, one journalist reported:

"This distance of twenty miles by water, is lessened to seven by the path on land. I say path, if path there is, for waggon never rolled its wheels through those impervious woods."

Harry Crosswell, 1810[171]

The navigation of this river is somewhat dangerous, on account of several rocky shoals, and the rapidity of its current; it, therefore, requires a particular knowledge of these places, in order to take a boat down safely.

Christian Schultz, 1807[172]

In the early morning hours of October 15th, the batteau of the expedition glided down toward Three River Point - an oasis of activity in the midst of what must have seemed a tractless wilderness.

At about eight miles from where we started is an island of considerable size, and covered with trees. A little beyond is the mouth of Seneca River, where there is a clearing and a good log house of squared timber, fastened with dove-tail joints.

Here we breakfasted with Major Bingham, the owner, who we hired as a pilot, to conduct us down the rapids that are somewhat dangerous to one not acquainted with the channel.

The Seneca River is the water route leading to the Genesee Country, and to all the western country now settling, and it is much navigated, as it leads into five lakes of considerable size. The Seneca Lake is also quite near to the Genesee River. By this stream all the salt made on the Onondaga Lake is brought down. This place is called "Three River Point", although there are only two, but the union of the Seneca and Onondaga rivers here takes the name of the Oswego River.

Arrival at Three River Point brought boatmen to the great crossroads of inland navigation. Behind was the return route to Albany, via the Mohawk. To the left one could run up the Seneca River to the Finger Lakes, and, most significantly, to the entrance into Onondaga Lake - the source of the salt being shipped throughout the Northeast in this era. And to the right, the combination of the Oneida and Seneca rivers created the Oswego River - passageway to the Great Lakes.

> "Three River Point is most eligibly situated on the left bank, at the confluence of the Onondaga, Seneca and Oswego Rivers. Although no town is laid out, as this place at present contains but a single house, yet, I do not hesitate to say, the time will shortly arrive when it will be the site of one of the most respectable inland towns in this part of the state... as it must always command a great share of trade, for all the goods bound to or from Oswego must pass by Three River Point, either in ascending or descending, exclusive of the whole trade of the Genesee Country by the Seneca River, as well as the salt trade to the upper country, which must also pass this Point on its way to the Mohawk. It has, likewise, nothing to apprehend from any rivalship from settlements on either of the two opposite points, as neither of these possess a sufficient elevation, being subject to be inundated by every rise of the river."
>
> Christian Schultz, 1807[173]

Although perhaps the most advantageous location for the establishment of a way station for boats, this place had but one house, and that less than inviting:

By a winding navigation of eighteen or twenty miles, we came to Three River Point. It is a place! Pray heaven I ne'er may see its like again! It was late before we left Fort

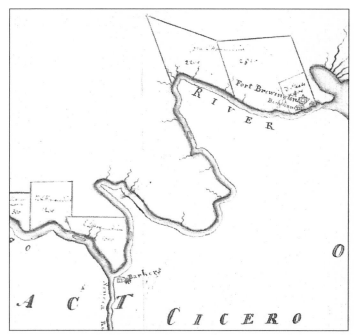

This 1792 map shows the navigation between Fort Breweton and Three River Point (Barkers).

Brewerton, or we might have arrived at this *omnium gatherum* earlier. There was no other house, except at many miles distance; and here, in spite of fleas, bugs, filth, and drunken boatmen, we staid all night.

Harry Croswell, 1811[174]

The aversion to lodging in public houses in the wilderness, expressed in many travelers' journals, appears to have been universal, and was applied to that at Three Rivers Point in particular:

All these people lay ill in the room where we were to dine and sleep; for it was the only room in the house. The newcomers, who brought with them a very tight tent, declared that they would rather pass the night under this tent, than breathe the noxious air of this house. Mr. VanAllen, struck with a dread of a relapse of the ague, ordered his tent, which consisted only of his sail, to be pitched on the banks of the river; and we wrapped ourselves up, as usual, in our blankets.

The spot, on which the inn stands, belongs to Squire Bingham, who also possesses a few acres contiguous to the building, and a comfortable quantity of land at some distance from it. All these lands would be tolerably good, but for their marshy, low, and flat situation, which exposes them to frequent inundations. The water is abominable; and the air bad.

Duke de la Rochefoucault Liancourt, 1795[175]

In spite of its marginal reputation, Three River Point became the place to wait while arranging for a pilot to guide one's boat down the Oswego River:

Next day about three in the afternoon we reached three-River Point, eighteen miles from fort Brewerton... One Barker lived at the east side of this point, whose chief employment was to conduct the Bateaux over the falls in Oswego River. He might have been independent, had he

Three River Point

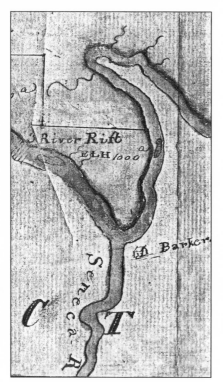

Detail of a 1795 map showing Barker's public house.

"Before sundown we reached Three-River Point. This place derives its name from the confluence of the Oneida and Seneca Rivers, and the river formed by this junction, is then denominated Oswego River. It lies in Cicero, on the south side of the Oneida River, is part of a Gospel lot, and an excellent position for a town. All the salt-boats from the Springs, and the boats from the Cayuga and Seneca Lakes, rendezvous at this place; and we found the house, which is kept by one Magie, crowded with noisey drunken people, and the landlord, wife, and son were in the same situation. The house being small and dirty, we took refuge in a room in which were two beds and a weaver's loom, a beaufet and dressers for tea utensils, and furniture, and there we had a very uncomfortable collation.

"Col. Porter erected his tent and made his fire on the hill, where he was comfortably accommodated with the young gentlemen. I reconnoitered up stairs; but in passing to the bed, I saw several dirty, villainous-looking fellows in their bunks, and all placed in the same garret. I retreated from the disgusting scene, and left Gen. North, Mr. De Witt, and Mr. Geddes, in the undisputed possession of the Attic beds. The Commodore and I took possession of the beds below; but previous to this, we were assured by an apparently decent girl, that they were free from vermin, and that the beds above were well stored with them. Satisfied with this assurance, we prepared ourselves for a comfortable sleep, after a fatiguing day.

"But no sooner were we lodged, than our noses were assailed by a thousand villainous smells, meeting our olfactory nerves in all directions, the most potent exhalation arising from boiled pork, which was left close to our heads. Our ears were invaded by a commingled noise of drunken people in an adjacent room, of crickets in the hearth, of rats in the walls, of dogs under the beds, by the whizzing of musquitoes about our heads, and the flying of bats about the room. The women in the house were continually pushing open the door, and pacing the room for plates, and knives, and spoons; and the dogs would avail themselves of such opportunities to come in under our beds. Under these circumstances sleep was impractical; and, after the family had retired to rest, we heard our companions above rolling about restless in their beds. This we set down to the credit of the bugs, and we hugged ourselves on our superior comforts. We were, however, soon driven up by the annoyance of vermin. On lighting a candle and examining the beds, we found that we had been assailed by an army of bed-bugs, aided by a body of light infantry in the shape of fleas, and a regiment of musquitoe cavalry. I retreated from the disgusting scene and immediately dressed myself, and took refuge in a segar.

"Leaving the Commodore to his meditations, I went out on the Point. The moon was in its full orb and blaze of unclouded majesty. Here my feelings were not only relieved, but my mind was elevated by the scenery before me. The ground on which I stood was elevated; below me flowed the Oneida River, and on my left the Seneca poured its waters, and uniting together they formed a majestic stream. Flocks of white geese were sporting on the water - a number of boats lying moored to the banks - a white tent erected on the right, enlivened by a blazing fire - an Indian hut on the opposite bank, displaying the red man of the forest, and his family, preparing for the sports of the day - the bellowing of thousands of frogs in the waters, and the roaring of bloodhounds, in pursuit of deer and foxes, added to the singularity of the scene. My mind became tranquilized, and I availed myself of a vacant mattress in the tent, and enjoyed a comfortable sleep of two hours."

DeWitt Clinton, 1810[176]

possessed virtue and strength of mind sufficient to take advantage of his situation.

Every Bateau bound to or coming from the Genesee - Onondago - Oswego - Catalaqui and Niagara stops here, and their crews would often deem it a happiness, could they there be supplied with refreshments of bread, butter and milk - of rum and gin. He knew scarce the first, so seldom did he see these articles, and the latter he wanted for himself exclusively.

A small patch of corn promised a good crop and a similar of summer wheat - which he said to have sown the first of May - had branched out its large ears.

We hired Barker at five shillings a day to bring us over the fall, and stay with us till our return.

Adrian Vanderkemp, 1792[177]

Whether one secured a guide at Three River Point, or embarked on one's own devices to descend the Oswego River, the challenges began immediately after departure:

Two miles below this is a rapid called Three River Rift, and very dangerous for batteaux in low water.

James Cockburn, 1792[178]

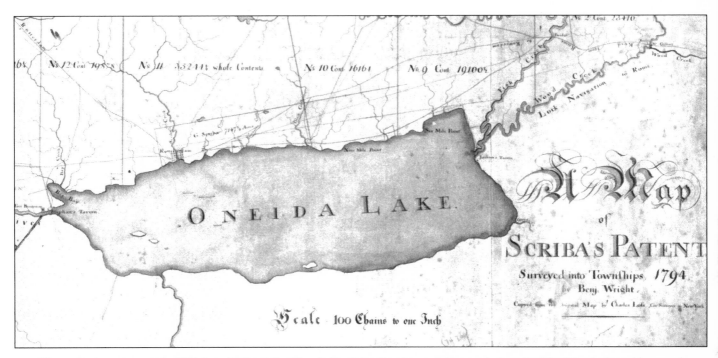

The navigation route west in 1794, from "Gilbert's" at Canada Creek junction (upper right corner), down the Wood Creek channel improved by the WILNC in 1793 to "Jackson's Tavern" at Oneida Lake, and along the north shore of Oneida Lake to "Stephen's Tavern" at the entrance to the Oneida River (far left).

CHAPTER TEN

The Oswego River

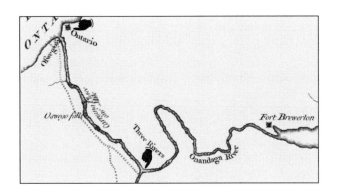

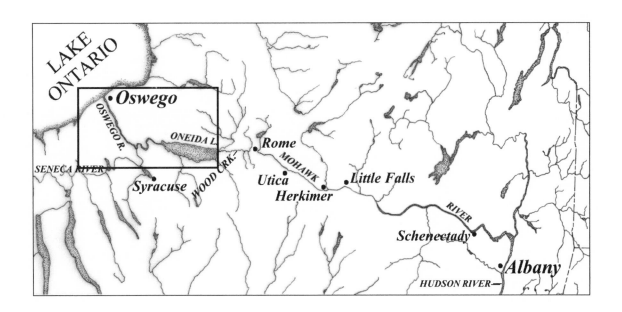

Stopping at Three River Point only long enough to have breakfast and arrange for a pilot, bringing the number in the batteau to eight, Pharoux, Desjardins, and Brunel started down the Oswego River on the last leg of their inland journey to Lake Ontario.

Soon after starting we saw a bear with two young crossing the river, and we hastened to overtake them by rowing, while three of us landed with axes and guns to intercept them, but they escaped.

Encounters with bears in this region were frequent. This party was fortunately spared the disaster that befell two other Frenchmen passing up the Oneida River that same summer:

As Mr. Stevens sat at dinner with his family, he was interrupted by a man, who came running to the door, almost breathless and dripping with water; stammered out with a tremulous voice, that he and his companion had been attacked by a bear in the river, and driven from their boat. He feared the bear would kill his friend, and wished Mr. Stevens to go instantly with his gun and kill the bear.

He started at once, reprimed his gun, and hastened with all dispatch to the scene of the disaster. When arrived, they found the remaining man on shore, wet through and through, moaning in the bitterest anguish the hardness of his lot.

The fact was; that as the two were proceeding up the river, the bear at the same time attempted to swim across. Upon seeing the bear, the boatmen resolved to have some sport and capture him. They rowed along side and aimed a blow at Bruin's head, which he evaded, and before they could recover themselves, scrambled over the side of the boat and drove the astonished Frenchmen into the river. They were forced to make a virtue of Necessity, and one ran for help, while the other watched the boat and its new occupant.

On the arrival of Mr. Stevens at the scene of action, his bearship was majestically seated at the stern, calmly surveying the scene, and quietly floating down the current, as undisturbed as a king upon his throne. A shot from Mr. Stevens' rifle bereft the monarch of his titles and his life at once. The boatmen swam to the boat and rowed up to the landing. When the prize was dressed, it was found to exceed three hundred pounds in weight.

Joshua Clark, 1849[179]

"The Oswego River is about twenty-four miles long. The fall from Three-River Point to Oswego, is about 112 feet. It contains a great many rapids, which I shall specify. Considering that it is constituted by the Oneida and Seneca Rivers, which proceed from the Oneida, the Onondaga, the Cayuga, the Seneca, the Canandaigua, the Oswego, and the Skeneatelas Lakes, it is surprising that it is not larger. It is about the width of the Mohawk, and appears like that river reversed. The river scenery is delightful. The large and luxuriant trees on its banks form an agreeable shade, and indicate great fertility."

DeWitt Clinton, 1810[180]

Not being accosted by the bear they saw, the party continued downriver.

The river is here quite wide, and we descended rapidly, the current bearing the bateau along with force. Near this we had to pass a second rapid, between two rows of stones piled up by the Indians for an eel weier, where the opening at the point is very narrow, and the water presses through with violence. On the right bank we noticed the fishing cabins of the Indians. At the opening of this passage they place their nets and take thousands of fish as they ascend from the lake or return, at the two fishing seasons.

Here was located the rapid known as "Three River Rift" [Phoenix], which had been, since prehistoric times, a favored fishing station of the Oneidas and their predecessors. It was a site of much activity in the season of fish migration:

Here were the Onondagos collected in large numbers - some fishing - some smoking in their huts - others from time to time arriving and passing us in their bark canoes, with much art constructed - so light and easily manageable that a squaw with her little daughter gained on us, and left us soon behind her by her velocity.

Adrian Vanderkemp, 1792[181]

An eyewitness image of Indians in a canoe, c. 1792.

Apparently Three River Rift was dangerous enough to warrant a pilot, notwithstanding the Oswego Falls to follow, as the one hired by the French party left after passage below that and the following rapid.

A little further down is a third rapid, but not more difficult than those of the Mohawk, and here our pilot left us. We noticed at the bottom of the water some little heaps of pebbles perfectly round, and in great quantity, the work of that industrious fish, the sucker, which there deposits its eggs, safe from the attack of its enemies the eels and pike.

These curious constructions drew the attention of several navigators in this period, none of which correctly identified the cause:

We observed in many places on this river, small hills of stones, - which, we are told, are thrown up by salmon, where they cast their spawn, to protect them from other fish.

Elkanah Watson, 1791[182]

Adrian Vanderkemp, passing this same spot in 1792, came closest to identifying the correct type of fish:

I had now an opportunity of examining and witnessing the truth of what the Baron had told me before of the curious manner by which the chubs (Tziobs) hide their eggs. They deposit these along the rivers of Oswego and Onondago on shallow spots, and cover these afterwards with small pebbles, heaped in a conical form, some what below the surface of the water, while others were prominent above it.

Adrian Vanderkemp, 1792[183]

It was, in fact, the Fallfish, a relative of the chub, that produced these pebble heaps. But even years later, the debate on their origins continued:

In Oswego and Seneca Rivers, and I think in Oneida River, considerable circular collections or piles of gravel are to be found, in the water near the shore, and sometimes on the margin of the water. Many are to be seen at very short distances, and they are evidently the work of some animal, exhibiting uniformity and design. As they appear the latter end of June, or beginning of July, when there are no freshets, and when the salmon and bass ascend, it is supposed they are erected by fish. By some they are called *bass-heaps*, and by others they are imputed to lamprey eels.

DeWitt Clinton, 1810[184]

The batteau, without pilot, continued on the river, running down with the current.

Between the two great rapids above mentioned, the bed of the river is paved by a mass of rock in one level, which further on forms a pleasant appearing island. On the left several creeks fall into the river, near one of which we saw an Indian family, who had some bear skins stretched on frames around their cabin, and a bark canoe on the bank.

Near this place the river forms another island. The sky was overcast through the day, with sleet from nine in the morning till sunset. After pitching our tent on the right bank, we noticed in the distance a fire, and heard a cow bell, from which we judged that they had already begun settlements in this secluded country.

This camp, marking the end of their second week on the journey, may well have been made in the same spot selected by Vanderkemp the year before, as he also had Major DeZeng as a guide in his passage down the Oswego:

We concluded to encamp about ten miles from three-rivers point, opposite to a handsome Island in the Oswego

river. The pickerel often weigh here thirty pound - pike is of a similar size. We took catfish of four span and a half - perch too; of which we obtained a few, is here in abundance.

Adrian Vanderkemp, 1792[185]

Early the next morning, the boatmen started down toward their inevitable encounter with the infamous Oswego Falls, or the "Falls of the Onondaga" if one called this river by that name.

Wednesday, October 16th. Started at half past six and soon came to an island on the right, and two locations on the left, and discovered the Oswego Falls, which are about eight feet high. The water is as still as in a basin, and the current is scarcely perceptible until just at the brink of the fall, which renders it easy to land, - usually on the right, where the portage house, and near it another, is built. On the left side is a house on the top of the bank, with clearings.

The river, which is quite wide above this perpendicular fall, flows over a bed of stone, perfectly level, forming several sheets following the irregularity of the edge and the crevices of the upper shelf, from which it falls with a loud noise, bearing along with it the debris of rock to the channel below, where the river forms a succession of rapids. The principal of these, and the one having the most water, is in the bend on the right side.

"Six miles below the point you arrive at the falls of Onondaga, which, more properly, should be called the falls of Oswego, as they are upon that river. This, however, I am told is in contradistinction to a very strong rapid, four or five miles below this, which is called the Oswego Falls. I had always been led to believe that what were called the Falls of Onondaga were nothing more than a mere rapid, therefore I was not a little surprised to find a perpendicular fall of the whole river for about ten feet, excepting a narrow channel of about twenty feet wide, worn by the constant friction of the water."

Christian Schultz, 1807[186]

On the same side we observed a cutting in the rock which they told us was the trace of a canal projected in the time of the French, but which we thought was only done to supply a mill, while the French had a fortified post on the top of the bank. This fort commanded the passage and closed it against the canoes of the Iroquois, who in wartime, at the solicitations of the English, took this route to molest our establishments in Canada.

The fort at Oswego Falls, 1794.

The Frenchmen were right to doubt their boatmen's tale of the old canal at this site, but wrong to understand the fort that stood here had been French:

The land by the falls is a state reservation - there is here a fine place for a mill - The British had a saw mill here and a fort to protect the

The Oswego Falls

The portage bypassing the Oswego Falls, 1795.

In the early years of the nineteenth century, the sixty foot long Durham boats became common in this region, particularly in the shipping of salt out of Onondaga Lake. Boats were rarely portaged around the Falls of the Oswego [sometimes called the Falls of the Onondago], unless they were small batteaux and lacked the assistance of a pilot. Such was apparently the case in one instance in 1810:

"The portage at the falls, is something more than a mile. We carried across, though we might have descended by water; but our boat must have been light, and our courage a little greater than any of us possessed at that moment."

Harry Croswell, 1810[188]

That same year, DeWitt Clinton, apparently traveling in a Durham boat himself, observed the situation surrounding the Falls in greater detail, noting the importance of the salt commerce here and the passing of unloaded boats down the rapids:

"In a smart shower we arrived at the celebrated Falls of Oswego, twelve miles from Three-River Point, and twelve miles from Oswego. There is a carrying place of one mile here, the upper and lower landing being that distance apart. At both landings there were about 15,000 barrels of salt, containing five bushels each, and each bushel weighing fifty-six pounds. It is supposed the same quantity has been already carried down, making together 30,000 barrels. The carriage at this place is one shilling for each barrel.

"Loaded boats cannot with safety descend the Falls, but light boats may, notwithstanding the descent is twelve feet, and the roaring of the troubled waves among the great rocks is really terrific. Pilots conduct the boats over for one dollar each; and being perfectly acquainted with the Falls, no accidents are known to happen, although the least misstep would dash the vessels to atoms. The Falls are composed of high rocks, apparently granite. The ascent by boat is impractical."

DeWitt Clinton, 1810[189]

After 1803, when the other improvements of Philip Schuyler's company had been already completed, this location remained the most difficult and dangerous spot on the inland navigation corridor. Its improvement remained within the mission of the Navigation Company until 1809, when all work west of Oneida Lake was abandoned. But in the end, it was never improved:

"The Western Inland Navigation Company are bound, by their act of incorporation, to erect locks at all the falls and obstructions on this route; but, in consequence of having expended their funds, they are unable to proceed with their improvements. The state has already made a purchase of this stock to a large amount, in order to give aid to the company; but it appears to be the general opinion, that unless it should take the whole into its hands, or give the proprietors some further and more effectual assistance, the establishment must inevitably fail, or at least, every thing will be suffered to remain in its present unfinished and obstructed state."

Christian Schultz, 1807[190]

portage which is two chains. But the rapid with dangerous rocks continues a mile below the carrying place, and is not to be attempted without a pilot.

James Cockburn, 1792[187]

This outpost, described in 1759 as a star fort of timbers fifteen feet high and a foot thick, was already in ruins a decade later:

...near them was formerly a Block house or advanced guard, from Oswego fort; but is now burned.

John Lees, 1768[191]

Vestiges of the fortifications here could be seen for a century after, but were not visited by this party. Perhaps it was the mill race mentioned by Cockburn that the journalists observed and took for an old canal.

Years later, DeWitt Clinton described a similar feature here that suggested to him the possibility of a canal yet to come:

> A little below the Upper Falls, a ravine, the ancient bed of a creek, appears, which falls in just below the Lower. Here a canal might be easily cut round the Falls.
>
> DeWitt Clinton, 1810[192]

In 1793, the passage of the Oswego Falls involved the combination of portaging boats and cargo as well as the piloting of empty boats through otherwise impassable rapids, to be reloaded below.

> *They slide the boats on rollers a distance of about sixty toises to the foot of the falls, from which point they are taken empty through the rapids about a mile, while the goods are loaded upon wagons, along a road upon the bank, to the point of embarkation. The price of the portage is four shillings, as at other places. We went this distance on foot. The soil next to the ridge of the fall is of moderate fertility. It is, however, cleared, and there is a new log house at the lower landing, where we again rejoined the four bateaux which we had overtaken, going to Canada.*

But passing even an empty boat was not always a simple matter:

> After the boat was unloaded, the captain determined to descend the falls in his empty boat rather than wait for the return of the teams to take it round over land. He urged me very strongly to make the descent with him, but as I should not then have had an opportunity of seeing the boat descend, nor of making those observations that I could upon the banks, I declined, and recommended my companion for his chief mate, but he likewise declined the honour, preferring a walk of twenty minutes by land, to a flight of two or three by water.
>
> The captain, and some of his men, then descended themselves, and, at the first pitch, nearly one-half of the boat disappeared; all the men fell down, while the countenance and conduct of the captain betrayed evident signs of the frolic not being quite so agreeable as he had expected; and, when we arrived at the landing place, we found the boat half full of water. Having repaired the boat, which had received some injury in descending the falls, our cargo was soon reloaded, and we continued our voyage.
>
> Christian Schultz, 1807[193]

"Here the river is about two hundred yards wide, and the water at one pitch all across the river, falls eight feet, and forms a strong, foaming rapid for one mile below. The banks of this river are low, and subject to be overflowed. The land apparently rich."

Jacob Lindley, 1793[194]

Perhaps to the good fortune of the French expedition, their pilot rejoined them unexpectedly just above the falls.

> *Here the river is quite wide, and from hence to the lake it forms several rapids so difficult to pass that we were again obliged to take a pilot. On again meeting Major Bingham, at whose house we had taken breakfast at Three Rivers, he offered of his own accord to conduct us down for a dollar. A major, skilled as a sailor and a pilot, for a dollar, gave us an idea of the importance of this rank in America.*
>
> *The view of the river is very fine, with its islands scattered here and there in a truly romantic way. The shores are low, but a little beyond rise into steep banks, but further down, as we approach the lake, they become higher, and we meet considerable rapids. Our major pilot took us through them all very skillfully, except one, called from its difficulty of navigation the <u>Devil's Race</u>, where we stopped upon the rocks. But our major, who was as intrepid in the water as under fire, threw himself into the river, and by his example induced our three men to do likewise, when by lifting with their shoulders, the boat passed over the shelf of rocks and glided again into the channel.*

"We passed a number of salt-boats. The commerce in salt is great between Oswego and the Falls. As we approached the former place the country bore marks of cultivation; the banks became more elevated, the current increased in force, and the rapids in number. About seven miles from Oswego we encountered a rapid called Smooth Rock Rapid. Six and a-half miles, the Devil's Horn; six miles, the Six-Mile Rift; then the Little Smooth Rock Rapid, the Devil's Warping Bars; four miles, the Devil's Horse Race; and one mile from Oswego, the Oswego Rift, a violent rapid, nearly as bad as the Oswego Falls, having a fall of at least five feet."

DeWitt Clinton, 1810[195]

> *The sight of the water plunging and boiling against the rocks, and of the other four bateaux, two of which passed safely while the others like ours were thrown upon the rocks, formed a scene rather exciting. As for the danger, there is none except that of bruising the bateaux, as the water is shallow, thus causing all the trouble with but little peril.*

The Durham Boat

A Durham boat underway, from an early woodcut.

By 1797 the several necessary portages along the Mohawk had been eliminated by the improvements of the Western Inland Lock Navigation Company. Various other obstacles to large boat operations had been overcome by the works in the Mohawk channel completed in 1799 and those in Wood Creek in 1803. It was then that the small, portable batteau was rapidly replaced by the long and narrow river craft known as the Durham boat.

The prototype of this boat in America had been the mid-eighteenth century iron ore boats of the Delaware River, which gained fame in transporting General Washington's troops across that river to attack the Hessians in 1776. Before the end of the century, they were as common in New York as they had been in Pennsylvania.

"The Durham boat, constructed something in shape like a modern canal boat, with flat bottom, and carrying from eight to twenty tons, took the place of the clumsy little bateau which had for more than fifty years superseded the Indian bark canoe. These Durham boats were not decked except at the front and stern; but along the sides were heavy planks partially covering the vessel, with cleats nailed on them, to give foothold to the boatmen using the poles. Many of the boats fitted for use on the lakes and St. Lawrence had a mast, with one large sail, like an Albany sloop. The usual crew was from five to six men. At that day, boatmen at Schenectady were numerous, and generally were a rough and hardy class; but from common labors, exposures and hardships, a sort of brotherly affection for each other existed among them which did not brook the interference of outsiders, and yet as a class they were orderly, law-abiding citizens.

"Boating at this period was attended with great personal labor. True, the delay of unloading and carriage at the Little Falls had been overcome, but it was found more difficult to force large than small craft over the rapids. In view of that difficulty, several boats usually started from port in company, and those boats first arriving at a rift, at a low-water stage, waited the approach of others, that their united strength might lighten the labor there. At high water, with favorable wind, they could sail the navigable length of the river; but when sails were insufficient, long poles were used. These poles had heads of considerable size that rested against the shoulder of the boatman, while pushing onward; as the writer has sometimes seen the shoulders of the boatmen become calloused by such labor, like that of a severe collar-worn horse. The toil of a boatman's life, when actually at work, was generally severe and trying; so that, in port, like the sailor, they were sometimes festive and hilarious."

John Sanders, 1876[196]

Christian Schultz, passing up the Mohawk River in 1807, gives a particularly accurate impression of these 60 foot boats; most dramatic to watch in operation for someone unfamiliar with shoal water navigation:

"It is not often, however, that a fair wind will serve for more than three or four miles together, as the irregular course of the river renders its aid very precarious; their chief dependence, therefore, is upon their pike poles. These are generally from eighteen to twenty-two feet in length, having a sharp pointed iron, with a socket weighing ten or twelve pounds affixed to the lower end; the upper has a large knob, called a button, mounted upon it, so that the poleman may press upon it with his whole weight without endangering his person.

"This manner of impelling the boat forward is extremely laborious, and none but those who have been for some time accustomed to it, can manage these poles with any kind of advantage. Within the boat on each side is fixed a plank running fore and aft, with a number of cross cleats nailed upon it, for the purpose of giving the poleman a sure footing in hard poling. The men, after setting their poles against a rock, bank or bottom of the river, declining their heads very low, place the upper end or button against the back part of their right or left shoulders, (according to the side on which they may be poling,) then falling down on their hands and toes,

continued on next page

continued from page 80

creep the whole length of the gang-boards, and send the boat forward with considerable speed.

"The first sight of four men on each side of a boat, creeping along on their hands and toes, apparently transfixed by a huge pole, is no small curiosity; nor was it, until I had observed their perseverance for two or three hundred yards, that I became satisfied they were not playing some pranks. From the general practice of this method, as likewise from my own trials and observation, I am convinced that they have fallen upon the most powerful way possible to exert their bodily strength for the purpose required. The position, however, was so extremely awkward to me, that I doubt whether the description I have attempted will give you an adequate idea of the procedure."

Christian Schultz, 1807[197]

A few days later, while traveling down the Oswego River, Schultz noted the treachery of operating these large river freighters in strong rapids:

"The navigation of this river is extremely dangerous, on account of the rapidity of the current, and the obstructions formed by numerous rocks, which lie hid in the channel. About five miles below the point our boat very narrowly escaped being stove to pieces, by being forced upon what is called Pilot Rock. The rapidity of the current here was so great, that the united strength and exertions of our whole boat's crew, nine in number, including ourselves, could not have prevented the boat from being wrecked, as we had become exhausted by fatigue, had we not fortunately met with assistance from five boats' crews, who were coming up the stream empty. These boats being very narrow, an expert pilot will conduct them with great judgement among the rocks; but, from their great length, (about sixty feet,) should the boat happen to strike any thing, or touch a rock on the bottom, the rapidity of the current sweeps the stern round with so much violence, that, should it come in contact with some projecting rock, as is not unfrequently the case, the boat is instantly dashed to pieces. The way of managing a boat on these waters, when she grounds forward, is to keep her in her position, and prevent her from springing with the current. For that purpose a couple of hands jump over the bows, and with hand-spikes set the boat back against the stream, until she regains the regular channel; but when once she swings in a very strong current, it is impossible for an ordinary boat's crew to check her, in which case, if she has room, and a clear bottom, no evil can result; but if, on the contrary, she strike a rock, ship-wreck becomes inevitable."

Christian Schultz, 1807[197]

Two miles below we landed on the left bank to relieve the bateau, on account of the shallowness of the river, which is here very wide. The banks are here formed of a greyish kind of clay, resting upon horizontal bed's and strata of alternately gray and brown stone.

By leaving their boat to lighten it, the French party missed the immediate experience of descending the final series of rapids leading toward the mouth of the Oswego River and Lake Ontario. The last of these, an extended rush of water often called the "Oswego Falls", but not to be confused with the greater falls above [Fulton], apparently could propel one's boat into the harbor below the walls of Fort Ontario with exceptional speed.

One traveler, who had the courage to remain within his boat on approaching Oswego, recorded his impressions:

For a distance of five miles below the falls there is a very strong rapid, the descent of which is probably not less than six or seven feet in each mile; this continues much the same until you arrive within one mile of the town, when you suddenly perceive a rapid increase of motion, occasioned by what are called the falls of Oswego.

The town and its shipping are now in sight; the current hurries forward almost with the rapidity of an arrow; and, although the water is perfectly clear and transparent, the bed of the river a smooth solid rock, and the water so shoal that you frequently feel the boat rub against the bottom, yet you are wafted along with such extreme swiftness that you can scarcely get a glimpse of the bottom as you glide over it; and, before you can imagine it, find yourself unexpectedly among the vessels of Oswego.

Christian Schultz, 1807[199]

CHAPTER ELEVEN

Oswego

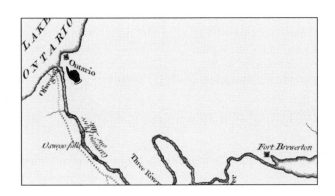

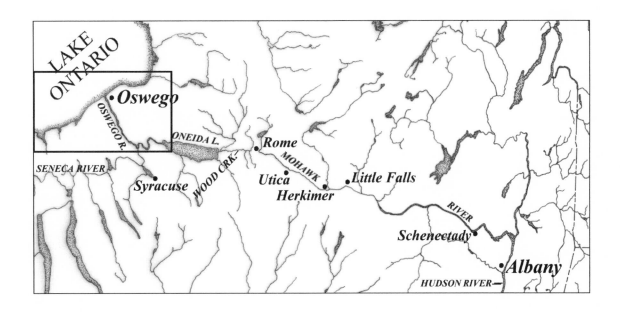

Having left their batteau in the hands of the boatmen, to run empty down through the last rapids in the river, the party approached the end of the inland route to the Great Lakes on foot.

In the distance we observed the lake, and Fort Ontario, now called Oswego. This fort, built by the French upon the right bank, is now occupied by the English, who have abandoned a site less advantageous on the left bank, which is now in ruins. We noticed that the soil is rocky and sterile, and the timber of meagre growth. We returned to our boat on approaching the fort, at the foot of which we landed, and presently an English inspector paid us a visit to see that we had brought no merchandize, as trade with Canada is prohibited. Finding nothing, he retired, and Major DeZeng went up alone into the fort to procure a government pass which he flattered himself that he could obtain, as the commandant, Captain Schroeder, was like himself a Hessian, and he had a letter of recommendation from Mr. Porteus his friend.

Oswego stood as a destination for most of the commercial and military batteaux traveling west from Schenectady. This expedition, however, was interested only in swiftly passing through this port and on to their lands to the northeast.

Yet without perhaps fully appreciating it, they had arrived at one of the most historic places in North America:

Oswego is a place celebrated in our colonial history as one of the great depots of the fur trade. It was strenuously contended for by the French and English, in their American wars. During the Revolutionary contest it was occupied by the British, who held it in defiance of the treaty of peace, until it was delivered up under Jay's treaty. As an important post, commanding the communication between the lakes and the waters that communicate with the Hudson, it must ever claim the attention of Government.

DeWitt Clinton, 1810[200]

The landscape here was dominated by the fort, which occupied a height of land on the east side of the river's mouth, and at its foot a small cove served as a batteau landing:

Oswego fort stands at the entrance of the river, which it commands... the fort is an irregular pentagon, and is garrisoned by a company of the Royal Americans and a few artillery men - It is in very bad repair and I am informed mounts not more than 4 carriage guns - at present the barracks is capable of containing a ridgement - there is no house or inhabitant without the fort - and a custom house officer resides in the fort to stop any prohibited articles passing from the States to the British colonies.

James Cockburn, 1792[201]

At this time (1793), the old civilian settlement on the west side of the river was in ruins. As observed by Philip Schuyler, civilian occupation had not re-established itself, even a decade later:

The fort on the north side going to ruin. Garrisoned by a Corporal & two men. Town lots are laid out on the south side and one tolerably good house & store house is erected by a Mr. Sharp who keeps a public house. There are besides three miserable huts - two wharves are constructed, at which there lay a sloop and two schooners ready to sail for Niagara and Kingston.

Philip Schuyler, 1802[202]

Five years later, in 1807, the marginal beginnings of a town were observed here by Christian Schultz:

This town was regularly laid out by the state...but, at present, it makes a very contemptable appearance, from the irregular and confused manner in which the inhabitants are permitted to build their houses and stores. Most of these are placed as suits the convenience or whim of the owners, in the streets or elsewhere, without any regard to the original plan. As the town is quite small, and there is no want of room, the inhabitants do not complain of this encroachment at present; but it certainly would be not only for their interest, but would likewise add much to the beauty of the place, were they to observe as much taste and regularity in their buildings as possible. This would obtain a favourable notice from travelers, and probably be the means of gaining settlers; whereas the present appearance of the houses and accommodations are really despicable.

Christian Schultz, 1807[203]

The major problem faced by navigators wishing to get by Oswego and into Lake Ontario in this period was the persistent British garrison here, a decade after the end of the Revolution, and the consequent paranoia about boats going to Canada.

> **"When we arrived at the Fort of Oswego on Lake Ontario, we were searched to see if we were not 'running goods' as they called it. This being adjusted without any difficulty, for we were neither spies nor smugglers, we were now ready to embark on the lake..."**
> **Rev. Elijah Woolsey, 1794[204]**

This situation also frustrated, and nearly aborted, the expedition of Pharoux and Desjardins to their lands along the Black River.

In the mean time Major Bingham, to conciliate the garrison in our favor, did them ample honors with our rum, and drank most cordially with his late enemies, while we passed the time in walking, and in examining the fort.

The ruins of many houses here convinced us that this place had been a small town in the times of the French. The soil is quite sterile. We noticed some very long saws, with which they employ the soldiers in sawing planks. The timber on both sides is cut off, having been used as fire wood, so that now the garrison find another occupation, in going out to cut at some distance from the lake shore, and loading it into large bateaux, which we saw lying in a cove that the river forms at the foot of the fort.

Oswego Harbor

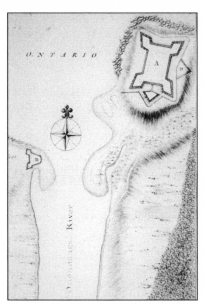

A 1758 view of the batteau landing below Fort Ontario.

At the mouth of the Oswego River, a harbor was formed by the intrusion, from either side of the river, of two substantial heights of land. The resistance of these bedrock elevations to the pounding seas of Lake Ontario had created an enclosure, within which the harbor would eventually develop.

On a broad elevation on the right bank, as one came down the river, stood Fort Ontario, a fortification begun by the British in 1755. This was to replace the earlier, and weaker, Fort Oswego, established on the left bank in 1727, and in ruins in 1793. Below the height on which the old fort stood was a low bench of land adjacent to the river, which provided some minimal space for the creation of a town, of sorts. Opposite, on the right bank, a small cove at the base of the cliffs leading to Fort Ontario served as a batteau landing and small harbor. It was here than the French expedition landed in October of 1793.

In 1756, Oswego fell to the French. But lack of forces to secure the port led to its recapture by the British two years later. In 1759 a new fort was begun on the right bank, built largely with wood, and it was this that the French party saw on their arrival over three decades later.

Oswego became the gateway to the Great Lakes for British North America until the American Revolution, and the treaty of 1783, placed the base on American soil. During this period, some attempts to establish a village on the west bank continued, but when the French batteau arrived in 1793, these attempts were a shambles, best described as ruins.

The harbor, standing at the western end of the great inland navigation corridor, continued to serve as the gateway to the west for the emerging republic, providing access into the Great Lakes and the heartland of North America until the completion of the Erie Canal in 1825.

Notwithstanding these employments, and the amusements of hunting and fishing, the garrison become exceedingly weary, with nobody to see in this wilderness, and the bleak winters to pass on the top of an isolated hill, exposed to all winds from every side. The garrison is relieved annually in May, and half of them have already deserted. Most of these troops are Germans and Scotch. They say that most of them are Catholics, and that they are very discontented here.

The fort is a polygon of four sides, and upon one of the bastions the fort, properly so called, is built, the remainder being only an earthen parapet with a palisade. It perfectly commands the lake and the mouth of the Oswego River, which is narrow and forms a natural harbor or bay on each side. There were no cannons, except on the bastion at the point, and this fort could resist nothing but a hand assault.

Seeing the commandant come out with Mr. DeZeng, we returned to our boat, least offense should be taken at our making observations, and Mr. DeZeng hastened forward to tell us that he had represented to the commandant that he was taking M. Pharoux to visit some lands which he had for sale; that M. Desjardins was the servant, and that M. Brunel was the secretary of Pharoux. He had done this to escape suspicions, and although we blamed him for not having told the simple truth, we were however obliged to accept conditions, so as not appear false.

M. Pharoux therefore advanced alone toward the officer, who, in an imperious tone, said he was astonished that Frenchmen should dare to venture near an English fort, that he could scarcely restrain himself from sending us prisoners to Quebec, and that his orders forbade him from allowing any Frenchmen from going into Canada.

"Fort Oswego is, at present, garrisoned by a captain's company of British red coats, in violation of the treaty of 1783; - but according to my calculations, this violent, and truly British aggression, will be of short duration. A high spirited, independent nation, will not long brook the insult."
Elkanah Watson, 1791[205]

M. Pharoux replied that, although French, our citizens could go upon the territory of their allies the Americans, and that we had no intentions of going to Canada, but to the Black River, which belonged to the State of New York, as did also the Oswego country where they then were, and as for the rest, he could well see that we came with no hostile designs, that we were only three men, and with no arms but our hunting pieces; and lastly, that he had no occasion to take offense at our visit.

The Commandant, having thus displayed himself before the soldiers of his garrison, returned majestically into the fort, followed by Major DeZeng, who continued his solicitations for a passport.

Fort Ontario

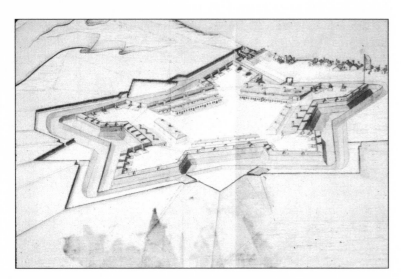

ort Ontario, often called "Fort Oswego" in the 1790s, stood on the east side of the harbor at the mouth of the Oswego River. Built initially by the British, it was captured by the French in 1756 and reoccupied by the British who held it to the end of the American Revolution in 1783. It was supposed to be turned over to the Americans in 1796, under the terms of the Jay Treaty, but was not in American hands until 1798.

The situation here in the mid-1790s is described by one observant traveler:

"Oswego is one of the posts, which Great Britain has hitherto retained, in open violation of the treaty of peace, though she will be obliged to deliver it up to the United States, in the course of next year [1796]. It is a miserable fort, which, in the year 1782, was built at a considerable expense by General Haldimand, at that time Governor of Canada. The river Oswego, at the mouth of which the fort is seated, is at present almost the only course for American vessels to Lake Ontario. The fort is in a ruinous state; one single bastion, out of five, which form the whole of the fortification, is kept in better repair than the rest, and might serve as a citadel, to defend for some time the other works, indefensible by any other means. The present garrison consists of two officers and thirty men, under whose protection a customhouse-officer searches all the vessels, which sail up or down the river. It is not lawful to import any other articles from the United States into Canada, but grain, flour, cattle, and provision, and no commodities are suffered to be exported to the United States, without the express permission from the Governor of Upper Canada; nay, this prohibition extends even to persons, who, if they intended to proceed to that country without such permission, would be imprisoned. As to the prohibited exports in merchandize, they are confiscated, without exception, for the benefit of the customhouse-officer, by whom they are seized...

"This officer... has not even a secretary. His pay is ten shillings a day, and a ration, which is estimated at two. He receives his pay all the year round, though the navigation of the lake is entirely interrupted for five months, and he himself is seven months absent from Oswego... The number of vessels, which ascend and descend the Oswego during the seven months the navigation is open, amounts to about thirty a month. By Mr. Mac-Donald's account far the greater number of them carry new settlers to Upper Canada, at which I am not astonished, it being a certain fact, that the emigration from the United States to Canada is far more considerable, than from the latter to the former country.

"Fort Oswego is the only settlement on the banks of the lake between Kingston and Niagara, excepting Great Sodus... Twelve miles behind Oswego, stands, on the river, the first American settlement. This fort must therefore shift for itself. The officers hunt, read, and drink; and the privates do duty, are displeased with their situation, and desert. For this reason the oldest soldiers are selected for the garrison of Oswego; and yet, though less open to temptation, they desert to the United States. This fort, which lies too remote for any communication with foreign countries, is for five months together completely cut off from the rest of the world; the snow lying then so deep, that it is impossible to go abroad but in snow shoes."

Duke de la Rochefoucault Liancourt, 1795[206]

We were soon after informed that we must go and encamp on the other side of the river, as Frenchmen could not be trusted so near the fort. We obeyed, although we were only three against sixty, and these well intrenched.

Earlier the same summer, a party going west, but lacking any Frenchmen on board, passed easily onto the lake:

> ...proceeded to Oswego garrison, held by the British. They expecting us, we were admitted, and dined with the commanding officer, Capt. Wickham. After dinner, we pursued our journey on the sea of Ontario...
>
> Jacob Lindley, 1793[207]

Having failed to clear the port of Oswego by late in the day, after extensive negotiations, the French party withdrew to the site of the old settlement on the west side of the harbor and prepared to remain the night.

Major DeZeng told us that he had hopes of getting the passport. Having crossed the river, we pitched our tent near the ruins of some chimneys, among the debris of former habitations, and found great difficulty in collecting wood enough for our camp fire for the night, as the four other bateaux, having no trouble with their papers, had encamped before us and gathered all the fuel on the ground. The night was very cold.

After some time, Major DeZeng came to inform us that the government had finally consented to grant a passport, but only for us two, and upon conditions that M. Brunel should remain a hostage until our return, as a guaranty that we should not go into Canada. M. Brunel generously offered to remain, and thus facilitate our journey, but he begged Mr. DeZeng to say that he would not give his parole, and that he would only stay upon condition of being shut up in the fort, instead of remaining alone on this desert side of the river. With this answer the major returned to sup and lodge with the governor, and we remained to council together upon our situation.

With their entire expedition in jeopardy, banished to the desolate ruins of the old town, with only the dim lights of the British fort across the harbor, and the campfires of the other batteaux, as evidence of human presence, the party was left to endure a cold October night, contemplating what the morning would bring.

> "From the mouldering parapet of the deserted Fort of Oswego, I beheld, for the first time, that vast expanse of water, which, forced by the rude winds, lashes the shore of Lake Ontario. The surf, 'curling its monstrous head,' rolled far on the beach, or dashed with fury against the adamantine rock. A lonely barque, ploughed through the unequal waves, greener than the waves of the ocean."
>
> **Harry Crosswell, 1810[208]**

But their night was further disturbed by an episode of serious trouble with the boatmen who had brought them here.

To crown our miseries, the boatmen, stimulated by the rum they had been served with so freely on account of the perils of the navigation, and through the liberality of Major Bingham, came to demand of us the payment of their accounts, saying that they would return in the morning on foot, leaving us and our bateau where we were. The fact was that the sight of a vast lake, and the diminutive size of our bateau, dismayed them. Moreover, seeing our difficulty with the governor, who would do nothing to protect the French, they thought it a favorable moment to show their rascality, without risk, by leaving us in this wilderness.

Such impending desertion was typical of batteau crews in this period, and often occurred in the face of deepwater navigation, here and at Oneida Lake. The best defense, in dealing with these kinds of insurrections, was often a strong offense.

> "We go on slowly, from some difficulty among the Batteaux Men—You know them to be a bad Set."
>
> **Charles Storer, 1793[209]**

We dismissed them to bed very abruptly, and made ourselves sure of our arms and effects by watching in turns through the night.

M. Desjardins, while off guard, went to visit the fires of the other bateaux parties, and there met a man named Amos Ainsley, a loyalist refugee from Kingston in Canada.

This man returned with him to our tent, and, after waking us all up, he gave us some very useful accounts concerning the Bay of Niaoure' and the Black River. He had become acquainted with the country by having traversed it several times, while trading in cattle between Kingston and New York, and trapping there for peltries. He made sundry offers of services, and promised to visit M. Desjardins next winter at Albany.

This encounter no doubt did much to alleviate a growing anxiety among members of the party. Traveling this late in the season, and with much exploration in the Black River country ahead of them, any substantial delay became critical. It was typical in the 1790s to have the inland navigation closed as early as the first week of December, due to "frost".

The next morning brought an opportunity to resolve their situation, which hinged on the demand of the Commandant that Brunel be left as a hostage to guarantee the return of the party to Oswego.

Thursday, October 17th. At day break Major DeZeng returned, saying that the governor would not hear a word about receiving M. Brunel into his fort, but that he might remain on the other side, and when he wanted anything, could fire his gun, and a man would be sent to ascertain what he needed, and carry it to him.

Mr. DeZeng had notified the Commandant that upon these terms he could answer for his hostage, and that probably he would return to Oswego Falls, and there await our return. From the portage to the fort it is about twelve miles, and half of the distance is a rapid. The major added that he had promised the governor our case of gin, and some powder and lead, and finally that the interpreter of the fort would come and search everything.

Upon this we held counsel.

It was determined that deceit would have to be used to avoid depriving Brunel of the opportunity of evaluating the lands this expedition was dedicated to examining, and a bit of rationalization was used to justify the deception.

M. Brunel felt himself released from parole, since he had only given it upon condition of being received into the fort. On the other hand, he disliked being turned back without finishing his journey, to spend a wearisome time in waiting at the falls.

We therefore resolved to pass him under our tarpaulin, (the number of our men being specified in the passport), from whence he could come out when we were out of sight of the fort, but again crawl out of sight should we meet any English vessels to demand our papers.

With this agreement, we waited for the interpreter until nine o'clock, when, seeing nothing of him, we embarked, ready to start. And at half past nine, our men were induced by Mr. DeZeng to return to duty, notwithstanding their dislike to the lake. M. Brunel, being laid under the tarpaulin, was not seen from the fort, and the sentinel allowed us to pass.

The wind being favorable we hoisted sail, and, coasting along, steered for Nine Mile Point. The sky was serene, the water smooth, and the wind fair...

"Lake Ontario resembles rather an open sea, than an inland reservoir of water. You look in vain for land to rest your eye upon."
Adrian Vanderkemp, 1792[210]

The expedition continued along the eastern shore of Lake Ontario and undertook their exploration of the lands to which they hoped to bring settlers and establish a community of French refugees in the coming years. As they returned along this same shore ten days later, landing to make camp for the night, an incident occurred that would add a new member to their party for the return trip eastward.

[October 27th] *Fortunately a bateau behind us, having seen us land, thought it was a good shore, and came to land by the side of us. It contained a Canadian named Silas Judson, and was managed by two Americans living at Three Rivers. These men, better fitted than ours for traveling in a wilderness, soon cut down a quantity of wood, and having piled a dozen logs on one another, we were soon basking before a most brilliant fire. After getting thoroughly warmed, we supped and smoked, and then looked after the safety of our boats.*

Having formed the acquaintance of our fellow voyagers, we agreed to continue together, and as Mr. Judson

was going to Albany, we promised to take him into our boat at Three Rivers, and bring him to Schenectady, without any pay, although he offered us money for the service.

This Mr. Judson was an American, native of Hartford, Connecticut, where he was going to visit his relatives and friends. Being a Royalist, he had emigrated to Canada, where the Government had given him a place at Elizabethtown, in the Township of Oswegatchie, three miles from the river St. Lawrence. He gave us some very useful accounts concerning Upper Canada.

On the morning of the 27th day of their voyage, the French party once again drew close to the western entrance to the inland waterway. Being unfamiliar with the coastline, they were stunned to find they had suddenly drawn in sight of the fort without taking precautions for the supposed hostage, Brunel, whom they were smuggling back into the country.

Monday Oct. 28th. ...came in sight of Oswego and the fort. We could scarcely believe our eyes, as it was but two or three miles distant. It became necessary to think of our friend Brunel, and we accordingly landed in the first bay, about two miles from the fort, and having given him some provisions, he set out, to travel through the woods and join us at the Falls of the Onondaga, this being the first place inhabited by Americans, as we come from the lake.

As we had reason to suppose that we had been seen from the garrison, we decided to continue our route on foot towards the fort, allowing our people to take the boat around to Oswego, where we would rejoin it by land. We thought to profit by the occasion, in observing the fort from a point of view we had not as yet enjoyed.

Our conjectures were not wrong, as they had noticed our landing, and had sent after our bateau, supposing that it had landed some contraband articles. But as they found all right, and as our men told them they had landed their passengers so that they could come by land, they allowed them to continue their route. An officer then came to meet us, and demanded who we were and why we had thus landed. We replied that we were the same Frenchmen who had passed some days before, to go and visit lands, that we were returning to Albany, and that it was so cold that we had landed so as to warm ourselves by walking to the fort. The officer then put on a more pleasant manner, and took us through the line of sentinels, chatting meanwhile on one thing and another.

He had traveled in France, spoke our language, and showed, by his sprightliness and polite address, that he really was the true gentleman that his manners indicated. This amiable young man, the son of Mr. Holland, Surveyor General of Canada, was killed eighteen months afterwards in a duel with his Captain, the same governor of Oswego.

It was perhaps fortunate that the party had on board Major DeZeng, who was acquainted with John Porteous, a friend of the Commandant. DeZeng was also familiar with the procedure of negotiating with the British and apparently felt comfortable in facilitating that process with some half-truths.

On arriving at the gate of the fort, which we went around, Mr. DeZeng went in to speak with the governor, while we walked down to the beach to rejoin our bateau.

An hour afterwards governor Schroeder came, and in a solemn tone enquired as to what had become of his hostage. M. Pharoux replied that he knew very well that it was impossible to subsist on the other side of the river, and that having been refused admission to the fort, he had probably gone back to the falls of the Onondaga, where he had been told that he might wait for our return, which was Jesuitically not telling a lie.

The governor, with all possible gravity, declared that he must retain us as prisoners, until the return of our hostage.

The comedy had begun to look serious, but was ended by Mr. DeZeng, who invited the governor to step aboard our bateau. There his Excellency was shown the famous case of gin, which had been promised him. He convinced himself, by tasting, that it could not be drunk, but as it had been purchased at the store of his friend Mr. Porteous, he could not impute any fault to us. He however contented himself with the powder and lead which we gave him, and loaded with these, he returned gravely into his fort.

He had scarcely turned his heels, when our boatmen hastened to set out, as when once out of range of his cannon he had nothing to say to us.

Brunel, who in the meantime was making his way through the woods in a wide circuit to the east of the fort, was at no small risk of being discovered, purely by accident.

We had noticed several patrols scouring the woods, and they told us that four deserters had escaped, and that they were trying to find them. While searching for these, the soldiers might come upon M. Brunel and bring him to the fort, and Monseigneur the governor might scarcely be willing to arrange this affair, without sending us to Canada. All this confusion was the fruit of Mr. DeZeng's subterfuge, for had he frankly stated the facts, we might have passed with the same, or at least with some little satisfaction.

But finally, the party re-boarded their batteau in the cove at the foot of the cliff on which the fort stood, and with an encouraging wind off the lake, began to retrace their journey back along the inland waterways to Albany.

CHAPTER TWELVE

Again to Three Rivers

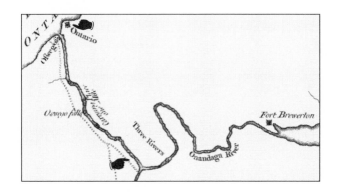

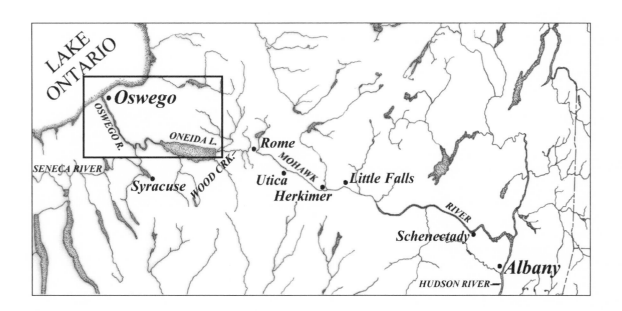

On their departure from the batteau landing at Fort Ontario, the French party immediately found that the current of the Oswego, which had hurried their craft down into the harbor only ten days before, now confronted them with an obstacle of potentially disastrous proportions.

We left the fort at two o'clock with a good wind, but the rapids soon prevented us from using the sail, and it would have been impossible for us to have advanced, had not the people in the other bateau lent us their aid by turning in to help us in passing one bad place after another. It was necessary, almost every moment, to get into the water, cold as it was. Our men would then drink rum to warm them. With great fatigue we were only able to make two or three miles in the course of the afternoon.

The rapids of the Oswego River presented a force much greater than that they had encountered coming up through the shallow rifts of the Mohawk, with the possible exception of Keator's Rift.

Running west from Fort Stanwix they had enjoyed the relative ease of navigating downstream. Now they had to backtrack up the current of each of these waterways, until they could enjoy the final downriver run on the Mohawk, far to the east. The fortuitous companionship of the crew of the other batteau possibly saved their expedition from disaster, or at least certain delay.

The labor was so great that one of the men in the Canadian bateau, named Armstrong, fell unconscious, overcome with the cold and the rum that he had drunk. We took him in charge, and, by forcibly compelling him to walk, re-established the circulation and saved him.

Exhausted by the ordeal of fighting their way up the river, the party decided to make camp. Pharoux, in spite of the misfortune previously associated with land travel on this trip, decided to go on up toward the falls on foot, in hopes of locating Brunel.

M. Pharoux, who was uneasy about M. Brunel, resolved to follow the path along the bank, in the hope of meeting him. We represented that he would fall behind, and that he ran a risk of getting lost himself, and of being obliged to sleep in the woods. Our people informed him that there was a path all the way up, that there were no creeks to pass, and that he had about ten miles to go. Upon this he left us at four in the afternoon. We prepared the tent, and as all our men were too fatigued for further labors, we resolved to remain till the morrow.

"At night we brought up the boat and made her fast to a tree. We then kindled a fire, put on the tea kettle and the cooking pot, boiled our potatoes, made our tea, and ate our supper with a good appetite and a clear conscience, and after smoking our pipes and chatting awhile, we ... laid ourselves down among the sand and pebbles on the bank of the river to rest; but I was so wearied with the toils of the day that I could not sleep much that night."
Rev. Elijah Woolsey, 1794[211]

Tuesday. Oct. 29th. Left at half past six, and, with much difficulty, overcame the other rapids. The greatest trouble arose from the low water at that period, so that we were obliged to push the bateaux by main strength over the rocks that formed the rapids, and at every moment they would touch bottom, and hang upon the points. We did not cease to be anxious about M. M. Pharoux and Brunel, whom we every moment hoped would rejoin us.

Finally, at half past two, we discovered M. Pharoux making signs to us, and we hastened to come and take him in. Instead of finding M. Brunel, he had gone astray, had passed the night in the woods, was chilled through and was nearly famished, as he had taken no provisions with him.

Finally, at four o'clock, we arrived at the portage of the falls, where we met M. Brunel, in good condition, except that he had galled his feet on the march. He had met one of the patrols from the fort, but by his presence of mind in answering him, had escaped suspicion, and slipped out of his hands. Not seeing our bateau, he had continued his route, had reached the log house, got his supper, and spent a better night than ourselves.

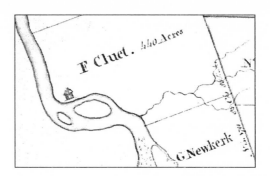

Brunel had walked from their lakeshore landing northeast of Fort Ontario to the lower landing at the Oswego Falls. It was here that the log house at which he sheltered overnight was located. It was perhaps this same house that was visited the following year by another party under less enjoyable circumstances:

Toward evening we saw a small log house, and went to it. We found the woman sick in bed, and the man in poor health. They had three children, and but very little to eat. Here we lodged all night. I laid me down on the stones of the floor which were very hard and uneven, but we kept a good fire all night, and I got into a perspiration which relieved me of my cold a little, so that in the morning I felt much better than on the preceding night. Brother D., being a physician, administered some medicine to the woman which greatly relieved her also...

This was the only time during our journey of nineteen days that we found a house to shelter us, and it was good for that family that they entertained the strangers, for we were in truth as angels of mercy to them. They must have suffered greatly had we not called on them at that time.
Rev. Elijah Woolsey, 1794[212]

Having been reunited at the falls, the expedition prepared to move to the embarkation point at the upper landing.

The Oswego Portage

Abatteau voyager, coming south up the Oswego River a couple years after the French expedition, stopped at the same log house in which Brunel had sought shelter in 1793. Here, at the lower landing of the portage, this traveler recorded the difficulties of the Falls and lack of reasonable accommodations:

"At the place, where the navigation is intercepted, we halted at William Shorten's. He keeps an inn, that is, he admits into one room of his house all the travelers, who desire to sleep there, and accommodates them with salt pork and rum; which is the most he is able to do. We arrived there, at nine o'clock in the evening, wet to the skin; for such of us, as had not been drenched by pushing and drawing the ship along, were soaked by the constant rain. We dried ourselves at a good fire; and a few slices of ham, we had brought with us, restored our strength...

"The portage, occasioned by the falls of the river Oswego, is about a mile in length. W. Shorten, at whose house we stopped, kept only a yoke of oxen, and our vessels were heavy laden. Each vessel was to be conveyed separately, and the cargo required four turns of the carriage. The Americans not being anywise remarkable for speed and agility, it was not until five o'clock in the evening, that our vessels had reached the place, where the navigation recommences, and where they were again to be loaded...

"This time we had not even a bed. Our party, our skippers, landlord, wife, sons and daughters slept all pell-mell in a room, which was about twelve feet square. And unfortunately we were not sufficiently fatigued, having traveled but one mile on foot and one mile and a half by water, to find the floor soft, and to be insensible to the stings of the musquitoes and the bites of fleas."

Duke de la Rochefoucault Liancourt, 1795[213]

This observer also noted the gap in the bedrock escarpment over which the river fell, and which provided in later years a convenient passage through the falls for the larger, Durham boats:

"The Oswego fall is about ten feet high; and the river nearly one eighth of a mile in width. The prospect is not without charms. A break of the bed of rocks, from which the river precipitates itself, and the irregularity of the form, produce a tolerably striking, but not a grand effect. On the right bank, near the water-fall, are found the traces of an ancient French entrenchment, and hard by them stands a small log-house, the proprietor of which is at present building a grist-mill below the fall."

Duke de la Rochefoucault Liancourt, 1795[214]

It was seven years later, when Durham boats routinely made this passage between the salt works at Onondaga and the harbor at Oswego, that Philip Schuyler remarked on the changing methods of passage through what had previously been an overland portage:

"From the head of the falls to the foot thereof is 49 yards over which the empty boats are drawn by horses or oxen and then put into the river in a current so strong that it is extremely laborious to bring an empty boat... to the foot of the falls. In going down, unless in very dry seasons, the boats can carry half of their lading. The other half is transported by land a little more than a mile. In coming up everything is taken out of the boats, which ascend empty to the foot of the falls where they are taken out and dragged to the head of the falls."

Philip Schuyler, 1802[215]

We had passed on foot the portage around the falls, where our bateau was taken in the evening. Here Mr. DeZeng showed some traces of ill feeling, instead of acting openly, but we had an explanation. It arose from our giving a dollar to the people in the other boat, to encourage them not to leave us until we arrived at Three Rivers.

The owner of the log house could not persuade us to quit our tent, where we preferred to sleep, notwithstanding the cold.

We met at the falls two bateaux with families going to Niagara, notwithstanding the lateness of the season.

Pharoux, Desjardins, Brunel, and their companions might well have celebrated their re-entry into the batteau above the Oswego Falls. If they did, no notice of it was made in their journal.

Wednesday. Oct. 30th. Left the falls at 9 o'clock, after they had finished the portage of our bateau by trucks. Passed the rapids as far as to Three Rivers with much trouble, notwithstanding the help of our fellow voyageurs, without whom we were assured we could never have got through, as our fresh water mariners had had no experience in overcoming such obstacles.

Apparently passing again Three River Rift [Phoenix], the journalists were fortunate to witness a variety of native activities along the shore.

We met several Indians fishing on the bank, and one of them was mending his broken bark canoe with other pieces of bark, threads of bark, and resin poured upon the seams. He had handsome silver rings in his nose and ears, and it appeared by the riches of this poor savage that he was some chief.

He so maintained his gravity that he did not quit his work, nor even turn his head, to look at us.

In one of the fishing cabins we saw some charcoal sketches, with very good representations of ships and a landscape.

> "...a great many animals tolerably well delineated with coal by the Indians on the boards of the house..."
> **Cadwallader Colden, 1721[216]**

Fishing cabins such as these, which had been observed on several occasions by members of the expedition, were inhabited seasonally as the fish migrated up and down the rivers. They were probably built on the plan of other Native American bark and sapling shelters recorded in contemporary accounts:

An Indian hut is built in the following manner: They peel trees, abounding in sap, such as lime-trees, &c. then cutting the bark into pieces of two or three yards in length, they lay heavy stones upon them, that they may become flat and even in drying. The frame of the hut is made by driving poles into the ground, and strengthening them by cross beams.

This frame-work is covered both within and without

with the above-mentioned pieces of bark, fastened very tight with bast or twigs of hickory, which are remarkably tough. The roof runs up to a ridge, and is covered in the same manner. These huts have one opening in the roof to let out the smoke, and one in the side for an entrance...

George Henry Loskiel, 1794[217]

The term "cabin" was not meant to imply a log house, and was often used by travelers in this era to denote the most temporary bark or brush covered lean-to, as described in 1783 along the north shore of Oneida Lake:

As night approached the crew landed half way down the lake, where they improvised a cabin with a good fire to dry their clothes.

Capt. Alexander Thompson, 1783[218]

Having reached the safe haven of Three River Point once again, the French party had an opportunity to rest and to observe the rudimentary operations of a regional commercial fishery.

On arriving at Three Rivers, the bateau in our company remained to fish and take in its load of salmon, which the men salt on the spot in barrels, and when they get a load, take them to Fort Stanwix to sell. The river is so full of fish that the night that M. Brunel slept in the log house at the portage, two men, who went out at eleven, returned at two o'clock with their boat full of salmon, having taken enough to fill two barrels.

> "We arrived at three river point about seven, discharged Mr. Barker, and pitched our tent in the vicinity of his house, crowded with travelers from several bateaux and canoes, which tarried there since yesterday. Barker had caught, by throwing a line behind the bateau, four large Oswego Bass, the smallest of a foot long, which was the best part of our supper."
> **Adrian Vanderkemp, 1792[219]**

This fishing is done as follows. They kindle resinous wood, placed in a little cradle made of strips of iron, fastened to a handle, which is fixed in the bow of the boat. The fish, attracted by the light, come and leap around the boat, and sometimes even spring into it, and the men have nothing to do but to harpoon them with spears of two prongs, fitted into a handle six feet long. Then going ashore the next morning, the fishermen open and clean their fish, cut off the head, and pack them with Onondaga salt, costing a dollar and a half a hundred, into barrels holding thirty four gallons. They sell these barrels at from two to three dollars, according to the supply. Those who buy the salmon usually smoke them, which is the best way of preserving them.

These men around Three River Point depended for their livelihood on their batteaux, easy access to the salt being boated down from Onondaga Lake, and the highly successful fish harvesting techniques they adopted from the Oneidas:

We were a little after sunset, suddenly surprised at a number of fires in a semicircular form on the lake. I numbered nine, others several more. These were made by the Oneyda Indians spearing eel. They are usually two or three in a canoe, one steersman, one, who spears in the bow, the third takes care of the fires, made from dry, easily flaming wood, in a hollow piece of bark, first covered with sand.

Adrian Vanderkemp, 1792[220]

Such ready access to subsistence without resort to agriculture apparently had a deleterious effect on these settlers, who carved out just enough riverside space in the wilderness to accommodate their cabins.

This facility of gaining a livelihood by hunting and fishing without care or labor renders the inhabitants who settle in these parts very indolent. We saw men sitting in the sun at the doors of their log houses, not yet covered with bark at the end of October, and nothing doing to plaster up the crevices between the logs. Instead of giving the least care in providing against the rigors of winter, they sat holding their children, and quietly smoking their pipes.

The profitability of this frontier fishing enterprise, as with all rural production in this period, depended on the ability to move produce from where it was plentiful to markets where it was not. In this instance, these fishermen depended on their own batteaux to move the salt-packed fish over 60 miles by water to Fort Stanwix, at the head of the Mohawk Valley, as no roads of any consequence yet served the area.

Passing the Three Rivers Rapid [Phoenix] two years after the French party, one traveler noted a newly arrived homesteader, struggling to eke out a subsistence from agriculture where none had previously applied it:

Mr. VanAllen, therefore, as well as myself, went on shore, and repaired to a small cottage, where we found a family, but very lately recovered from the ague, and at present busied in mowing a meager looking field of wheat. These good people, who have no neighbors, are necessitated to do everything themselves. Of eight children, who compose this family, the oldest, who is nine years old, is alone able to assist them a little. They have neither rakes, harrows nor scythes; and yet it is better to sacrifice three fourths of their harvest, than to lose the whole.

These poor people, who have lived here a twelvemonth, were constantly troubled with the ague. They possessed one thousand two hundred acres of land, six hundred of which were, by the state of New York, given to the husband, who had served in the army, and the other six hundred he purchased two years ago for ten shillings an acre, but was compelled by extreme distress to sell again three hundred, with the small profit of two shillings per acre.

The good people cultivate a garden; they exchanged some vegetables for a few pounds of pork... They seem to be good and industrious people; the wife, though mother of eight children, and scarcely recovered from the ague, is yet handsome. They presented me with some potatoes and cucumbers, and declined accepting any payment.

Duke de la Rochefoucault Liancourt, 1795[221]

Yet settlers along this frontier, who did not exhibit the agricultural prowess familiar to the travelers who passed through the region, frequently drew the contempt shared by the French journalists. Often they were seen as the unsavory cutting edge of civilization, described by Isaac Weld as he traveled through western New York a few years later:

...in general they are men of a morose and savage disposition, and the very outcasts of society, who bury themselves in the woods, as if desirous to shun the face of their fellow-creatures; there they build a rude habitation, and clear perhaps three or four acres of land, just as much as they find sufficient to provide their families with corn: for the greater part of their food they depend on their rifle guns.

These people, as the settlements advance, are succeeded in general by a second set of men, less savage than the first, who clear more land, and do not depend so much upon hunting as upon agriculture for their subsistence.

A third set succeed these in turn, who build good houses, and bring the land into a more improved state. The first settlers, as soon as they have disposed of their miserable dwellings to advantage, immediately penetrate farther back into the woods, in order to gain a place of abode suited to their rude mode of life.

Isaac Weld, c1797[222]

CHAPTER THIRTEEN

Return to New Rotterdam

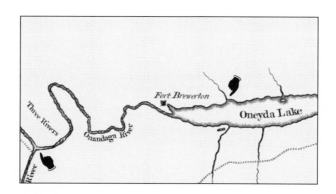

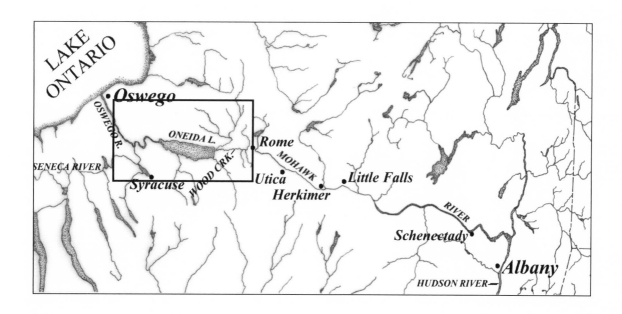

aving overcome the most arduous portion of their return journey, and leaving behind the Canadian batteau whose crew had helped them overcome the rapids of the Oswego River, the expedition turned eastward into the Oneida River and began a relatively peaceful navigation up to Oneida Lake.

After warming ourselves, and eating a little at the Major's house, we took Mr. Judson into our boat and encamped and slept four miles beyond, in a very pleasant spot at the mouth of a creek, on the point of a bend in the Onondaga.

Apparently the party encamped, at the end of their 30th day, at the outlet of "Pieter's Hole", a swamp of monstrous proportions. Its prominence is clearly evident on many of the 18th century maps of the province.

This expanse of low water was located at the apex of a sharp northward bend in the Oneida River. Although the swamp itself, and its immediate margins, would have represented anything but a pleasant campsite, there was an elevated levee, formed by the river, that separated the swampy land to the north from the main channel, broken only by the narrow outlet of a creek. This levee would have provided, in a season of cold weather, a dry and insect free camp, memorable by comparison with most on this route.

Thursday. Oct. 31st. Started at six o'clock with a fine navigation, and the river wide and without rapids until the entrance of Oneida lake, where we could scarcely get through on account of a bar of gravel. We landed on the site of Fort Brewerton and warmed ourselves at a log house, where the inmates - father, mother and children - were shaking with fever. We walked a mile from thence to

"Pieter's Hole"

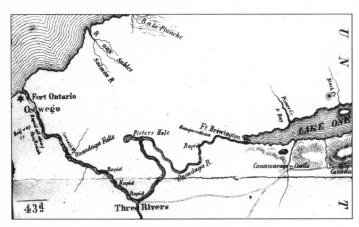

The location of Pieter's Hole, c. 1779.

On several late-eighteenth century maps of the region east of Three Rivers, appears a vast section of inundated lands standing on the north side of the Oneida River, usually denoted as "Pieters Hole." In more recent times, this wetland has been designated "Peter Scott Swamp."

A most plausible explanation for this latter name is given in 19th century histories:

> "Six-Mile Creek, mentioned above, which flows through Gilbert's Mills and the west part of the town, is properly Peter Scott's Creek, so called from the fact that after the close of the war of 1812-15 Col. Peter Scott was sent with his regiment from Oswego to Albany, and arriving at the mouth of this stream, his boats

were frozen in the ice and the troops were compelled to remain there through the winter. Northward along this creek, varying from half a mile to a mile in width, is Peter Scott's swamp, some of which has been reclaimed to cultivation by artificial drainage."

John Churchill, 1895[223]

Were it not for the half century time difference, one might suppose it was this same Peter Scott whose name gave rise to "Pieter's Hole", which appears as early as the 1770s.

But reference to James Cockburn's journal, kept during his 1792 field survey of the Roosevelt Patent, unlocks the mystery:

"About four miles from Three Rivers is a creek called Peter's Gaats, the country hereabout is swamp..."

James Cockburn, 1792[224]

The Dutch term "Gaat", which is pronounced "got", denotes a passage or "strait". This is similar to the English term "gut", which is often taken to indicate a narrow water passage. It may have well been the narrow outlet connecting the swamp to the Oneida River that was intended to be described as the "Gaat". At any rate, the Dutch terminology seems appropriate to the spelling "Pieter's" that appears on maps of the feature, even though Cockburn gives it an Anglicized phonetic spelling. It is clear that the original "Pieter's Gaat" became, phonetically, "Peter Scott."

If, in fact, a Col. Peter Scott was frozen into the mouth of this creek decades later, as suggested by the published accounts, it would be one of the most bizarre coincidences in New York history.

reach a point on the lake, where the bateau could come and take us, in order to aid in lightening the load in passing some other shoals.

In just seventeen days time, the situation at the Oneida Lake outlet by Fort Brewerton had deteriorated significantly. The Steven's family, often noted for their hospitality, had fallen victim to disease, perhaps brought on by the increasing cold. As well, the water level over the bar had dropped sufficiently to require the boat to run up empty, and to continue for some distance into the lake to find sufficient water to permit reloading.

The soil was very sandy, and sterile, and only fit for herbage in the low places. We found on the banks a quantity of fresh water shells, piled up by the fishing birds as they gathered their food and brought it to their nests. We were obliged to wade out in the water among the rushes to reach our bateau, the shore being too shallow to land, even on this point. This is the greatest difficulty on the north shore, where they have scarcely found five or six places where they could land in the whole course of the lake.

The weather being calm, and then the wind contrary, we were compelled to row, and finally at nightfall arrived at New Rotterdam, having met five bateaux under sail towards the other end of the lake. Landing at half past five, we met this time with Monsieur and Madame Desvatines, and improved a day's rest in visiting a saw mill lately erected. The dam not having been substantially built, we presumed that it would soon give way, when the waters arose in the spring time.

Major DeZeng, who now traveled with this party, had accompanied Adrian Vanderkemp on his exploration of the area the year before. In examining the location at the mouth of Bruce's Creek, to be occupied the following year by Scriba and dubbed "New Rotterdam", DeZeng had spoken glowingly of the possibilities:

...but do you not reflect on the advantages of that creek; art thou not convinced by what you have seen, that, with small exertions to improve it, full-laden Batteaux may go in and out - may do it actually now. Did your eye not discover the mill-seats on this creek?

Adrian Vanderkemp, 1792[225]

The imperfect attempts to establish a water-powered mill complex here, observed by the journalists in 1793, were still little advanced two years later:

A dozen poor houses, built almost entirely at Mr. Scriba's expense, constitute all there is of the city of Rotterdam... The dams for the use of the mill that he has built have cost much money, and being always poorly built, he has been obliged to recommence them several times. The grist mill is not yet built, and the dam appears too feeble for the pressure it will have to sustain. Some work and considerable money has been expended at the mouth of the creek to make a landing, but the accommodation is very poor.

Duke de la Rochefoucault Liancourt, 1795[226]

However, being perhaps the most dramatic attempt at establishing a full-scale commercial and industrial community on the western navigation route to Lake Ontario, New Rotterdam deservedly attracted the attention of the French travelers.

We supped and lodged at the log house of Mr. Scriba. At midnight we were awakened by Mr. Vanderkemp, a Holland clergyman lately established four miles from New Rotterdam. He had returned from across the lake, where he has been to look for limestone suitable for building, the rock here being only a ferruginous sandstone. He had found some near the mouth of the Canaseraga, a considerable river that forms the boundary between the military lots and the Oneida reservation, and that flows into the lake nearly opposite to New Rotterdam.

Vanderkemp, a native of Holland, had come to New York in 1788. After exploring much of the inland route in 1792, he had settled at a site a few miles to the east [Cleveland] earlier in 1793. His search for building stone, a commodity of considerable rarity along most of the waterways west of Fort Stanwix, had begun the year before.

"Towards the south the Canoserago creek, rich in fish, falls in the lake. The bottom of the Lake at the south side is a greystone - which extends to the shore - and seems divided in oblong squares. There are appearances, and very strong indeed, of rock iron, which ore in some parts is extending for a considerable length on the shore..."
Adrian Vanderkemp, 1792

The batteau landing here remained in poor condition, and the dream of a bustling port, connected with Lake Ontario by a transportation corridor that

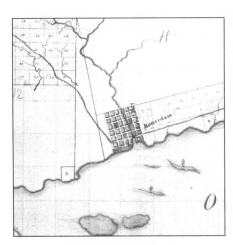

by-passed the tortuous journey via Three Rivers and Oswego, never materialized. But a unique and unprecedented local industry developed in the mouth of Bruce's Creek in 1792:

We arrived safe in the creek at Mr. Bruce's - in former days a Connecticut merchant, now an Independent Inhabitant of the Oneyda Lake, maintaining himself by the chase and fishery, and what he earned from a small potato spot.

He fetched directly, upon our arrival, a fine cat-fish from a *reservoir*, constructed from saplings and twigs, so well twisted, that no escape was possible. He praised himself not a little on his invention, as this magazine supplied his wants by foul weather, or, as he said, when Bruce was too lazy to go in quest for other food...

Adrian Vanderkemp, 1792[228]

"Desvatines"

It is perhaps interesting to examine the fate of Desvatines and his family, who had previously inhabited "Frenchman's Island" and were just becoming established at Rotterdam in 1793. Although by no means typical of the settlers who were attempting to gain a foothold around Oneida Lake in the 1790s, at least in terms of their noble background, they were bravely facing some of the same trials and sobering realities, with a poverty of resources off-set only by the company of others.

Two years later, another Frenchman touring the region visited with Desvatines, who apparently survived the winter of 1793 at New Rotterdam. He had gained by then a reputation as an accomplished gardener, and was encountered gathering in his potatoes and onions. In recounting to this visitor his past misfortunes, Desvatines exhibited "in his countenance and manners some air of distinction."

"He had for the past three years lived around Oneida Lake, spending one with the Indians, whom he highly extols. He then settled on an island in the middle of the lake, where he lived alone with his wife and cleared some twenty acres of land, but for the last fifteen months, he has resided at Rotterdam, where Mr. Scriba has sold him a hundred acres of land on very easy terms. The instability of character in M. Vatines, according to his own admission, has more influenced his changes of residence than any reflecting calculation. He is a man some thirty years of age, gay, active, always laughing, accustomed to labor, and complains of nothing, but has taken a dislike to Americans because he says they are faithless in their bargains, and above all that they are always solemn. He lives, however, on good terms with all the inhabitants of Rotterdam, although he found some among them worse than others. He aids in their labors, and is helped in turn, and he sells to them as dear as possible, the products of a little garden which is well cultivated with vegetables.

"His pleasure on seeing his fellow countrymen was extreme, and he wanted to give us everything in his garden, without receiving a sol. He dreams of nothing but France, and of the moment when peace will permit him to return to a country that he prefers to all others, though he should there eat nothing but bread. He would rather live miserably there, than to dwell in any other country, however rich he might there be. This feeling is common with all Frenchmen.

"He had some books, of which the selection showed to his advantage... He had first sold his jewels, then his garments, then his linen, and finally was obliged to part with his library, and this at less than half of what it would have brought in New York or Philadelphia, because the store keeper was the only person within two hundred miles who could procure the sale, and they went to the benefit of a rich Hollander, who has settled some miles from Rotterdam.

"We wished to see Madame de Vatines, who is a woman of twenty four years of age, lively, good, and has eyes of peculiarly sweet and agreeable expression. Like many other ladies, she appears to love her husband with more tenderness than she receives. I would not be surprised if there was a little jealousy in play. The light and flippant tone of her husband might give occasion for this which does not however prevent him from appearing much attached to his wife. She is the mother of three children, of whom the oldest is some ten years old. She appears bright and intelligent, makes hay, bread and soap, and does the kitchen work. Yet her hands are yet delicate. She is at least as tired of America as her husband, and especially is weary of Oneida

Lake. They entertain a project of going to live with some French families. They received us with infinite pleasure, and were more confident and more at ease with us, they said, in a quarter of an hour, than they would be among the Americans, although they should live ten years with them. This kind of disgust for Americans, is a very common trait with the French, whom we meet in this part of the world."

Duke de la Rochefoucault Liancourt, 1795[229]

Although this account suggests the family may have been planning to join Desjardins and Pharoux in Castorland, it has been suggested by other sources that this family did, a few years later, return to their native France, to a fate unknown.

This primitive fish hatchery began a tradition that has lasted, on this very spot, for over two centuries.

In addition to an extended visit with Mr. Scriba, it certainly must have been a novelty for the Frenchmen to also observe the Oneida Lake legend of the Desvatines family in the making. Perhaps the members of this expedition saw in the plight of this French family, thrust into the heart of the American wilderness, something of the romance and adventure of the New World that may have more than a little motivated Desjardins and Pharoux.

M. Desvatines presents another example of the class of Frenchmen who are not enough guarded against ill fortune in this country. Arriving in America seven years ago, with over $40,000, a sum which is a fortune in the United States, where money is scarce, he had gradually wasted his funds in traveling, and in buying farms for which he paid two or three times their value.

Seeing his fortune reduced at the end of two years, he resolved to invest the remainder in trade in order to gain a fair return, but one fine morning his partner was gone, carrying money and accounts, leaving him only the movable goods of himself and wife. The Chevalier De Goyon advised him in his distress to repair to an island in Oneida Lake, which was beautifully located, although uninhabited, and there to form an establishment by himself.

Being without resources, he followed this advice, came to the island, and began a clearing. He had sold the most of his furniture, which would have been useless in the woods, but reserved his library.

He took his wife among the Indians to pass the first winter, and there spent his time. In the second year his log house was built, and about six acres cleared, which promised him support, when Mr. DeZeng, from whom he had three years before refused to buy a farm, came in the name of the Roosevelt Company and informed him that the State had sold these islands, with the land, to this company, and that he must quit them.

In the meantime, Mr. Scriba, one of the interested parties, had offered him a lot of land at New Rotterdam, for which he might pay when able. Our French Robinson Crusoe, being forced to abandon his island, accepted this offer, with thanks, and began anew here this last summer.

His house was not quite covered, as no one cared to help him, because they knew that he had not a single dollar at his command. This unfortunate man had taken incredible pains in clearing and building, but altogether single handed; his wife and children, however, in the mean time enjoying good health.

Desvatines apparently did not benefit from the reputed community spirit of the early American frontier, but was reduced to relying on the labors of himself and his family. When observed by the French party late in 1793, his log house was as yet not roofed with bark, but presumably not from the lack of energy and initiative observed elsewhere in the West.

> "The squares of our houses were up but there was no roof on them. In the course of ten days we had our log houses fix't to move into, a blanket for a door and table cloths for glass to cover the window holes. We moved in as they were, and we were happy."
>
> Lewis Beers, 1797[230]

As Desvatines needed to journey eastward to trade, the members of the expedition looked forward to having further discussions with him during the remainder of the voyage across Oneida Lake.

M. Desvatines proposed to go with us in the morning, in his canoe, to Fort Stanwix to buy corn. M. Desjardins paid him four dollars for the skin of a bear, which he had killed a little time before.

Before they could set out, however, a turn in the weather afforded the party an extended opportunity to examine the fragile beginnings of the emerging settlement of "New Rotterdam."

Friday. Nov. 1st. Mr. DeZeng, having some business to finish with the Rosevelt Company, the wind being ahead and the lake rough, we concluded to remain, to the great contentment of our boatmen. Mr. Vanderkemp spoke a little French, and we soon formed an acquaintance.

In the morning we were witness of a scene between Mr. Scriba's people and M. Desvatines. They abused his sad condition, while he, soured by misfortune, did not fail to throw back as much, but we, with Mr. DeZeng, endeavored to conciliate affairs as well as we were able. We then went with him into his log house, which was as open as a cage, and found his wife and three little children as jovial as cupids. They made the most they could of their poor barrack, where they would be obliged to spend the winter, as from all appearances it could not be finished this season.

We then took a view of the site of the future Rotterdam. It is upon a moderately elevated sandy plateau, with a view of the lake and the islands, and at present consists only of a saw mill and three log houses, but its location is favorable. Mr. Scriba intends to open a road from this place to the Little Salmon Creek, which is twenty four miles by land, will save more than sixty miles by water, and the tedious navigation of the Onondaga. It is probable that this will become the route of trade from the lakes, which cannot fail to give it importance, especially if the Little Salmon Creek is navigable, so as to reduce the portage to six or eight miles as they assured us. The only trouble is in the landing place, but some piers would remedy this, and timber is plenty.

In spite of the lobbying efforts of George Scriba during the coming years, the old inland route to Lake Ontario via Three Rivers would remain the only one viable, until the opening of the Erie Canal in 1825.

Although it would never be the international port envisioned on that first brisk day in November, 1793, Rotterdam [Constantia] would grow into the only settlement of substance on the interior of Oneida Lake in the coming years.

From thence we went to see the reserved lands beyond the creek, which are very good for this country. In the course of our walk we visited the labors of M. Desvatines, his future house, and his lot, which is not a bad one. We encouraged him as much as possible. He has a couple of cows, which Mr. DeZeng bought for him with

Rotterdam Landing

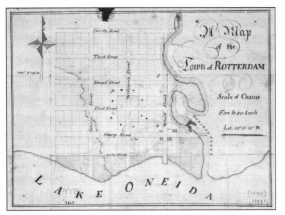

The settlement at Rotterdam, with new street plan suggested, 1797.

It was not because of the land that George Scriba selected the mouth of Bruce's Creek for his settlement of "New Rotterdam", although suitable land for agricultural production was to be had in the immediate area. Nor was it primarily the potential mill sites just north of the creek's entrance into Oneida Lake that attracted him, although industrial development here was clearly to the advantage of any subsequent settlement.

Scriba had visions of a landing here at Rotterdam, connected by a series of navigable waterways and canals to a comparable landing on Lake Ontario, some thirty miles to the north. It was a vision shared with Adrian Vanderkemp by Frederick DeZeng as they viewed the creek's mouth in 1792:

"...can you not see Bateaux ascending Bruce's creek, and descending the Salmon creek? - can you not see the furs and other valuable produce of Canada brought hither, through the canal? ah! do you not see already various stores and magazines crowded with merchandize..."

Adrian Vanderkemp, 1792[231]

Yet three years later, little could be found here to support this vision:

"The money, which Mr. Schreiber has expended on buildings and roads, is estimated at eight thousand dollars. If they were constructed on good principles, this money would have been well spent. He is now building a handsome house of joiner's work, where he intends to keep a store, in company with two partners... A store or shop affords here, as indeed it does all over America, the best income which a man can procure, who incurs a considerable expense in forming a new settlement. Mr. Schreiber, by means of his store, obtains all the money back, which he expends for his building, etc. He sells his brandy for four shillings and sixpence, flour for sixpence a pound, and ten dollars and a half a barrel, for which he pays no more than seven dollars. The profit he obtains by the sale of other provision, is still more considerable. The land, which eighteen months ago he purchased for one dollar an acre, costs now three, but is not much sought after. The present settlers come from New England and the environs of Albany."

Duke de la Rochefoucault Liancourt, 1795[232]

Scriba's most ambitious, and perhaps most immediately promising, endeavor was to create a land and water route to Lake Ontario that would by-pass the river navigation down to Oswego past Three River Point:

"Mr. Schreiber, a rich Dutch merchant, possesses a large tract of land, extending from Lake Ontario to Lake Oneida. He fixed upon the mouth of Bruce-creek as the site of the chief place, and another settlement he has formed on Little Salmon-creek, two miles from Lake Ontario. Bruce-creek continues navigable some miles farther up. Mr. Schreiber has made a road from Rotterdam to his new town; but all these settlements are yet   of no importance."

Duke de la Rochefoucault Liancourt, 1795[233]

This roadway, in many ways similar of those being constructed in the more settled areas to the east, was a typical "one-rod-road", supplied with the essential log and brush "causeys":

"...it is however understood that the road must be cut sixteen feet wide and to be cleared of all logs, stumps, etc. which the passage of the width of sixteen feet might obstruct, and the sticks of the causeways well and closely laid and so as not to endanger any horse or cattle which passes over the same."

George Scriba, 1804[234]

The success of this venture depended somewhat on improved navigation west from Fort Stanwix to Rotterdam; a navigation continually frustrated by the twisting shallows of Wood Creek. Scriba took an active interest, therefore, in the developments proposed by the Western Inland Lock Navigation Company, and had suggested, to the Directors of that company, a couple routes for canals to by-pass that stream altogether. These schemes never were accomplished, and Scriba's shortcut to Lake Ontario, via the Salmon River, never came to be.

the proceeds of some embroidered clothing, which he had left for sale at General Schuyler's. His poultry yard contained a few fouls, and this was all he possessed. He gave us a piece of bear meat which he had killed, and which was cooked for our dinner. It is very fat and delicate, but a little unsavory, yet we found it excellent, as we had not tasted of fresh meat for a long time. It is a favorite with the Indians.

Although the fishponds established at Rotterdam in Bruce's Creek saved their owner the trouble of harvesting fish in more traditional ways, there does not appear to have been a particular shortage of the catch. When DeWitt Clinton passed along this

shore a few years later, just east of Rotterdam, he reported the successful use of nets and what may have been the first use on the lake of an artificial lure:

As we approached Rotterdam, we saw a seine drawn at the mouth of a small cold brook, and six salmon caught at a haul. A kingfisher, as large as a hawk, was also flying about for prey. We amused ourselves on our voyage over the lake, by trolling with a hook and bait of red cloth and white feathers, and caught several Oswego bass, yellow perche, and pikes.

DeWitt Clinton, 1810[235]

The Batteau

"**B**atteau", a French word for "boat", came to mean in the late 18th century any flat-bottomed craft that was pointed at both ends - the type of boat commonly used in the inland waterways of northeastern North America. Here, frequent shallows required a boat that drew little water, even when fully loaded, could be deftly maneuvered through rapids and around rocks, and was light enough to be lifted out of the channel and carried over the several portages that blocked navigation into the interior.

The batteau was the mainstay of inland shipping, particularly for the military, until the end of the 18th century. During the French and Indian War, and later the Revolution, fleets of these craft were constructed at the boatyards in Schenectady, Albany and along the shores of Lake George and Lake Champlain.

Batteaux (the plural) came in different sizes, known generally as 3 handed, 4-handed or 5-handed, according to the men needed to propel them. There were undoubtedly many variations in design, but all were characterized

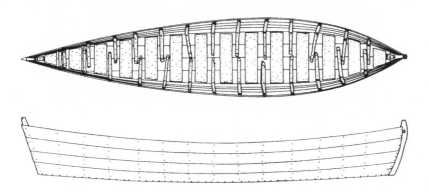

by a flat bottom of pine boards laid lengthwise, with battens (cleats) nailed across to hold them together. Oak frames (ribs), usually made from natural crooks, fastened the bottom to the pine planks which formed the sides of the vessel. Being so commonplace a vehicle, built by eye, not from plans, very little detailed information has been preserved regarding batteaux. Although they occasionally appear in contemporary paintings, batteau images are sufficiently vague to preclude drawing very specific conclusions about design and construction.

Archeological remains of military batteaux sunk in Lake George in 1758, consisting primarily of bottoms, fragmentary frames and a few planks, suggest a boat about 31 feet long and 4 1/2 feet wide on the bottom with a fairly blunt stem and only a moderately raking stern - similar to the drawings above, which were recreated from remains of one such boat.

During the Revolutionary War, reference is made to batteaux as generally being "thirty six feet long and about five or six broad in the center, tapering to both ends almost to a point" with sides "about three feet deep" and attached by "slight knees of timber." These craft were carvel built, with the boards abutting each other ' caulked with oakum and pitch. However, a significant qualifier was then quickly added: "There is no other batteaux used in America except on the Mohawk River from Schenectady to Oswego, which is a bad and shallow navigation. A smaller boat is used, which carries seven barrels, navigated by two and sometimes three men."[236]

continued on next page

continued from page 103

The "new threehanded batteau" purchased at Schenectady by Philip Schuyler on August 21st, 1792, by which he would conduct his survey of the Mohawk, would appear to be the direct descendant of these "smaller" boats which sixteen years earlier had already been established as a unique sub-species of batteau.

An examination of the navigation between Schenectady and Oswego as it existed at the close of the 18th century reveals the limiting characteristics of the waterway that directly influenced batteau design. There were over 90 separate and occasionally extensive rifts or rapids on the Mohawk alone, often as shallow as a foot and frequently under 18 inches. The rivers west of the Mohawk contained still more. The falls at Little Falls and near Oswego, and the Great Carrying Place at Rome, required lifting the boat out of the river and carting it overland for distances of up to three miles. The twisting, narrow, and extremely shallow channel of Wood Creek, between Rome and Oneida Lake, could stop a long or deep drafted vessel in its tracks.

Thus a boat in the range of 20 to 30 feet and 4 to 5 feet wide on the bottom would seem to be representative of a Mohawk River batteau. The interior depth was probably fairly shallow, if for no other purpose than to lighten the craft for portaging. A high-sided boat would not only be unnecessarily heavy, it would impede the work of the boatmen in the bow, poling the boat upstream. There was little function to a 36 inch deep vessel when it rarely was able to draw over 15 inches because of the shallow river.

References made by 18th century Mohawk travelers to the batteaux they traveled in are rare. Where they do exist, however, they suggest a boat less than 30 feet long and barely 24 inches deep. Two construction scows ordered by Schuyler in 1796 to haul lime to his canal works on the upper Mohawk were to be only "22 or 24 inches high."[237]

Commercial Mohawk River batteaux probably had more graceful lines than suggested by the sunken remains of military batteaux in Lake George. The few 18th century illustrations available, of which almost none are from New York, suggest at least a moderately raking stem and stern. Perhaps the most relevant illustration of this vessel is found on the seal of the Western Inland Lock Navigation Company, carved in 1792. (right)

An illustration of a large Durham-type freighter and what appears to be a double-manned batteau, observed and recorded on the Mohawk in 1807 (front-cover), reveals craft that are shallow and have an observable pitch to the stern and stern posts. Certainly the working batteaux of the later 19th century, represented primarily by the logging batteaux of the St. Lawrence region and interior New England, had dramatically raking stems and sterns. These boats were particularly well suited to river running and easy handling.

Whether we see the Mohawk River commercial batteau of the 1790s as part of a continuum from the blunt-nosed military craft of the 1750s to the sleek working boats of the 1890s, or as a design that undeveloped in reponse to the most restrictive heavy traffic navigation in the Northeast, we may assume a craft of modest but pronounced rake, stem and stern, with overlapping side planks a lighter but still strong construction.

Seal on 1792 stock certificate of the WILNC.

CHAPTER FOURTEEN

Excursion to Oneida Castle

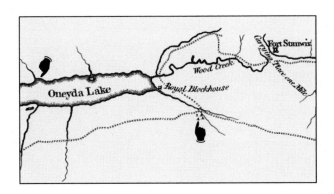

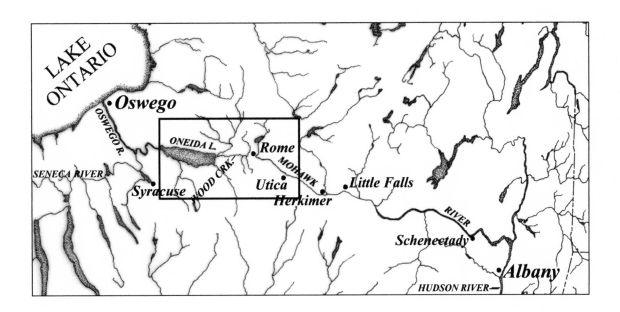

Being delayed half the day at Rotterdam, and notwithstanding having been afforded the chance thereby of making some educating observations on shore, the party embarked from the mouth of Bruce's Creek at noon on November 1st, sailing toward the entrance of Wood Creek at the east end of the lake.

Having had an early dinner, we set out at noon, attended by M. Desvatines in his little canoe, which was broken at the end and took in water from every wave that passed, the lake being still somewhat rough. He had with him two men belonging to the settlement, who improved this opportunity to go and look after some cattle that had strayed eight days before, and were said to have been seen at Nine Mile Point.

Besides Mr. Judson, we had in our bateau one of Mr. Scriba's carpenters, who had asked passage for payment as far as Fort Schuyler. We told him we did not want his money, but that since he was sick and wanted to go home, we would cheerfully take him along. He seemed astonished at our refusing his money, and we soon had occasion to witness another trait of this character in Briton, one of our boatmen.

On our return across the lake he had taken a hard cold, and this had gained upon him on the river. With his half a dollar a day all summer he had bought nothing, and his pantaloons of coarse stuff were badly torn, so that he was in fact nearly naked. M. Brunel had a pair still very good, which he gave him. He was astounded at the word <u>give</u>, and asked him to repeat it several times. Nor would he accept the garment until, in the presence of the two other boatmen, M. Brunel had declared that he <u>gave</u> them to him, and that he <u>would never ask anything for them</u>. Then, being sure of two witnesses, he accepted the gift, without thanks and staring at him as a prodigy - nevertheless he afterwards threatened to quit us on the way.

Traveling in company with Desvatines, who carried the two farmers from Rotterdam in his canoe, the party of nine in the batteau pushed on, and made plans for a detour by land through Oneida country.

By constant rowing we reached Nine Mile Point, where we encamped. We had resolved to land the next morning at the mouth of Wood Creek, and go to visit the Indians at their village at Oneida. M. Desvatines induced us to this course, and gave a note to M. Perrot, a Canadian who had spent some time with him on the island and who was now living with Schenando, an Indian chief.

Being sure of finding an interpreter in the place, we were decided upon going. From thence we would rejoin the bateau at Old Fort Schuyler, at the house of Mr. Post, whose address Mr. DeZeng gave us.

M. Brunel undertook to keep with the bateau to look after our goods. It was very cold in the night.

On the morning of the 32nd day of their voyage, the expedition prepared to divide into two parties, while Desvatines and his two passengers continued along the north shore of Oneida Lake in search of the missing cattle.

The boatmen, with DeZeng and Brunel, would retrace their navigation of the previous month by passing up the twisted channel of Wood Creek to the tavern at Canada Creek, then overland to Fort Stanwix and the Mohawk River. They would next run down that river to Old Fort Schuyler [Utica], tying up at Post's Tavern to await the arrival of the land party.

Saturday. Nov. 2nd. In the morning the New Rotterdam men, not having found their cattle, engaged M. Desvatines to take them further. We accordingly separated, bidding them have patience and courage; qualities very useful in this country. Started at six, with the wind ahead but slight, and therefore had to row the nine miles. It was well that we arrived, for the wind and the waves arose so that our oarsmen could scarcely gain upon them. We passed the bar with difficulty, the water being very low, and at half past nine landed at the mouth, quite chilled through.

In the mouth of Wood Creek, the separation took place. As the batteau drew out of sight, Pharoux and Desjardins, with Judson and the carpenter from Rotterdam, turned southward along the beach to begin an exploration on foot, deep into Oneida country.

We had much trouble in getting fuel enough together for a fire. Being at length warmed, and having breakfasted, we bid adieu to our people, who continued their voyage by water, while we went back about two miles on foot along the sandy shore of the lake to the mouth of Oneida Creek, a considerable stream.

Attended by Mr. Judson and the carpenter, we followed along up the stream, crossing it at one place where we found a canoe fastened to the bank, and on the other side a bear's head and other traces of a feast, suspended to a large tree. This was to indicate that there was a council and a great festival at the village, and some hatchets and blankets hung up also, signified that there was to be a treaty. The whole were sheltered by branches of evergreen trees.

The route to be followed ran alongside Oneida Creek, which entered the southeast corner of Oneida Lake a couple miles south of Wood Creek. This creek was navigable by canoe, and perhaps light batteaux, up as far as Oneida Castle, the village of the Oneidas in this period.

Although this party used a small canoe to cross the stream that intersected Oneida Creek, they proceeded on foot, following paths that ran alongside the waterway.

This pleasant invitation led us to follow the path half a mile further, when we came to the house of Colonel Lewis, an Iroquois Indian from Canada, who having taken part with Congress became a colonel. He has settled at Oneida, where he has an establishment as well fitted up as the best farm in the country. In fact, we found some Americans there with pack horses who had come to buy wheat and corn. His oxen, cows, and horses were well kept, and his clearing was fine, but we did not find the owner at home. He had gone to St. Regis, a village of Christian Iroquois on the St. Lawrence, forty miles from our lands and the place of his former home. We were the more disappointed because he spoke French, and in going frequently to Canada had often traversed our possessions, and might have given us some very useful information, and which in part we had come to obtain.

"For the first time we went into an Indian's house and were surprised at the degree of comfort and convenience it exhibited. They are longer than broad and through the building is a large entry or hall on each side of which are the beds of the family exactly resembling the berths of a ship. Overhead on poles is hung their Indian corn to dry and all round the building the skins of different animals. At each end of the entry is a fire which they burn Winter and Summer and in the middle a pot hangs filled with a soup made of Indian corn. From this any one who is hungry satisfies himself, they having no stated meal. The only ornament I observed was a panel opposite to the Suppaan pot on which were painted very rudely some animals and flowers. On the front of the house similar figures are painted."

William Morton, 1798[238]

Although disappointed at having missed the opportunity to consult with the elusive Col. Lewis, the party must have been heartened, in this strange land, by the welcome they received.

After resting for a time at the house of these kind Indians, who welcomed us as Frenchmen, we continued our journey, and three miles beyond came to Oneida Castle. It is on a great cleared plain almost entirely surrounded by the river, and the entrance is quite narrow and closed with a barrier. It would be an excellent place for natural defense against Indians. On this plateau we found some American farms and Indian cabins, into some of which we entered to enquire for the house of Schenando.

"Col. Lewi"

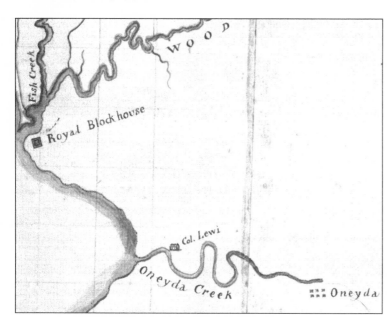

The homestead of "Col. Lewi" in 1795.

The Canadian Indian "Colonel Lewis", whose house was encountered along the bank of the Oneida Creek by the French party on their way to Oneida Castle, might have yielded a very interesting commentary in Desjardins' journal, had he not been away from home on that November afternoon. His name crops up sporadically in the historical record, bearing such various spellings as "Col. Louis", "Col. Lewi", "Col. Lue", and "Col. Looey", confirming its French pronunciation.

His name is recorded elsewhere as "Louis Cook" and his military denotation was not merely happenstance, nor honorary. It was formally earned in service to the American forces during the Revolution. Cook, a Caughnawaga [Mohawk] chief named Atyatoghhongwen, or Atayataghronghta, was living at St. Regis [Hogansburg], on the St. Lawrence River, surrounded by a native population in self-imposed exile from the Mohawk Valley and loyal to the British cause. Yet he was dedicated to the American rebellion and was successful, in the late 1770s, in recruiting Mohawks to come to Albany to join the American campaign. In the succeeding years Cook became one of Gen. Schuyler's three leading Indian officers and received a commendation from Gen. Gates for his leadership against Burgoyne in 1777. It was Schuyler who commissioned Cook a Lieutenant Colonel in 1779.

continued on next page

continued from page 107

Cook, often mentioned only as "Col. Lewis" in the documentation, commanded the Indian force under Col. Willett in 1781 that chased down and killed, along Canada Creek north of the Mohawk, the infamous Tory Walter Butler, who had pillaged and burned throughout the Mohawk Valley during the later years of the Revolution.

Cook was listed at the Treaty of Fort Stanwix in 1784 as "Lieut. Colo. Louis or Atyaoghharongevia". It was the year before, in 1783, that Cook may have formed an attachment with the Oneidas, who were then living as refugees along the banks of the Mohawk in Schenectady, for by the mid-1780s he was, in many respects, a member of their society. "Col. Lewis" was also present in Chief Schenandoah's house in 1788 when the infamous "Plan of Government" was ratified, and which he signed as a witness. He was held in such esteem by the Oneidas that they appointed him one of the two men to act for their nation in executing the terms of The Plan.

> "Col. Louis Cook, or Atyatoghhongwen, was a St. Regis Chief, who from hatred to the English, took a decided stand in favor of the colonies in the revolution, and led off quite a number of Caughnawaga and St. Regis Indians. He lived with the Oneidas several years, but when tranquility was restored to the northern border he returned to St. Regis. He participated in all the treaties made by the Canada Indians relative to lands in New York, and was employed the greater part of his life in the public service of his people. In the revolutionary war, he received a commission as Lieutenant Colonel. He again entered the service in the war of 1812-15, at an advanced age, and died of sickness near Buffalo towards the close of the war."
>
> Franklin Hough, 1883[239]

But this story of exceptional accomplishment for a Native American leader in the closing decades of the eighteenth century takes on even more interest when we read that Cook may not even have been an Indian:

> "On the south side of the lake the Indians, as they are commonly called, or rather the natives of America, still possess a considerable stretch of land on Oneida Creek, which forms their border to the east. The place where they reside is called Oneida Castle. Although they live right in the middle of civilized people, come in contact and do business with them almost daily, they nevertheless still remain true to their old dress, lifestyle and customs. Their dress consists of a linen smock or Beiderwand, which is very similar to a German coachman's smock; around the loins they wear a flap of blue woolen cloth 15 to 18 inches wide, and that is their summer wear. They cover their hair, which hangs down straight in their faces, with neither hats nor caps; however, I did see some few of their women wearing round felt hats, and draped with blanquets (woolen blankets).

> "The king [chief], I was told, was bred by a white - a German to boot - and a Negro in Canada; and is consequently a mulatto. However, he conducted himself so well in the war that the Indians elected him to this important position. His name is Lewis or Louis."
>
> Friedrich Rohde, 1802[240]

The historian, Hough, confirms the African-American heritage, but claims it was a St. Francis, not a German, who was his mother.

The farm of Lewis Cook stood on the bank of the Oneida Creek, near its mouth, and apparently served in the 1790s as a batteau landing and trading site, where settlers around Oneida Lake could obtain corn and produce from the Oneidas.

Today the only remnant of the presence of Col. Lewis at the east end of Oneida Lake is "Lewis Point", on the south shore near the mouth of Oneida Creek. The derivation of that feature's name had eluded local historians until a clipping was found which revealed the connection:

> "Lewis Point...of this romantic place, too much cannot be said in its favor. Lewis Point was named after a French Indian, Leweye, afterwards called Lewis."
>
> Madison County Times, July 23, 1876[241]

The richness of that association was not elaborated, as it apparently was unknown.

This map covers the route of the expedition from Oneida Lake (top) up the Oneida Creek to the Oneida Castle (bottom, left). The "Colonel Lewis" homestead is indicated near the mouth of Oneida Creek.

GÄ-NÓ-SOTE

Bark-sided Indian cabin.

In this period, Native American houses had begun to evolve from the bark-covered longhouse, built of saplings, to the type of log cabins often associated with White settlement. The mixture of houses probably seen by the party at Oneida Castle that November afternoon undoubtedly represented both kinds, as observed further to the west that same year:

> The Indian houses are about twelve feet square, built some with bark and others with wood, as we build our log huts. Many of them have chimneys, in which they can keep comfortable fire, while others retain their ancient custom of having the fire in the center of the house.
>
> Gen. Benjamin Lincoln, 1793[242]

Traditional "cabins" could, however, still be seen in the vicinity of Oneida Castle three years later, when Jeremy Belknap had one pointed out to him by the interpreter "Mr. Dean." This was the same Dean who had been flooded out of his homestead at "Dean's Landing" on the lower end of Wood Creek:

> ...viewed a house which our interpreter, Mr. Dean, said was a complete specimen of Indian architecture. It was made of two rows, each consisting of five posts set in the ground, which supported the roof. The beams were fastened by withes to the posts, and the rafters lay on the beams, projecting downward to stakes fastened in the ground, which formed the side of the building, and there fastened with withes. The roof was covered with bark.
>
> At each end of the house was a separate apartment; one of which served as an entry, the other as a store-room. In the store-room was a vessel as big as a barrel, and in that shape, made of bark; also another in the form of a bread trough. There was also a mortar and two wooden pestles.
>
> In the entry was a pig's trough, and a few other things of little worth. Their corn is hung on poles inside. There were four bunks, or raised platforms, on which they sleep; and two places in the middle where they make the fire, over which were two holes in the roof for the smoke to go out.
>
> Jeremy Belknap, 1796[243]

As they entered the village of the Oneidas, the Frenchmen were able for the first time to observe a Native American community in the marginal region between the wilderness to the west and the White settlements to the east.

> Those whom we saw were wretchedly clad, in a blanket of coarse blue woolen, and were warming themselves around their fires. Their children were entirely naked, and their figure is exactly like that of the Chinese whom we see selling curiosities in France under the name of Pagodas, and they are of the same copper color. They have their ears cut, and their arms covered with figures made by pricking with needles and filling with gun powder.

Earlier that same summer, a party of Quakers, en route to Ohio to observe an Indian treaty conference, encountered a delegation from Oneida Castle at the mouth of Wood Creek, including Col. Lewis and Chief Schenandoah:

> This evening, a number of Indians came to our camp, viz. Col. Lewis, Capt. John, and a very old chief, named Beechtree, or Kind Doe, and several young warriors painted red, with black streaks. Some had their ears cut in strings, with trinkets in them; and they mostly had bobs of wampum, metal, or bright shells, hung in their noses.
>
> They had two of their wives with them - each had a child laced with its back to a board - the front side made of skins, lined with soft flannel, and a canopy of curious work like embroidery, overhead - of like workmanship, were the laces and bandages with which the infant was fastened in - these they loose with great facility, and take out the babe. The whole has the appearance of a case, narrow at bottom, and widens upwards - it is about two feet in length, and has a bow to the front side of it, to go over the mother's breast, when she carries the child.
>
> Jacob Lindley, 1793[244]

An 18th century image of decorative ear slitting.

109

The scattered settlement of Oneida Castle was nestled in a bend of the Oneida Creek. To reach Shenandoah's house, which was located a short distance to the east, the party had to pass through the village and along the north side of the creek.

The land that we traversed forms a part of the 240,000 acres which the Oneidas have reserved, and which are the best in this part of America. The vegetation is really superb, and we can trace the remains of orchards, and even of ancient clearings, in places now lying waste. This country, formerly well peopled, does not now actually have a hundred Indian families.

After passing through a luxuriant herbage, we arrived at length at the house of the aged Schenando. Father Perrot, the Canadian, was no longer there, but we were not less cordially received as French, and we claimed to be acquaintances of M. Desvatines. Mr. Catheliu, a minister whom the State of New York has stationed among these people to convert them to Christianity, came in soon after. He treated us kindly, and offered to serve us as interpreter. He informed us that Mr. DeWitt, the Surveyor General, and the State Commissioner, were then at Oneida for the purpose of holding a treaty with the Indians concerning the sale of a part of their lands, and for the opening of a road with proper accommodations from the Mohawk River to the Genesee.

Although they had missed both Col. Lewis and Father Perrot, the members of the expedition would not be disappointed in their encounter with the great leader Schenandoah, and the visitors who were constantly drawn to his house.

Schenando and his wife did their best to entertain us and set before us corn cakes filled with beans of every color, so that when cut they appeared marbled; squashes, a kind of little gourd cooked in water without butter or salt; and beans cooked with the same sauce. In spite of all our French politeness, and our appetite, the odious savor of these dishes did not allow us to taste them. We had noticed some great wooden dishes full of excellent milk, and upon asking for this, they gave it freely, and this, with some very fresh butter, enabled us to master the cakes.

Fortuitously, Desjardins and Pharoux met, in quick succession, several people who were able to offer them insights into the land situation to the north, particularly wilderness areas bordering the St. Lawrence region and the eastern margins of Lake Ontario.

Soon after, there came to the cabin two half breed Indians, sons of a Canadian, who spoke a little French and gave us some account of our lands, as also those which the Oneidas had given to one M. Penet, who some years ago, with other Frenchmen, had settled at

Schenectady. Having gone through the Indian villages, he had made magnificent promises of a profitable trade, but had left America without paying his debts, and the very lands they had given him had been seized and sold at the rate of ten cents an acre, *although of the best quality, and the best located of any in the country. Schenando showed us some property of Penet's, and told us that we should sleep in his bed, which had been left at his house.*

The story of this mysterious figure, Penet, perhaps interested them, he being also a Frenchman and having been granted, by the Oneidas, a vast tract of land bordering the proposed settlement of the French Company represented by this expedition.

But if this tale drew their attention more than most, it was not revealed in the journal, perhaps because the diversions attending their visit at Schenendoah's cabin continued to increase.

A short time after, an Indian came in, and crouching down before the fire, said quite bluntly, "bon jour Messieurs." Ah, ah, said M. Desjardins, you speak French very well. "Aussi: le suis je," he added. We would not have suspected him, for not only his equipage, but also his gestures, and even his color, which was very swarthy, would have passed him off for a native, born from the deepest woods. He told us that he had come over to Canada as a soldier, and that the same year, in an engagement on Lake Champlain, he had been taken a prisoner by the Oneidas, who had adopted him. He had remained with them more than forty years, and lived very contentedly the life of an Indian. We improved the occasion to obtain some information concerning our purchase. Schenando, an old man of seventy six years, congratulated himself on the prospect of having Frenchmen as neighbors, and told us that the lands along the Black River were very good, as were also those on the Bay.

The Canadian's son traced for us, with coal upon a plank, the three routes we might choose in going to Fort Schuyler on the morrow.

As they stared at the map of the roads running east down to Old Fort Schuyler, sketched in charcoal on the board, the party might have begun to turn their thoughts toward departure and their reunion with the batteau at Post's Tavern.

But in the meantime, an evening of hospitality awaited them.

At night Mr. DeWitt sent us a quantity of beef for supper, and invited us in the name of the Commissioners, and of himself, not to leave in the morning without taking breakfast with them. The sight of a quarter of beef was extremely pleasant to our hosts. We cooked it, ate a part for supper, and made a feast to them of the rest. After which, we slept in M. Penet's bed. They gave a bear skin for Mr. Judson and the carpenter.

During the night, we were somewhat disturbed by the noise made by the women in pounding their corn in mortars. Such is the work of these beauties, who having toiled all day, spend half the night in this tedious exercise, while their husbands lie sleeping at their ease, having smoked all day long.

Oneida Castle

Three years after the French party visited the village in the bend of the Oneida Creek, Jeremy Belknap recorded his impression of the settlement, and of the home and hospitality of Chief Schenandoah:

"We arrived at Oneida Castle - so called, though there was no appearance of a fortification - about three P.M., and went into the house of John Skanandogh, an old chief aged seventy-six. His house is built in the English, or rather the Dutch style, and warmed in winter by a fire made on one side like the Dutch houses, with an open space all round, and a kind of funnel above to let out the smoke...

"The chiefs had notice of our coming, and began to assemble in their meeting-house, which is built of logs and covered with bark. About four o'clock they blew the horn as signal, and we met them. They were not quite so formal as the chiefs at New Stockbridge, and were willing to enter on business immediately. We held a conference of two hours, and had several examinations, which we minuted in writing. A tin kettle of water and a small tin cup served us for refreshment during the conference...

"This village is situate on a high plain; and Skanandogh's house, on the south edge of it, commands an extensive and grand view all around. Were the country in a state of cultivation, nothing could be more charming than such a prospect; but it is melancholy to see so fine a tract of land in such a savage state. There are in this village a considerable number of huts, most of which are of logs, some few framed, and several of them have covered stoops or piazzas in the Dutch style. In the late war their village was destroyed by the Indians and Tories in the British interest. They had a decent church with a bell, which was built with charitable donations. This was destroyed. The whole nation removed down the Mohawk River, and encamped on the plain of Schenectady above the town, where they lived several years, and were supported by the United States. After their return to their own country, they rebuilt their houses chiefly after the manner of the Dutch, and carried home some of their customs...

"Lodged this night at old Skanandogh's on a mattress. Had a supper of tea, milk, Indian cake, fried eggs, and strawberries. The Indian cake is made by soaking the corn in ley, which takes off the hull; then it is pounded in a mortar; then mixed up with water into the form of a biscuit, and boiled till it becomes of the consistence of a dumpling."

Jeremy Belknap, 1796[247]

One might suspect that the "Dutch" design noted in Schenandoah's house resulted from the influence of their exile near Schenectady, where such houses were prevalent. However, a pre-exile journal indicates otherwise:

"...Chief Scanindoe who lives in a good house built in the Dutch fashion..."

Joseph Bloomfield, 1776[248]

"Of all the languages I have ever heard, none strikes my ear so pleasantly as the Indian, especially from the mouth of a female. Their accent is harmonious, soft, and full of music, - swelling, and descending, in a manner grateful to the ear."

Elkanah Watson, 1791[246]

During their sleepless hours in the cold darkness of Penet's cabin, the party might have pondered the differences between Native society and that of their homeland. This contrast was certainly well noted three years later by another traveler in the same locale:

On the way observed several Oneida ladies preparing to go out into the fields with their hoes to work in the cool of the morning whilst their husbands smoke their pipes at home. On the road we met four or five women, with each a bag of corn on her back, which they had been to Stockbridge to buy. The bag was hung by a strap round their forehead.

When the man and woman go together to buy corn, the woman carries the load; and, if they have a horse, the man rides it with a bag under him, but the woman goes on foot with her load on her shoulders. The women are strong and patient and very laborious. Some few of the men, however, do work in the field, and the women work with them.

It is to be observed that, in the Indian husbandry, the huts are placed in the centre of an inclosure, which is greater or less according to the number of the inhabitants. This inclosure is a common pasture, in which all their horses, cows, and swine feed together. Beyond the fence is the planting ground, and there is no fence between that and the woods. Some exceptions, however, there are to this general rule. The Indians of New Stockbridge make their fences, and separate their fields from their pastures in the English mode.

Jeremy Belknap, 1796[249]

"I visited some of the huts of the ordinary tribesmen and returned there later ... but we found only women about. To them is left all the work of the fields and all the domestic chores. We saw very tall and beautiful girls digging potatoes and carrying them to their cabins. The men do nothing but rove about the woods fishing, hunting bears, deer, raccoons, squirrels, etc. They also make distant expeditions to the lakes."

Julian Niemcewicz, 1805[250]

This imbalance of specialized labor was frequently cited in travelers' journals of the period:

As we passed through their villages, we saw some women employed in works of husbandry, but very few men. Among the Indians the husband does not work at all; all laborious services are performed exclusively by the wife. She not only transacts every part of domestic business, but cultivates the ground, cuts wood, carries loads, etc. The husband hunts, fishes, smokes, and drinks.

Duke de la Rochefoucault, 1795[251]

The next day, having enjoyed a more fruitful visit than they could have ever expected, the party prepared to depart for the Mohawk Valley. But first, Pharoux and Desjardins determined to take advantage of the offer of breakfast in the Surveyor General's camp. Perhaps they hoped to gain some advantage or additional insights by this consultation with the man more responsible than any other for the surveying, mapping, and eventual allotment of lands in the unsettled regions of the west.

The building in which this breakfast took place was no doubt the Oneida meeting house, which stood in the center of the settlement on lands that would later be reserved as a village square.

Sunday. Nov. 3rd. In the morning we left our two fellow travelers at Schenando's, and accepted the invitation of the State Commissioners. The house where they were holding the council was on the plain about a mile from our host's.

Mr. DeWitt presented us to Mr. Caldwell and the other Commissioners, who made us briefly relate the incidents of our journey. These gentlemen flattered themselves that they would be able to conclude terms with the Indians, but Schenando had assured us that his advice, and that of the old men, was to sell nothing, and that the Americans would never be satisfied until they had seized their last acre; that some drunken chiefs had been gained over, but that the great majority would hold fast.

We informed these gentlemen what we had heard, but they replied that this would not prevent them, and that they had the King, a great chief, on their side. In fact, a moment after, his Oneida Majesty made his appearance, without bearing any marked insignia, and clad in a blanket like the poorest of his subjects. The Commissioners had us shake hands with his Majesty, who drank a glass of rum to the health of the French. They then sat down to breakfast, in the American style, and it was very well served for the woods. His Majesty, and two or three lords of his court, modestly seated themselves at the end of the table.

Mr. DeWitt brought us news of the family of M. Desjardins, who had finally found a house that could be hired, and gave us the address, for we did not know where to stop on our return.

The wilderness hospitality proffered the Frenchmen by DeWitt would not be as forthcoming the following year, when they visited him in his Albany office:

I saw Mr. DeWitt, the Surveyor General, and having showed and explained to him the plan, expressed our fears and our grounds of hope. I also asked his advice, as to our contract which I showed him, but observed that he avoided committing himself on this subject as much as possible, which I attributed to a fear that he might get compromised with our grantors, who are Americans, while we are foreigners and can neither be to him so useful or injurious.

Simon Desjardins, 1794[252]

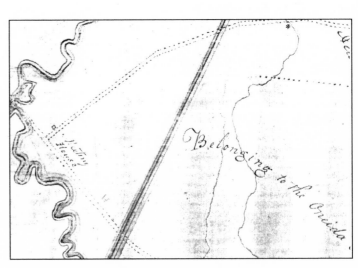

The Meeting House at Oneida Castle.

CHAPTER FIFTEEN

The Road to Whitestown

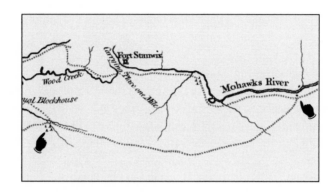

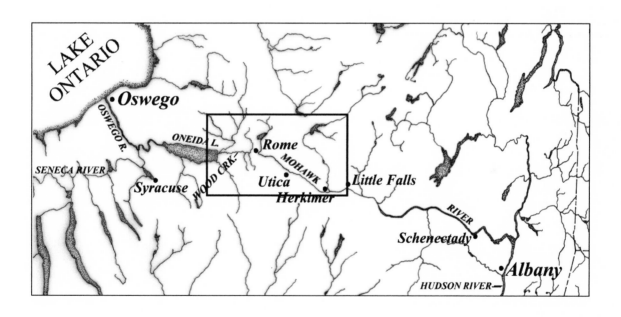

With what was perhaps the richest and most colorful twenty-four hours of the entire journey behind them, it was now time for the French party to concentrate on getting back to the waterways and their rendezvous with the batteau at Old Fort Schuyler.

After breakfast, Mr. DeWitt returned with us to the house of Schenando. Not finding him, we begged Mr. DeWitt to oblige us by giving him for us something for our expenses. We then left with our two men, and bade them all adieu.

These men would not again meet with Chief Schenandoah [Skan-an-doa = "Hemlock"], even though he remained a figure of considerable impact in the region, in spite of his age:

In appearance he was noble, dignified, and commanding, being in height much over six feet, and the tallest Indian in his nation.

Pomeroy Jones, 1851[253]

He died almost a quarter century later, in the spring of 1816, at the estimated age of 110.

"I am an aged Hemlock; the winds of an hundred winters have whistled through my branches; I am dead at the top. The generation to which I belonged have run away and left me. Why I live, the Great Good Spirit only knows. I pray to my Jesus that I may have patience to wait for my appointed time to die."

Chief Schenandoah, c1816[254]

A selection of three roads heading to the east had been offered the party the day before. The choice of one, and the location of its point of beginning, depended on one of the Frenchmen's newly acquired acquaintances.

On meeting with the Canadian Indian, he guided us to the bridge at the Oneida corn mill, where, after showing us the road, he left us, with many thanks for the shilling that we gave him.
It was about ten miles from the Oneida Castle to the first American settlement. The Indians have no accession for roads, and never do anything for them. The State has not yet undertaken any, and this route is therefore almost impassable. It could scarcely be traced through the woods by some trees marked here and there; the streams had no bridges, the swamps no causeways, and the oft used stepping places were nearly impassable. Yet this is the great route to the Genesee, and to all the western country.

Roads, particularly roads in relatively unsettled regions such as this, were often little better than paths through the woods. Travel, under the best conditions, remained an ordeal.

The traveling in the country in the spring and fall of the year is very unpleasant, as your horse is often from his knees to his body obliged to founder on through mud and

mire, owing to the depth and richness of the soil, its uncultivated state, and the want of proper roads.

J.A Graham, 1797[255]

The Old Genesee Road was certainly no exception to this rule. Even as late as 1799, one year before the improved Genesee Turnpike replaced the Genesee Road, travel here remained potentially a nightmare:

...ten travelers came in from the west... the roads, they informed us, were worse than they had ever been. Their horses were drenched in the mire to the hips and shoulders; and the riders were pale, and broken-spirited, with excessive fatigue.

Timothy Dwight, 1799[256]

This road, as impoverished of improvements as it may have been in the 1790s, represented the best land route to the west for immigrants landing in batteaux at Old Fort Schuyler. Access to the Finger Lakes and the margins of the Genesee River could be obtained by this path, without the difficulties of the Upper Mohawk, the Oneida Carry, Wood Creek, and the Oswego River.

The majority of the people using this road were moving west, perhaps never to return to what was then the hub of westward migration - Whitestown:

The "Genesee Road"

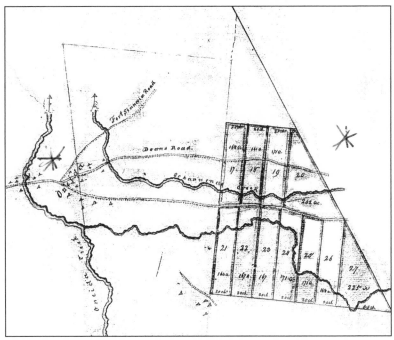

A 1790s map showing the three roads leading east out of Oneida Castle. The middle one was taken by the expedition in 1793.

In 1793, little more than a path connected the batteau landing at Old Fort Schuyler [Utica] with the western territories of New York:

"An Indian road being opened from this place (now Utica) to the Genesee country, it is probable the position at Fort Stanwix, and this spot, will become rivals, as to the site of a town, in connection with the interior, when it shall become a settled country."

Elkanah Watson, 1791[257]

Yet for over thirty years prior to that, a road, or trail, had run from the batteau landing at Old Fort Schuyler [Utica] to the Oneida Castle and points further west. It and appears on nearly every map of the region from 1756 on. Evidence suggests that this road followed the line of what would later become the Seneca Turnpike, and is today State Route 5.

But in 1793, the road which the French party followed was well north of that alignment, for they stopped at the Dean's Tavern on the way, in what is now Westmoreland. This confirms that they followed the "Great Genesee Road" between Oneida Castle and Whitesborough, on the Mohawk; the middle of three major routes in the 1790s that went to Fort Stanwix, Dean's Tavern, and Utica respectively. This middle road was later labeled the "Old Genesee Road" on a map of Oneida Castle, and is clearly located north of the Seneca Turnpike, also indicated on the 1813 map.

By early fall, 1793, Simeon DeWitt, the Surveyor General of New York, was making preparations in Albany for negotiations with the Oneidas and Onondagas for cessions of land for the new Genesee Road, that would allow for a more effective land transport between the Mohawk Valley and new settlements west of the Finger Lakes. From his correspondence we can detect some anxiety about being able to complete these negotiations before winter. At the end of September, arrangements were being made for supplies of flour to be given to the Indians, as an incentive, with Mr. Porteous at Little Falls the likely contractor.

An initial meeting at Oneida Castle was held the first of October, but by mid-month DeWitt was back in Albany, asking his nephew, Moses Dewitt, for assistance in scheduling another meeting with the Oneidas on the same business. Although Moses, who lived at Onondaga, had been entrusted with obtaining "supplies of flour & beef," his uncle states "Our intention is (unless you have already made provision for it) to employ one of our batteaux, after our arrival at Fort Schuyler, for transporting the flour we shall want at Oneida."

Two weeks later, and only two days before the arrival of the French party, Simeon wrote from the Oneida village:

"I have already by my letter dispatched this morning informed you of our arrival. We got some of the Chiefs together to announce ourselves and inform them that as soon as our batteaux arrived, we would be ready to enter on business. This afternoon our young gentlemen arrived from the batteaux, having left them at Loues's place. Tomorrow morning two canoes with Indians go down to fetch up the baggage we shall want here.The event of our business is doubtful. We will have strong prepossessions (the result of former councils & instigations of malicious Whitemen as we conjecture) to combat with. But we will, as is our duty, try to effect our ends. We have both Deane & Kirkland as interpreters who we hope will render us all the service in their

Continued on next page

continued from page 115

power. We would all be glad of your company. Possibly your council may assist in forwarding our views & facilitate our business."

Moses DeWitt, 1793[258]

It was clearly out of this stock of flour and beef, initially brought to Col. Lewis' landing near the mouth of Oneida Creek, that the "quarter of beef" was taken that DeWitt sent to the cabin of Chief Schenandoah and the French visitors. And it was apparently at the Oneida meeting house, which stood in the central commons of the village, that the State Commissioners held their negotiations and to which our journalists were invited to breakfast on the 3rd of November.

On November 7th, DeWitt wrote his nephew at Onondaga indicating their business with the Oneidas was completed and that they would shortly journey on westward by land to begin their negotiations with the Onondagas near Syracuse.

As a result of continuing negotiations during the coming year, the Oneidas ceded much of their reservation to the State of New York in 1795, and in 1797 construction on the new Genesee Turnpike was begun. This road [now State Route 5] ran from Utica, across lands formerly owned by the Oneidas, ending in Geneva on Seneca Lake. The opening of this improved road west from the batteau landing at Old Fort Schuyler [Utica] in 1800 not only facilitated land travel west, in direct competition with the old navigation route to Oswego, but it promoted Utica as the destination for emigrants coming upriver from Schenectady, thus weakening the pre-eminence of Fort Stanwix [Rome] as an inland navigation terminal.

After breakfast several of us went 4 miles up the river on foot to Whites Town... it is quite a new settlement but has the appearance of becoming a place of note, being situated in a fast improving Country, and has already in it large Stores, and the finest Pot Ash works that we have yet seen...

William Hartshorne, 1793[259]

"I met on the road to Whites-borough, a group of Oneyda Indians - some of them on horseback, others walking and jumping - the one with a bottle, another with a jug or small keg with rum - for the most part merrily jolly - some deeply soaked by the beverage, distilled from the cane. Their numbers increased in proportion I approached nearer Whitesborough. There I saw about two hundred of every age and of both sexes around their fires near the road, eating, drinking, smoking, singing, laughing, all then in perfect harmony together, though many a little before had tried their strength and agility upon one another.

"The occasion of this unusual concourse was, that they came to receive the corn from the State, which had been stipulated in one of the articles of the late Treaty. But they soon changed this corn, certainly for a large part, by the merchants for money, which they changed again for chintzes, silk hankerchiefs, linen, &c."

Adrian Vanderkemp, 1792[260]

It was along this miserable route that the party of four picked their way. The degree to which the experience was bleak may be inferred from the lack, in the journal for this period, of the characteristic descriptions of the flora and fauna along the wayside.

Three years later, Jeremy Belknap made his way along this road in summer, when conditions were more favorable. He accordingly had more to offer in his journal:

...the weather very hot, but when we got into the woods the shade was very agreeable. On our way picked several flowers and got specimens of some vegetables not in flower... Found the ginseng and maidenhair in great plenty in the Oneida woods; also a substance much resembling hops, growing on trees. Met with the prickly ash, not in flower, and passed by many others which our time and circumstances would not allow us to take.

Jeremy Belknap, 1796[261]

Approaching Oneida Castle, Belknap noted the infrequent depredations of the Gypsy Moth and its impact on the maple sugar production:

Rode through twelve miles of woods; very fine land, but excessively bad road. In this route the first runs of water fall into the Mohawk; the latter into the Oneida Lake, and so into Ontario. The growth was sugar-maple, beech, elm, walnut, and oilnut, - the trees very tall and straight; in the latter part much eaten by caterpillars. When this is the case with the maple, no sugar can be made from it the next season. Last season very little, because the caterpillars devoured them last summer. This has not been known since the English settled here, but the Indians remember it before.

Jeremy Belknap, 1796[262]

Traveling on eastward along this rudimentary road, without benefit of horses or guide, and no doubt wishing for the relative ease of batteau navigation once again, the party approached a tiny oasis of civilization located in a swale along a creek, roughly at the halfway point of their arduous journey.

M. Desjardins, overcome by the fatigue of travel, and by a fall which abraded his leg against a tree that lay in the road, could scarcely go farther. We took dinner and supper at once, at a place called Dine's tavern. This Mr. Dine, seeing how much M. Desjardins needed a horse, refused to hire him one for the remaining twelve miles for less than two dollars, and M. Desjardins, exasperated at this renewed

Whitestown

The thriving settlement observed at Whitestown in 1793, did not even exist ten years earlier. It had begun with the arrival of Judge White in 1784:

"Hugh White...came by water to Albany, crossed by land to Schenectady, where he purchased a batteau, in which he made passage up the Mohawk River, to the mouth of the Sauquoit Creek. Immediately after the revolution, Judge White became one of the purchasers of Sadaqueda Patent, jointly with Zephanial Platt... Ezra L'Hommedieu, and Melancthon Smith. By an arrangement between the proprietors, it was agreed that they should meet on the land in the summer of 1784, and make a survey and partition. Upon the arrival of Judge Platt, at the mouth of the Sauquoit, a bark shanty was erected for a temporary residence. During the summer the patent was surveyed into four sections, and the particular section of each owner was decided by lot."

Pomeroy Jones, 1851[263]

Even the year before, its astounding rate of growth had been noted:

"I next passed through Whitestown. It would appear to you, my friend, on hearing the relation of events in this western county, that the whole was fable. And if you were placed in Whitestown or Clinton, ten miles west from Fort Schuyler, and could you see the progress of improvement, you would believe it enchanted ground. You would there view an extensive, well-built town, surrounded by highly cultivated fields, which spot in the year 1783 was the 'haunt of tribes' and the hiding place of wolves, now a flourishing, happy situation, containing about six thousand people."

Capt. Charles Williamson, 1792[264]

The influence of geography on development in this period was so profound that one could travel just a days ride west, toward Oneida Castle, and find a significantly more primitive situation, even over a decade later:

"We left early and came into completely new terrain. Here in the midst of forests, the enormous height and thickness of whose trees filled us with astonishment, we came from time to time upon clearings. In these one sees only the stumps of trees with a little cabin and, in the center of the clearing, on soil the surface of which was scarcely scratched, a few potatoes, some corn, a few chickens and pigs. It was quite surprising to see coming out of one of these huts good-looking and well dressed women whose white hands draw water from a hole which serves as a well. When a traveler arrives in this place two or three years hence he will find a fine house, well-cultivated fields, and all the amenities of life."

Julian Ursyn Niemcewicz, 1805[265]

It was in this same area, that one observer noted in some detail the process by which the virgin forest was initially rendered livable at the hands of isolated families in search of land:

"When a family have come to a resolution to settle in this country, the husband, that latter end of summer, repairs to the spot where the settlement is to be made. The first thing he does is to cut down the small trees on one or two acres; he next barks the larger trees, and then sows a little rye or wheat. Of the wood he has felled,

continued on next page

continued from page 117

he constructs a small house, and makes suitable fences around it; a labor, which may be performed in about a month's time. He then returns to his former habitation; and, at the beginning of spring, he brings his family and the best of his cattle to the new settlement. His cows cost him little, being turned into the woods to graze: he then finishes his house, plants potatoes, sows Indian corn, and thus is enabled to provide for the first year's maintenance. While thus employed, he is at the same time clearing more ground, burning the trees he has already felled, and, as far as may be, even those which he has barked. By this process the roots of the bushes are in great measure destroyed; yet they require to be more carefully grubbed out of the land, which is to be thoroughly cleared. The ashes afford a very useful manure, and, in the opinion of the best judges, are employed this way to much greater advantage, than when converted to pot-ash...

"Thus, within the space of twelve months, a man may clear fifteen acres; and few families cultivate more than thirty... The stumps of the felled trees, generally two or three feet high above the ground, hardly rot sooner than the barked trees, which have been left standing on the lands. The dwellings of new settlers are commonly at first set up in a very slight manner; they consist of huts, the roofs and walls of which are made of bark, and in which the husband, wife, and children pass the winter, wrapped up in blankets. They also frequently construct houses of trees laid upon each other; the interstices of which are either filled up with loam, or left open, according as there is more or less time to fill them up. In such buildings as have attained to some degree of perfection, there is a chimney of brick or clay; but very often there is only an aperture in the roof to let out the smoke..."

Duke de la Rochefoucault Liancourt, 1795[266]

exhibition of avarice, resolved to go on foot in the morning as far as the next place, where he might hope to procure one. The usual hire of a horse is four shillings a day.

Here they had crossed again the trail of James Dean, the interpreter. Eight years earlier Dean had been flooded out of the grant of land given him by the Oneidas on Wood Creek. It was there, at what was thereafter always known as "Dean's Landing", that Pharoux and Desjardins had bid farewell to the contractor for the Western Inland Lock Navigation Company, whose batteau had helped them get over the shallows coming down from Canada Creek.

It was to this parcel here on the Genesee Road that James Dean had relocated in 1786, having secured a generous grant from the Oneidas to replace the one on Wood Creek. And it was his brother, Jonathan, who had built across the stream and now maintained a tavern on the spot.

It was probably no accident that this stream, thereafter known as "Dean's Creek", included a waterfall, which was shortly developed by Dean into a mill site. The grist mill which he operated here, coupled with his occasional services as an Indian language interpreter, provided him with relative wealth and a measure of political power.

"Mr. James Deane, who lives at Westmoreland, four miles this side of Oneida, is a man of education, sense, and independent way of thinking; has spent many years among the Indians; is personally acquainted with the principal Oneidas. ...In estimating his opinions, some allowance must be made for the influence of that disgust which he appears to have taken against the aboriginals. If Mr. Deane will be interpreter, he will be accurate and faithful, or, if he cannot act himself, he will tell of a good one."

Samuel Kirkland, 1796[267]

Forced to endure a night under the roof of a tavern keeper of dubious hospitality, but the only one in the vicinity, the party pushed on the next day along the unfamiliar route.

Monday. Nov. 4th. Started in the morning, but M. Desjardins, who was suffering from his leg, could scarcely get two miles to the next house, where we stopped for breakfast and procured a horse for a dollar and a half. Our shoes were torn in the woods so that they would scarcely stay on our feet, and we had to tie them on with straps of Moosewood bark.

As we advanced, the country was better settled, and the inhabitants had from necessity made the roads more passable. The bridges over the creeks, and log causeways across the marshes, rendered the road, if not good, at least passable.

It may have been well that these improvements were recently made, as maintenance was often neglected.

In addition to all these evils, the causeys, which I have heretofore described, abound, of course, on every miry surface. These, you will recall, are made of round, smooth poles, and therefore furnish, at the best, a very imperfect footing. Some of them are soon displaced, and others broken. The inhabitants, in the mean-time, are so few, so poor, and so much occupied in subduing their farms, and in providing sustenance for their families, that it is often a long time before these bridges are repaired. Such, upon the whole, was the state in which we found them....

Timothy Dwight, c.1795[268]

As the party of four continued walking northeasterly along the Genesee Road, with the injured Desjardins on horseback, they began to see evidence of the expanding settlement that was pushing westward from Whitestown, on the Mohawk.

We traversed the greater part of the Whitestown settlement, which was begun only seven years ago, and has already more than seven hundred houses. The log houses already begin to give place to houses of light carpenter work, lined with plank and again covered; a very good substitute for stone. They are painted externally in oil paints. These slight dwellings are cheap when saw mills are near, and they present a very neat and cheerful appearance. Their only inconvenience would be that they could not keep out the cold in winter.

We passed a number of saw mills, on the Oriskany Creek and other little streams, a forge, and several potasheries. The latter, with the saw mills, have contributed wonderfully to the growth of these settlements. The soil monly good, but not extraordinary for fertility.

The improvements extend about seven miles in length, along the road leading to the chief place. We crossed the Oriskany, on a bridge of solid timber work. The soil here changes its quality, and spreads out into a wide sandy plain, nearly level, and crossed on one corner by the streets of the future town, that already begins to be adorned with houses scattered here and there, among which may be seen the Court House, Presbyterian Meeting house, the houses of Judge White and other founders of the place, all of whom are Yankees, or men from the New England States.

We stopped at a tavern of very neat appearance, where we drank rum mixed with milk. They call this drink Milk Punch, and as lemons are unknown in the country, it is the great beverage of the inhabitants. We did not, however, find it much to our taste.

119

CHAPTER SIXTEEN

At John Post's Landing

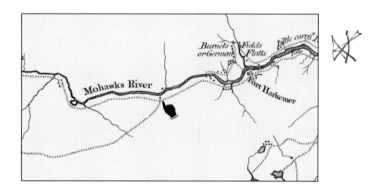

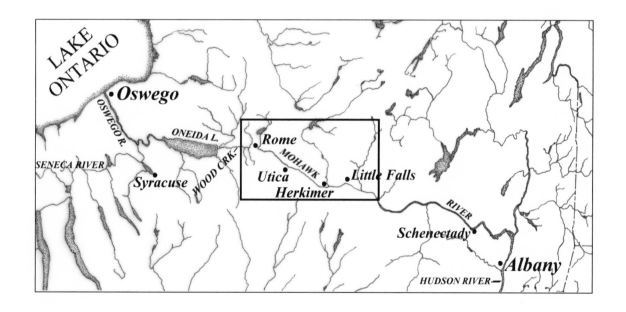

After a grueling march over the Old Genesee Road that had lasted a day and a half, the four men gazed off to the north to see the glistening ribbon of the Mohawk once again. Although it had been just three days since they had left the rest of their expedition at the mouth of Wood Creek, the richness of their experiences, coupled with the hardship of their overland excursion, must have made it seem like a week.

They were undoubtedly anxious to be reunited with their batteau and to spend the rest of the journey sitting in a boat that would glide effortlessly down the Mohawk to Schenectady. They were also undoubtedly surprised to find that, in spite of their arduous detour through the forests of the Oneida Reservation, they had still arrived at the landing ahead of their boat.

At two o'clock we arrived at the house of Mr. Post, at old Fort Schuyler, four miles from Whitestown, at the place appointed for our rendezvous. Our bateau had not yet arrived. We took dinner and supper at this place, and looked into his store, which was well stocked and a favorite place for tipplers and customers.

As with many settlers who chose to build at strategic points along the inland waterways in this time, John Post had thrust upon him the role of tavern keeper. His daughter, years after, recalled this circumstance:

As ours was the first house which could accommodate travelers, a sign was put up, though reluctantly, and my father kept tavern no longer than until some one with means could be prevailed upon to leave a more privileged place to settle here, for the sole purpose of keeping a tavern.

Mrs. Petrie, c1851[269]

Post had come here by batteau, with his family, in the spring of 1790. Previous to that, he had been in partnership with a Schenectady merchant, and engaged in trade with the Indians for, among other things, Ginseng or "Mandrake". This wild root, which was often encountered in the woodlands to the west, was a valuable export commodity in the 1790s, particularly to China, where it reportedly was considered superior to their local variety.

"The lands through which we passed this day are all highly cultivated, and loaded with a luxuriant growth of wheat, rye, oats, and peas. Hops grow wild along the margin of the river and run over the bushes. There is a fruit called mandrake, very plenty in all this tract and above. It grows on a stalk from twelve to fifteen inches high, under a canopy of leaves. It has a fine smell, and some people are fond of it. Gooseberries and black currants are also very numerous. Some of the gooseberries are half ripe and have prickles on the fruit."

Jeremy Belknap, 1796[270]

The grassy riverbank between Post's cabin and the batteau landing served, throughout this era, as a sort of camping place and staging area for people disembarking from their boats here, and for those going and coming between this place and Fort Stanwix. Desjardins and Pharoux availed themselves of this area twice more, the following year, as they passed between Schenectady harbor and their lands on the Black River:

At five in the evening, we finally arrived at the bridge at old Fort Schuyler, where I unloaded the batteaux and pitched the tent on the river bank in Mr. Post's yard. The batteaux returned at once to Schenectady, so that they might be ready for the surveyors on their arrival. The tent being pitched, we changed our linen, but not without annoyance from curious spectators, who came to look into the tent, and under the sails and tarpaulins, with which we had covered our provisions. When wearied with this impertinent curiosity, I asked them what they wanted. They very quietly replied, "to see."

...we pitched our tent on the bank of the river, to store our things and lodge ourselves, preferring our own blankets and a board, to the tavern beds, where filth and vermin reigned.

Simon Desjardins, 1794[271]

By coincidence, the party in 1793 met someone at the tavern who was very familiar with the lands along the Black River.

He introduced us to Mr. Boon, a Hollander, who had been some time in the country, where he has bought some patents near the Baron Steuben, and not far from our lands. He informed us about the Steuben road, which runs within three miles of the Black River, and said sixteen miles had been built, but that the route was in a very bad condition. The Baron had, a little before, gone down to New York, and we therefore gave up the journey, but resolved to make the acquaintance of our estimable neighbor in New York. He assured us that much expense had been incurred on these patents, and that all the lands were good.

Exactly one year later, in October of 1794, the Frenchmen would have an opportunity to visit Boon's settlement [Boonville], some 30 miles to the north, and be impressed by its progress:

Boon's... We found this settlement greatly advanced, and his house of five windows in front and two stories high is entirely finished, wainscoted, glazed, etc. The farm buildings, gristmill and sawmill are finished, and sixty acres of land cleared: all the work of eighteen months, but at an abundant cost of money.

Simon Desjardins, 1794[272]

Their interest in Boon's lands derived from their proximity to the headwaters of the Black River and the proposed French development. They might have wished to consult with von Steuben about his road, which could serve as an alternate route into their lands, by-passing many long miles of difficult navigation. The Baron was then the most famous, and perhaps influential, landholder in the region they hoped to inhabit.

Frederick William Baron Von Steuben had acquired the land grant north of Post's landing in 1786, in recognition of his service during the Revolutionary War. Known as the "Drillmaster of the Revolution", he was credited with introducing the discipline that turned the American rebels into an army. By 1793 he had established

"Old Fort Schuyler"

From the time of the French and Indian War, and no doubt long before that, a ford across the Mohawk River existed where Utica would later be located. In 1758 Fort Schuyler, named for the uncle of Philip Schuyler, was erected just below this point to guard the crossing, which provided access from the trails which came down from the west to the road which ran along the north side of the river toward Albany. The site of the fort here had long served as a landing place, but it was many years before a commercial building was erected:

> "At Utica there was a small frame store of old John Post, an Indian trader, and a large log house kept as a tavern."
>
> Jared Broughton, 1790[273]

Post was one of several merchants who in this period established frontier trading posts as western –extensions of commercial enterprises operating at the port in Schenectady:

> "John Post, the first merchant in what is now Utica, was engaged for some years previously to 1790, in connection with Mr. Martin, of Schenectady, in trading with the six nations, particularly in the purchase of ginseng, then exported in large quantities to China, as a supposed remedy for that fatal disease the Plague.... In the spring of 1790, having purchased and leased real estate near old Fort Schuyler, upon Cosby's manor, he removed thither. With his wife and three infant children and a carpenter, placing a stock of merchandize, furniture, provisions and building materials in boats, he embarked upon the Mohawk at Schenectady, and in eight or nine days landed at his new home. So deep was the mud in the road, now Genesee Street, that the children had to be carried to the log palace previously erected, where they all arrived cold and uncomfortable...
>
> "At first Mr. Post kept his goods for sale in his dwelling, but in the next year (1791) he erected a building for a store, where he had extensive trade with the Indians and the early settlers of the surrounding country. Of the Indians he purchased furs, skins and ginseng in exchange for rum, paints, cloths, powder, shot, ornaments of various kinds, beads, small mirrors, etc., etc. It was a common occurrence that thirty or forty Indian men, women and children remained at his house through the night, and if the weather was cold they occupied the floor in front of the immense kitchen fire of logs, but in the summer they lodged in the barn, or... lay upon the grass plats by the side of the log and brush fences..."
>
> Pomeroy Jones, 1851[274]

Years later, Post's daughter recalled the mode of the accommodations offered by her father:

> "In those days men in that business were very independent, and if travelers or 'movers' wished to 'put up' at a tavern, they had to help themselves, water their own horses or oxen, harness or yoke them again, and if they asked to be served with aught, the landlord or his family would sometimes ask 'who was your waiter last year?' Sometimes, if persons did not look well to themselves, they received rough words and usage from these back-woods landlords."
>
> Mrs. Petrie, c1851[275]

continued on next page

continued from page 123

At the close of the eighteenth century, Post had become well established, and was engaged in running a line of Durham boats on the Mohawk:

> "Mr. Post erected a warehouse of wood, three stories high, upon the river, and afterwards another of brick, which stood a few rods above the Mohawk bridge... He owned several boats which were employed during the season of navigation in taking produce, etc., to Schenectady, and bringing back merchandize and the families and effects of persons removing into the new country. After a while he fitted up three stage-boats, the Accommodation, the Diligence and another, with oil-cloth covers, seats, etc. for the accommodation of travelers between Utica and Schenectady, who preferred this mode to wagons and afterwards stages, over rough and muddy roads."
>
> Pomeroy Jones, 1851[276]

These converted Durham freighters were the forerunners of the Erie Canal packet boats to ply this route some years later. Although most accounts suggest they only made round trips between Schenectady and Utica, at least one primary source indicates they could go as far as Montreal. Their description matches the woodcuts in an 1815 advertisement printed in Schenectady (below):

> "I will add, as a matter of curious history in the travel of the Mohawk Valley, that about the year 1815, Eri Lusher established a daily line of packet boats which were constructed after the model of the Durham boat, with cabin in midship, carefully cushioned, ornamented and curtained, expressly calculated for and used to carry from twenty to thirty passengers at a time, between Schenectady and Utica, making the passage between the two places down the river in about thirteen hours, and up the river, with favorable wind and high water, within two days."
>
> John Sanders, 1879[277]

In spite of his strategic location and his diversification into shipping as well as trade, Post's unprecedented enterprise on the bank of the Mohawk was not without risk:

> "July 13, 1792, Mr. Post purchased ... eighty-nine and a half acres... and he had a lease of twenty-five years of a small piece... where his store stood. Doing an extensive business, he was apparently prosperous, and doubtless in a few years amassed a considerable property. He had taken as a partner his son-in-law... and in making collections they had received a large amount of wheat, pork, etc., to take to market, with which, and a large sum of bank notes, they intended to purchase largely for their several stores. This was in 1806 or 7, and a most disastrous fire swept away the whole, goods, money, etc., in a few minutes. Not more than $100 of the whole was saved, and Mr. Post was ruined..."
>
> Pomeroy Jones, 1851[278]

NEW LINE.

THE subscribers inform the public, that they have established a line of *STAGE BOATS*, to ply between this city and Utica, for the accommodation of passengers from the latter place, and to carry up such valuable articles of merchandize, &c. as require the utmost care and dispatch. One Boat will leave Utica every Monday and Wednesday morning, and Schenectady every Wednesday and Friday morning. For passage at Utica, apply to A. Van Santvoord & Co.

THE OLD LINE CONTINUED,

From Schenectady for Oswego, Cayuga, and Seneca Falls. One Boat will start regularly every Saturday, during the season. Goods received between Saturday and Tuesday evening, to be forwarded beyond Utica, will be put on board the *Stage Boat* of Wednesday morning, and will overtake the Saturday's boat, at Utica, where they will be put on board and forwarded as directed.

Wagons will, as heretofore, be kept in constant readiness to transport from the city of Albany to Schenectady, or any part of the United States and Canada. Gentlemen who reside at a distance from the water communication are informed, that their goods will be delivered from the boats at any place they may think proper to designate; and at the Seneca Falls, to avoid delays, wagons are provided to convey the property, if required, to its place of destination.

The subscribers consider themselves the actual carriers, and responsible for all property passing through their hands, unavoidable accidents excepted.

Eri Lusher & Co.

Schenectady, May 1, 1815.

RIGGS & STEVENS, Printers—Schenectady.

This broadside advertises the new service between Schenectady and Utica using converted Durham boats.

Baron von Steuben's cabin as it appeared in the 1790s.

a homestead with a modest cabin, and a water-powered mill, and had hopes of inducing other homesteaders to settle around him.

Although he held no lands along the Mohawk River, by 1793 von Steuben had established a temporary batteau landing a short distance west of Post's, apparently in the mouth of Nine-Mile Creek. Its existence above Whitestown was recorded in the account of a traveler passing up the Mohawk a few months before the French expedition:

> After breakfast several of us went 4 miles up the river on foot to Whites Town... At 4 P.M. stopt at Baron Steuben's Landing on the north side of the river, from which to his house we were informed the distance was 7 miles and 9 to Fort Stanwix.
>
> William Hartshorne, 1793[279]

The opportunity to meet with Von Steuben to discuss matters of mutual interest appears to have been lost, as on November 28th of the following year he passed away.

The Frenchmen may have wished for more information about this landing, and the road that ran north to the upper fringe of the Black River watershed. But for the time being, they had to confine themselves to more immediate problems.

> *In the evening, a Canadian named Francois Sabourin, who was working for Mr. Post by the month, came to seek our aid. He could not speak a word of English, and was accused by an enceinte girl. We took much pains to console him on this taint attached to his honor, and finally he consented to remain with Mr. Post and let the charge rest, although he could hardly persuade himself that this would be the last of it.*

It is unfortunate the journalists, forced to spend an evening at the landing, did not record more in detail of the place. Their attention was entirely drawn to the new bridge crossing the Mohawk; a novelty in this region as well as a structure of potential service to them in the future.

> *Tuesday. Nov. 5th. We began to be uneasy about our bateau. Went to look at the bridge built over the Mohawk opposite Mr. Post's, and which leads to the road going to the Baron Steuben's settlement, and consequently to the*

> *Black River.*
>
> *This bridge, built after the English manner, is the arc of a circle with a very moderate curve, and is supported by beams made like a St. Andrew's cross, and covered above with plank. The bridge has already bent from the curve first intended, and inclines to the oval, an effect due as much to the framing as to the quality and smallness of the timbers, which are of pine and fir.*
>
> *The main support, which they have put in the middle, would rather tend to its entire destruction, when the ice is going off. The abutments are of timber and are also settled, from miscalculation of the resistance, the one on the south side being built upon ground that is full of springs.*
>
> *This bridge has been built but a short time, and was erected by a country carpenter. We asked Mr. Post why, when they had such a work to execute, they did not employ an engineer or architect to draw a plan and the details, which a carpenter might then easily execute. He replied that this was not the custom, and that no carpenter would be willing to work after the plans of another man. He however appeared mortified at the probable fall of his bridge which we predicted. It had indeed cost but little, thanks to his management, but economy in such a work is not always reasonable.*

Another, less critical, viewed this same bridge a short time earlier with a kinder opinion:

> At Fort Schuyler we found another bridge thrown across the river, which is here about one hundred and twenty feet wide when the waters are within the banks. The workmanship of the bridge does great credit to the ingenuity of the workman, as the arch extends from shore to shore.
>
> Gen. Benjamin Lincoln, 1793[280]

Before the discussion with Post regarding the ad hoc engineering of the new bridge could get any more heated, the batteau arrived from the west, bearing DeZeng and Brunel and the crew of three.

This bridge might well have interested Brunel further, as he was versed in the mechanics of construction and would later become one of the leading engineers in England. He may well have concurred in the opinion of his friends that this bridge was poorly built and at risk of failure.

All had the bitter-sweet satisfaction of having their suspicions confirmed when, the following spring, the bridge did collapse and had to be entirely rebuilt.

But the delays imposed by the late arrival of the batteau prevented any further examination of the structure during this trip.

> *Our bateau finally arrived at ten o'clock, and M. Brunel informed us that he had experienced the greatest difficulty in ascending Wood Creek, where there was so little water that they had been obliged to drag the bateau along the channel with oxen.*

Had the journalists remained with the batteau at the mouth of Wood Creek, we may have gained some telling insights into the near impossibility of ascending the channel late in the year, when lack of rain reduced the waterway to a few inches over logs and bars.

Such was the fate of any boat coming up Wood Creek in the low water season:

> Batteaux which ascend the creek, at this season, are dragged by horses, traveling in the water, and frequently the descending boats; which is a work of incredible fatigue and difficulty
>
> Elkanah Watson, 1791[281]

The ordeal of getting the boat from the east end of Oneida Lake to Post's, via Fort Stanwix, no doubt was related to Desjardins and Pharoux in some detail by Brunel. It apparently made an impression. Although the party again used batteaux to transport their baggage and equipment up the Mohawk from Schenectady the following year, they disembarked at Post's Tavern and, using the landing there as a staging area, proceeded north by wagon to their lands.

The delays in ascending Wood Creek were increased as the larger Durham boats began to come into the system after the opening of the Rome Canal in 1797, which eliminated the portages along the Mohawk route. These boats came east from

The Wood Creek Locks

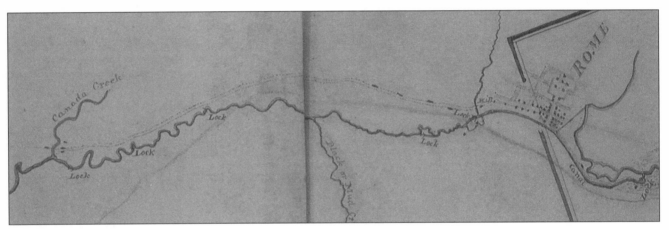

Detail of map showing the locks on Wood Creek between the Rome Canal (right) and Canada Creek junction (left).

The problems encountered by the French party, in bringing their boat eastward up Wood Creek, were typical of those experienced by navigators in this period:

> "...the difficulty of ascending was still greater; the boat was unladen at Canada creek, and, as the state of the road would not admit of its conveyance by land, oxen were applied, and by main strength dragged it along the bed of the creek, to the great detriment and injury of the boat."
>
> Western Inland Lock Navigation Company, 1798[282]

The conditions of passage on Wood Creek continued to frustrate navigators until 1803, when the Western Inland Lock Navigation Company began installation of four wooden locks between Rome and the Canada Creek junction. Schuyler himself made the initial inspection the previous year:

> "I left Canada Creek, on the 25th of last month, and aided by a flush of water from the canal at Rome, I reached the Oak Orchard at half past ten, after a tedious passage of two hours and a half, and notwithstanding the increase of water from the canal at Rome, I found the intermediate distance so shallow, and the bed of the Creek so filled with sunken timber as fully confirmed me in the opinion I have formed on a former view that locking it was the only efficient means of rendering it a competent navigation.
>
> "From the Oak Orchard, to the [Oneida Lake]... the shallowness of the water in the creek, the sunken timber, and the many sand bars, I found almost infinitely beyond what I had been led to believe. If the sunken timber was taken out of the bed, if the heaps of it, which are collected in many places, were removed, several of the sand bars would be carried into deep pools (which are frequent) when the freshets prevail, the navigation would be so improved as to afford a passage for half laden boats only to ascend to the intended lock at the Oak Orchard in all

continued on the next page

continued from page 126

the months subsequent to June, and until the autumnal rains prevail, and swell the waters of the Creek... when they might again bring full cargoes, but as the large Durham boats and batteaus of equal burden, now come fully laden from the falls between the Cayuga and Seneca Lake, and from the salt works at Onondaga at every season, as far as Dean's Landing, the ascending from thence with only one half of their cargoes to the intended Lock at the Oak Orchard, when that shall be completed, and then returning to bring forward the remainder, will continue a charge on the transportation very much beyond such a toll as would be an adequate compensation to the company for passing the Locks. If Wood Creek was locked in all its extent, from Dean's Landing to the canal at Rome, I am therefore clearly of opinion that it is equally the interest of the company, and of the country, that two more locks should be constructed, between the intended one at the Oak Orchard and Dean's Landing. This done, with the trifling expenditure herein after mentioned, on the Onondago and Seneca Rivers, we should have a compleat navigation for fully laden boats, even larger than the largest Durham boats now in use, from the falls between the Cayuga and Seneca Lakes.

"On the 30th I crossed the Oneida Lake and ascended Wood Creek to a hut, four miles from the lake. On the 31st at day break we began the arduous task of ascending the Creek.. In doing this the boatmen were for a great part in water, dragging the boat, and altho aided by a flush of water which met us when we arrived at the Oak Orchard & which had been sent down with two descending boats. It was near six in the afternoon before we arrived at Canada Creek having stopped only one hour to breakfast, the distance come 13 1/2 miles."

Philip Schuyler, 1802[283]

Over a decade earlier, Watson had suggested dam and lock combinations as part of the solution to the myriad problems of navigating Wood Creek:

"From a superficial view of this important creek, it appears to me the great difficulties may be surmounted: - first, by cutting away all the bushes and trees on its banks. Second, by cutting across the necks, and removing all sunken logs and trees; - and lastly, by erecting substantial sluices, or inclined planes, at given distances, so as to continue a head of water from sluice to sluice. This creek, in its present state, may be considered a natural canal, from ten to twenty feet wide. If sluices were erected only to the height of the banks, with small locks, or inclined planes, it is probable they would be sufficiently high, and they could be well done, I am persuaded, for fifty pounds each."

Elkanah Watson, 1791[284]

Even with the virgin timber right at hand at each lock site, one might wonder why wood was used here, in 1802, when in the same year the decayed wooden locks at Little Falls were being replaced with stone. DeWitt Clinton, in retrospect, suggests an answer:

"In a well timbered country, a wooden lock of the usual size can be constructed for $150 a foot... Wooden locks will last 15 years - besides their great cheapness, they are preferable on account of their being susceptible of repair in winter and of being rendered perfectly water tight."

DeWitt Clinton, 1825[285]

But these wooden locks were not the first such devices to be placed in Wood Creek to overcome the obstacles to navigation it presented. During the French and Indian War (1758-63) a series of timber dams, with gates, allowed the fleets of military batteaux to pass the shallows above Canada Creek:

"We passed, on the north side of the creek, the appearance of an old fortification, called Fort Bull. The remains of an old dam, to impede the passage of a hostile fleet, and to assist the operations of the fort, were also to be seen. Although there is now a road on that side of the creek, yet in those days there could have been no marching by land with an army. The transportation of provisions must have been impracticable by land; and, indeed, the general appearance of the country exhibits a sunken morass or swamp, overgrown with timber and formed from the retreat of the lake."

DeWitt Clinton, 1810[286]

Seneca and Cayuga Lakes, and out of Onondaga Lake loaded with salt.

Sensitive to the adverse impact poor navigation would have on his dreams of a commercial center at New Rotterdam, George Scriba petitioned the Directors of the Western Inland Lock Navigation Company in 1805, using examples from his own experience:

I ascended Wood Creek with a three handed batteau having four hands on board. We left Jackson's [Sylvan Beach] at six o'clock in the morning, and although the

The "Shunpike" Schemes

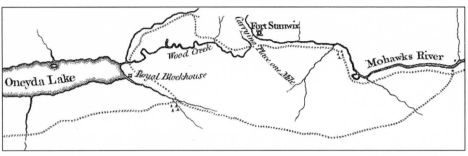

Shippers could choose the WILNC route up Wood Creek, the Rome Canal and down the Upper Mohawk to Utica (top), or the bypass route up Oneida Creek and over the new Genesee Turnpike to Utica (bottom).

From the earliest years of the turnpike era, people devised by-pass routes called "shun-pikes" that departed from the main road and followed a detour to avoid payment of tolls on the improved highway. It was in the opening years of the nineteenth century that a form of waterway "shun-pike" developed east of Oneida Lake, following a route similar to that taken by the Frenchmen on their foot expedition in 1793.

Boatmen running east over Oneida Lake after 1800, to avoid the frustration of Wood Creek and the tolls of the Rome Canal, conspired to take their boats up Oneida Creek, which was sometimes navigable as far as Oneida Castle. Here they could off-load cargoes into freight wagons, which used the newly completed Genesee Turnpike [State Route 5] to run these goods down to the landing at Utica. There, the Durham boats that regularly ran between Utica and Schenectady took on the freight and completed the shipment:

> "The canal at Rome is expected to become completely abortive and useless... from a concerted plan by Mr. Williams & others of diverting ... the navigation of boats coming from the West into the Oneida Creek, which is a good boatable stream, to unload near the Oneida Castle - their cargoes to be transported thence over the Turnpike to Utica 25 miles."
>
> Elkanah Watson, 1800[287]

Even those boatmen using Wood Creek, and coming up as far as the Canada Creek Junction at Gilbert's Tavern, found ways to avoid full payment on the Rome Canal:

> "...from the exorbitant tolls and ... from the impossibility of proceeding with loaded boats from Canada Creek to the said Canal ... most of their cargoes have been transported that distance (viz 6 miles over land) by Mr. Gilbert, and unloaded 1 to 2 miles below the lock on the Mohawk River ... so that the greater part of the boats have passed through empty, and paid accordingly, and the company in consequence deprived of the tolls... A remedy must be applied - or this noble canal must be abandoned altogether, and with it an immense expenditure. The canal at the Little Falls and consequently the one at German Flatts must also become useless, and totally unproductive unless immediate measures are taken..."
>
> Elkanah Watson, 1800[288]

This network of land and water forwarding, made possible only by the new turnpikes, threatened the commercial viability of the canal company, thus necessitating the further improvements in Wood Creek in 1802 and 1803. But even after these improvements were made, the rest of Wood Creek continued to be a bottle neck for shipping:

> "By information which I obtained the next year, sudden freshets having come on destroyed several hundred barrel salt and flour left thus in Wood Creek. On the 12th October of the same year, after having had previously several heavy rains, I ascended Wood Creek with a three handed batteau having four hands on board. We left Jackson's at six o'clock in the morning, and although the water was tolerable good in Wood Creek, we did not reach the Oak Orchard before five o'clock PM. Fine weather and moon shine at the time brought us at 9 o'clock that night at Gilbert's.
>
> "These difficult passages down & up Wood Creek every year experienced, and the heavy complaints of that so difficult navigation which with a cargo of from 12 to 24 barrels makes it still worse, and takes much longer time - drew my attention to investigate these difficulties with more attention.
>
> "In the year 1803 I again descended from Gilbert's to Jackson's through Wood Creek, and found the same difficulty in the month of September, and even more so than in the preceding year - I was obliged to hire more hands in Wood Creek to bring me through to Jackson's that night; and I was for the distance of about 17 miles and a half (the distance of that creek from Gilbert's to Jackson's) from the morning 6 o'clock til 9 at night on

continued on next page

Continued from page128

my voyage with an empty six handed batteau, drawing not two inches water: this boat was an Onondago salt boat which had to carry 36 barrels salt to Rome, and the batteauxmen assured me that they had been obliged to leave two thirds of their cargo about a mile above Dean's Landing, and they had to go three times up and down to bring these 36 barrels to the lock at Gilbert's, and then to ascend with the whole to Rome, which had occasioned them ten days and a half time to do it before they came with these 36 barrels salt from Jackson's to Gilbert's with five hands on board. I did not ascend the Creek in October 1803 which I intended to do, but being advised by boatmen who came down that it would take me full two days to go from Jackson's to Gilbert's, I came by land.

"In August 1803 there were not less than 500 barrels flour & salt at Jackson's landing, which were left there by boatmen unable to proceed with their cargoes up Wood Creek.

"Upon my return last up Wood Creek on the 2nd of October last, I met about four miles from Jackson's two Durham-boats which drew but little water, each fifty barrels flour on board, on a sand-bank about four miles up the creek, where they had lain 36 hours, coming from the Seneca mills. This was on a Tuesday morning, and on the Thursday a week following being the 11th of the same month, the boats had not passed the locks at Rome, to descend the Mohawk for Schenectady; being ten days since I left these boats about four miles on their way up the creek."

George Scriba, 1804[289]

Such intolerable conditions motivated shippers to try the "shunpike" route and look to the emerging turnpikes for at least partial relief.

water was tolerable good in Wood Creek, we did not reach the Oak Orchard before five o'clock PM - fine weather and moon shine at the time brought us at 9 o'clock that night at Gilbert's [Canada Creek].

In the year 1804, (last year) I again went by Wood Creek to the lakes, and returned by the same route. I found the navigation much in the same situation, and *rather worse*. On my descending I met two batteaux with five hands each, and half a load on board (being 21 barrels salt) at the Oak Orchard about 11 o'clock in the morning; I asked them as common, how is the water? They answered, bad enough. I then asked the boatman or captain, How long passage from Jackson's? to which he replied two days and a half. By inquiring of our boatmen how they had the water from Gilbert's to the Oak Orchard, and being told but so, so; I heard them say, we shall not see Gilbert's before tomorrow night.

George Scriba, 1805[290]

This account was but one of a series that Scriba had accumulated, sometimes the result of his own attempts to survey and document these conditions, and to beg for their improvement.

"In the year 1802 I descended Wood Creek from the locks at Rome, to the Oneida Lake, with an empty fourhanded batteau; in order to make all possible speed I engaged four hands: two other boats, lay loaded with furniture, and families ready at the locks to descend with us, when we passed through the locks and by my watch it was then seven o'clock AM: by eleven o'clock, with much difficulty, we reached Fort Bull; there myself and company (all four in number) stepped out to walk the other distance to Gilbert's, at the junction of Canada & Wood Creeks, where we arrived about one o'clock that day; the empty boat did not arrive till late at night at Gilbert's: from thence I went on board the batteau next morning at five o'clock, and with the greatest labour and difficulty we reached Jackson's at the mouth of Wood Creek on Lake Oneida at eight o'clock at night. The loaded boats did not pass the lake till the fourth day following, consequently had been from Rome to Jackson's five days on their route through Wood Creek.

"The boat in which I was, did not draw two inches water, and I can say with confidence, which the gentlemen in my company will attest, that we set fast on sand banks and other obstructions on that creek, more than fifty different times with this empty boat, and at each time the boatmen were obliged to get out of the batteau, and lift & drag the same over the sand bars, etc. to deeper water; at that time I counted upwards of three-hundred barrel of salt and flour, left at different places, which were hove out by the batteauxmen to lighten their loads, unable to ascend Wood Creek with their full loads coming from Onondago Salt-Springs, and the Cayuga mills, with from twenty to thirty barrels, and who found it impractical to come by such shallowness of water through the creek to Gilbert's."

George Scriba, 1802[291]

129

CHAPTER SEVENTEEN

Little Falls Revisited

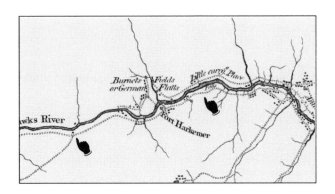

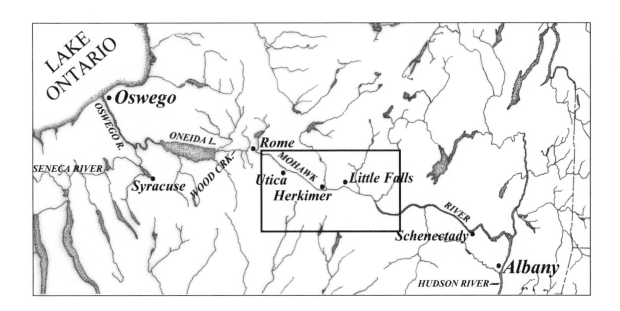

With little more time than it took to climb back aboard the batteau, the reunited expedition pushed away from the landing at Post's [Utica] and headed down the Mohawk. This was the first downstream navigation Pharoux and Desjardins had seen in ten days, and in contrast to their recent experience with foot travel, must have seemed superb.

It was this advantage of travel by boat over land travel, in that period, that made the works of the canal company so significant in the growth of national transport.

We left at once, and by night arrived at the rapids of the German Flats, where there is a good tavern, and Mr. DeZeng urged us to stop, not wishing to go down, but we hoped to get through without much difficulty, but from want of water were forced to stop a mile beyond, it being then dark.

It was this complex of shoals and gravel bars that made up the obstruction at German Flatts called "Wolf Rift." Avoiding this rift, and the one just below, known at one point as "Knock 'em Stiff Rift", was the intent of the German Flatts Canal, completed in 1798. Prior to that, as was often the case, a public house was situated at the head of the rift. Here that public house was Aldridge's, a place of relatively good repute, and undoubtedly the one at which DeZeng had hoped to spend the night:

Dined at a good house, Aldridge's, near Fort Herkemer, on the edge of German Flats.

Jeremy Belknap, 1796[292]

The following year, while making a run back to Schenectady from the Black River country, Desjardins, his judgement perhaps tempered by this experience, did stop at Aldridge's for the night, but without comment.

Prevented from making a quick downstream passage of Wolf Rift by the combination of low water and darkness, the party was reduced to searching for hospitality among the scattered homesteads that stood inland from the river.

Mr. DeZeng conducted us to a farm house, quite high up on the bank and at a considerable distance from the river. We made our supper on Sopane, (corn meal boiled in water, and eaten with milk) a German dish - and we slept with our feet to the fire. Mr. DeZeng hired a horse of a farmer and went on to his own house, as we were only five miles from the Little Falls.

With the departure of DeZeng, the party was left to enjoy a modest night out of the elements, and to prepare to navigate the remaining few miles to the Little Falls in the morning.

Wednesday. Nov. 6th. Left at half past six and arrived at the Little Falls at half past eight.

Went to see Mr. Porteus and to examine the grist mill, fulling mill, and saw mill, which he had built at the falls. The grist mill has four pair of stones, driven by two wheels. The stones are of small diameter, which renders the movement so swift that the meal would get heated if

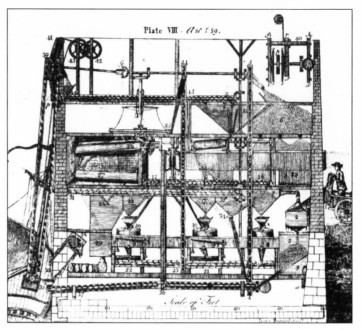

A cross-section of an 18th century grist mill.

they did not take measures to cool it. There is a mechanism by which the meal is raised to the upper story as it leaves the millstones, and spreads it into a trough where a roller covered with flat pegs scatters, stirs and cools it by introducing air among it. They call this machine an Elevator.

The machinery of the mill also drives a fanning mill and screen, so as to save as much as possible the hand labors so dear in this country. These mills are perfect in their kind. The saw mill is double, is driven by two wheels, and has two common saws.

The house and store of Mr. Porteus are very finely located, overlooking the falls, while the future canal passes below them.

The interest Pharoux and Desjardins took in this complex of water-powered industry at Little Falls went beyond the casual curiosity of tourists, and was more than a courtesy to their guide, DeZeng. They knew that their settlement on the Black River would depend on similar establishments, and the observation of these, which appeared so successful, was insurance against their own future efforts.

They were far less impressed by the canal, which DeZeng might well have suggested was the more noteworthy undertaking here.

We examined the canal more in detail and were pained to see the incompetence of the Directors, who, according to all appearances, had never seen nor known any thing about this kind of labor. Incredible as it may appear, they had no plans. Mr. DeZeng was quite surprised to see that we admired nothing, and when asked the height of the falls, he replied, "about forty feet." The word "about," in a matter that should have been determined with the greatest precision, surprised us in turn.

"Supaan"

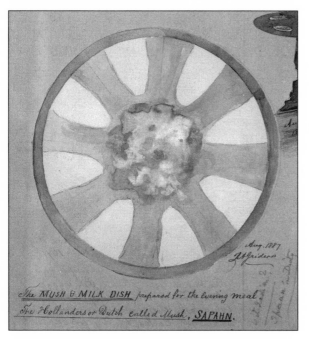

The "Sopane" served to the members of the expedition on the evening of November 5th was a boiled cornmeal dish commonly found at homes throughout the frontier. They might have eaten a similar dish among the Oneidas, as well, but it certainly was a staple among the settlers of the middle Mohawk valley:

"Supaan is the name among the Germans and Dutch, by which Indian pudding, usually called mush or hasty pudding among the English, is known."

Jeptha Simms, 1845[293]

Rufus Grider's painting of a supaan dish
with its "ponds" of milk, 1887.

A detailed description of not only the preparation of the meal, but the presentation as well, is provided in a retrospective look written a generation after it ceased to become commonplace:

"Until about 1830 to 1840 the inhabitants of the rural districts of Schoharie - which were settled by the Dutch & Germans - eat their meals from a large pewter dish placed by the housewife in the center of a round top table... I lately measured one of 20 1/2 in. in diameter, or 2 in. larger than the head of a large barrel head. Mush was prepared in the fall & winter of the year... it was boiled in the afternoon & about one hour before meal time poured from the iron pot into the pewter dish & set in a cold place, cooling stiffens it.

"Near meal time the housewife made as many excavations as there were guests - piling or heaping up the centre. As many pewter table spoons as milk ponds were supplied. After grace was said by the head of the family, everyone began to diminish the banks & increase the size of his white lake by feeding on its outer banks and center - but there were limits beyond those no one could go - if for instance anyone tapped his neighbor's milk pond it was ill manners - if children did so the penalty was finger clips.

"Persons at this time do not know why such a method was practiced? We answered - because china was scarce & high in price, & the people were poor in money - altho many had much land but little cash. Pewter plates cost from 50 to 75 cts each, by making such ingenious arrangements answered every purpose & saved much dishwashing and labor."

Rufus Grider, c1896[294]

We asked him how they expected to pass the creek near Mr. Porteus', which must be of considerable size in freshets, and was bounded by a rocky chasm. He answered that they did not intend to turn it nor to open any passage above, but simply allow it to run into the canal. We judged from this that our questions were useless, and he readily saw that our surprise was not admiration.

He confessed to us that with all surplus affairs he had nothing to do, and that he was only charged with carrying out the views of General Schuyler, the President of the Company, who did not like to be contradicted in his opinions, and drew a thousand pounds a year as the head of the enterprise. This did not keep us from remarking that these thousand pounds might have been better spent

in paying a European engineer, and that the country should have known better than to give such a sum uselessly to one of the richest citizens of the State, by whom the confidence of the company should be borne as an honorary office.

It would scarcely be believed in Europe that in building a navigable canal, they had laid up dry walls of broken stone, five or six feet high, without any widening at the base, and with only six feet of sandy soil on the outside. More than this; at the lower end of the canal, where most of the locks will be placed, and where the solid rock offered naturally a work of great solidity, although long in cutting, the locks should have been made in the rock itself.

The Little Falls Canal

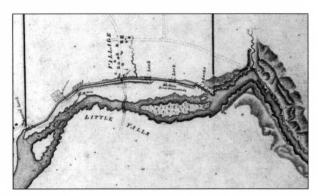

The Little Falls Canal in 1803.

The construction of the Little Falls Canal between 1793 and 1795 never failed to draw the attention of travelers along the Mohawk Valley:

"For these three years past, the people have been busied in constructing a canal, which runs along the banks of the rapids, and is intended to remove the impediments, that interrupt the navigation. A company of gentlemen of considerable property, supported by a great number of subscribers, have entered upon this undertaking, and but very lately obtained a powerful aid from the Legislature of the State of New York, which has subscribed largely for this enterprise. The canal, it is assured, is to be finished this year; and we are assured that it will be accomplished very soon.

"The work is, however, in my judgement, but little advanced; although the whole length amounts to no more than three quarters of a mile; the progress is very slow; and a rock is to be cut through. The stones, which are dug out, are partly made use of for erecting a wall three feet in height on both sides of the canal. This wall is again covered with earth, which is also thrown against it on both sides, so that it forms a dam, the top of which is eight feet in width, and the slope about thirty. As neither mortar nor any other cement is used in erecting the wall, it remains with me a matter of doubt, whether the water will not find its way through the dam, and do mischief.

"At the beginning of the canal two locks have been constructed, which are completely finished, except that the doors are not yet hung. These locks are built all of wood, the foundation as well as the sides, and the workmanship as far as I am able to judge, is very good; but I am at a loss to conceive, why no stones are made use of in the construction of this work, as they abound in the surrounding country.

"Two hundred and fifty workmen are constantly employed at the canal, who receive each six shillings a day, without board. These workmen are divided into certain companies; a great number of them are inhabitants of the neighborhood, but many are also Irishmen newly arrived, nay Irish convicts, whose conduct is far from being beneficial to the country."

Duke de la Rochefoucault Liancourt, 1795[295]

The impressions formed by members of the French expedition during their initial inspection of the canal in 1793 were little improved during subsequent visits:

"...and I, to examine the labors on the canal, which I found but feebly advanced. The proprietors have now an Irishman, who appears to me more intelligent in the construction of wooden locks, for, in the way it had been begun, it would cost large sums to make them of masonry. They are now under the necessity of building in the excavation of the rock, locks of carpenter work, covered with plank, pitched, and the intervals and seams between the rocks and woodwork filled with broken stone, which will render the work passable, but not durable.

Simon Desjardins, 1794[296]

"...arrived at Little Falls... we visited the works on the canal, and observed a continuation of the same ignorance in their operations: the oversight bad, and the work insecure. We thought they would scarcely be able to finish the structure at the close of the coming season, at the rate they were going on."

Simon Desjardins, 1794[297]

continued on next page

continued from page 134

Even after it was completed, the canal failed to impress them:

"...we arrived at half past four at the canal at the Little Falls, and spent an hour in getting through, on account of the small experience of the lock tenders, and the little depth of the water. On getting out of the canal, it was dark, and having imprudently let the boat go before the lock was empty, we were thrown by the violence of the rush upon a rock, where we thought we were injured..."

Simon Desjardins, 1795[298]

"Our boatmen not coming, we went to the canal, where we found our boat which they had passed. The locks require a considerable time to fill and empty, as the water wastes on all sides, through the joints of the planks, and the earth supporting the sluices, and forming the banks. Beside this, the gates do not close perfectly. They have not yet blasted the rock away at the outlet of the canal, and almost all the batteaux strike there, with more or less peril. When some accidents have happened, they will attend to this. We escaped with a violent shock and a broken boat hook."

Simon Desjardins, 1796[299]

It was shortly thereafter that Schuyler hired William Weston, a British engineer with canal-building experience, to supervise these and subsequent works of the company, with very appreciable results. For now, however, skilled engineering was clearly lacking, and the apparent irrationality of constructing wooden locks in cuts made in solid bedrock was duly noted by the journalists:

They have, however, done nothing of the kind, but after blasting the rock here and there, without plan or system, so that the excavation looks like a huge trough, they have built the locks of carpenter's work, and the spaces between the cheeks of the locks and the rock are filled, after General Schuyler's economical style, with broken masses of loose rock, without mortar - for cement is an article unknown in these parts.

Elkanah Watson, viewing the canal seven years later, when it had been completed for five years, had a higher opinion of its workmanship, but still cautioned the use of wood in its construction:

The canal at Rome & the German Flatts do honor to the efforts of the Directors & talents of the engineer; & is not inferior to some of the best works of the kind I have seen in Europe...

The canal at the Little Falls may be pronounced permanent - but the guard lock and the 5 other locks at this place, being unfortunately constructed of timber, cannot exist above 2 or 3 years more.

Elkanah Watson, 1800[300]

Watson's predictions were correct, and in 1803 all of these wooden works were entirely rebuilt in stone. The Frenchmen noted that excavations made across the portage here were in exceptionally hard rock, and required significant amounts of blasting with black powder.

The rock is of a greyish color, strikes sparks with steel, has a glistening fracture, and is often found crystallized.

We dined at the house of Major DeZeng, and bought of him a hundred pounds of maple sugar. We then bade him adieu. Our first pilot having left us, Mr. Judson undertook to supply his place, and Briton and Newton, who wished to return to their own country, agreed to improve this opportunity by going with us, at only half a dollar a day.

At the portage they robbed us of two little turtles, of very handsome shells bordered with bright red, which M. Brunel had found in his course on the Onondaga and took a fancy to carry to Albany, being of a kind very rare, even in this country.

The open criticism recorded in the journal of the canal over which their guide DeZeng would serve as superintendent was perhaps stimulated by the insights of Marc Brunel, who might have enjoyed remaining a while longer to inspect these experimental efforts at American civil engineering. But after some rearrangements were made to accommodate the change of personnel, the expedition prepared to undertake the final leg of their journey; a simple downriver voyage back to the harbor at Schenectady from which they had embarked 35 days earlier.

"The Inland Lock Navigation Company was incorporated in 1792, and had capital of $450,000, of which the State owns $92,000. They have five locks at the Little Falls, two at the German Flatts, and two at Rome, besides their works in Wood Creek.

"All their improvements might now be done at less than half the original expense. General Schuyler, the original superintendent, was inexperienced. The locks at the Little Falls were originally built of wood, which rotting, stone was substituted; and those at Rome were made of brick, which not standing the frost, were replaced also by stone. There is a fine stone quarry a mile and a half from the Little Falls, of which the locks were made; and they were first built of wood from ignorance that the country contained the stone. This quarry is no less curious than valuable. The stones divide naturally as if done by tools. The wooden locks here put the Company to an unnecessary expense of 50,000 dollars - 10,000 dollars a lock. An old church at the German Flatts was built of stone taken from that quarry, and yet this escaped the notice of the Company.

"The artificial bank of the canal was supported in the inside by a dry wall which cost 15,000 dollars. This is found worse than useless. It served as a sieve to carry off the water and to injure the banks, and it has become necessary to remove it. The bridges of the canal are so low that we were obliged to take down our awning."

DeWitt Clinton, 1810[301]

CHAPTER EIGHTTEEN

Passage to Schenectady

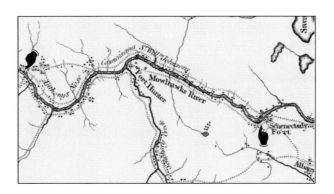

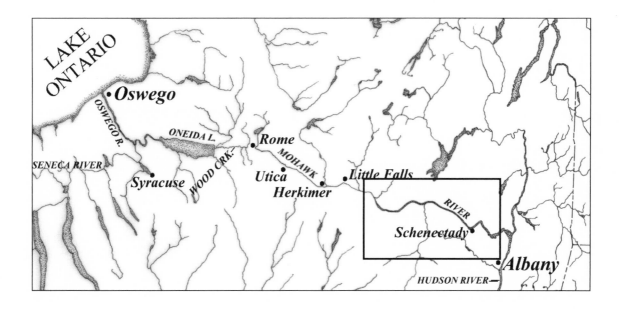

As the party left the portage at Little Falls behind them, late in the afternoon of November 6th, they looked forward to an easy passage down the lower Mohawk, helped along by the current, and even an occasional following breeze. At this point they might well have considered the major challenges of their momentous, if not monumental, expedition to all be behind them.

Yet the weather soon conspired to tarnish their expectations, forcing an early end to the day of travel.

We re-embarked at half past four, and at six a violent rain compelled us to land at a point five miles from our place of starting. We hunted for a path, and came to a log house on a hill at some distance from the river, where we were cheerfully received, and aided in bringing up our packages. We took supper, and spent part of the evening in singing and dancing with these gallant people. The father's name was David Heiss, of German origin, who, persecuted in the revolution, had sought refuge in Canada. On the restoration of peace, he had been obliged to begin again entirely anew. His large family were polite in their manners, and of fine spirit. He spoke with M. Desjardins about buying a farm that was for sale near him, as he wished to have French for neighbors.

By chance, they had fallen in with people with surplus real estate for sale. For whatever the motive, Desjardins was interested enough in the possibility of buying a Mohawk Valley farmstead to examine the parcel the next morning. Perhaps the ordeal of the journey, coupled with the ambiguity of the project on the Black River, induced him to consider other options. Or perhaps he was just curious and polite.

Thursday. Nov. 7th. In the morning, M. Desjardins went to look at the farm that was for sale. It consisted of eighty acres of low ground, on the banks of the Mohawk, and the farm house, situated on a height, needed rebuilding. It had adjoining it some sixty large apple trees. There were seventy acres of upland, which was very rocky and only fit for pasturage and fire wood. They asked for the whole two thousand dollars, which is not a dear price, and M. Desjardins took the address of the owner. On his return we set out.

This modest farmhouse appeared to provide an opportunity for the Frenchmen to observe the reputed benevolent American character that had so often, on this journey, alluded them.

Our generous host would not take any money for our entertainment, but we gave a few shillings to his little ones. This was the first house in which we had experienced any of the American hospitality so highly extolled, and soon after leaving we discovered that they had stolen a cake of maple sugar.

Disillusioned again, the party pushed off into the river, where the cold night had reduced visibility to nearly zero.

The morning was foggy, and we safely passed the rocks of a rapid, almost without seeing them; the noise of the water only notifying us of the danger.

The blind navigation of furious rapids may well have caused the three Frenchmen to call up their reserves of courage, for this is the first instance recorded in this journal where they so fully entrusted their boatmen with their lives.

Boatmen on the Mohawk, as those on the great western rivers a half century later, usually knew the river channel by heart and boasted of their ability to run at night.

Two years later Desjardins and Pharoux passed this same stretch of river on their way to Schenectady. It was early December, and pressed for time they determined to make a night passage:

...took council as to whether we should continue on the route in the dark. The <u>ayes</u> prevailed; so I wrapped myself in my cloak, as the cold was piercing, and abandoned myself to Providence, who allowed us to pass in the darkness all the rapids, where we might have been broken and drowned a thousand times. We went ten miles further, and our boatmen glorified in their skill in running the batteau where they could not see their course. We slept on the floor of a very good log-house.

Simon Desjardins, 1795[302]

Emerging from the morning fog, the batteau ran quickly down through the valley. In this one day they had traveled a distance that had taken over twice as long going up, and passed such landmarks as Hudson's Tavern, Spraker's Tavern, and the Noses.

Finally we came, with new pleasure, to some agreeable habitations on the river bank. We especially admired the District of Canajoharie, and the picturesque location of Fort Plain.

"At a distance of forty-two and a-half miles from Schenectady, passed Fort Plain on the south side and in Minden. It derives its name from a block-house which was formerly erected here."
DeWitt Clinton, 1810[303]

At the close of the day we landed above the Schoharie rapids, and M. Pharoux, attended by Mr. Judson as an interpreter, went to a fine brick house which they took for a tavern. The mistress told them that it was not one, but that they and their companions could stay there. Upon this we landed, and were received in silence before a good fire.

Their happenstance landing had brought the expedition into the home of one of the Mohawk Valley's most colorful residents, Col. Visscher, who lived on the north side of the Mohawk, roughly opposite the mouth of the Schoharie Creek at Fort Hunter.

His grand house represented the emerging reconstruction of pre-War society in the valley, which had suffered so greatly the devastation of the Tory and Indian campaign:

This extent was the scene of the British and savage cruelty during the late war, and they did not cease while anything remained to destroy. What a contrast now! Every

River Wrecks

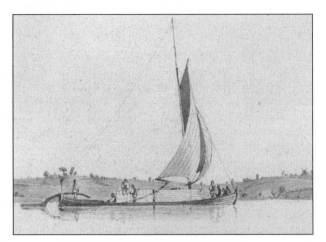

A Durham boat under sail, c.1810.

Frequent accidents no doubt occurred to those who navigated small batteaux along the inland waterways in the closing years of the eighteenth century. However, little mention is made of these in surviving accounts. Perhaps the captains of these light, maneuverable craft were skilled and experienced enough to avoid serious mishaps

But in the opening years of the following century, as the large Durham boats took over the bulk of Mohawk River transport, incidents of death and destruction increased, at least in the historical record. Boatmen, competing with the emerging turnpikes for business and struggling against the vicissitudes of the river, pushed the system to its limits, often running the river when the water was dangerously high in order to make one or two extra trips.

It is not unexpected, therefore, that some of the most dramatic river boat accidents on record occurred in those closing years of the river navigation era just prior to the opening of the Erie Canal [c. 1825]:

"At the upper end of the island, [around 1820] some two miles west of Fort Plain, near the Palatine shore, a man at a setting pole, on a Durham boat, lost his footing and fell into the river. The current there was quite strong, the man could not swim, the boat fell below him and he was drowned. ...In 1823....Ezra Copeley ran a Durham boat on a rock in Ehle's rift, below the Fort Plain bridge. It was loaded with wheat in bulk, was stove and filled with water. The wheat was taken to Ehle's barn and dried, the boat was repaired, reloaded, and went on to its destination."

Jeptha Simms, 1882[304]

But the most spectacular and interesting accident on the river befell the great Durham freighter "Butterfly" in the Spring of 1823:

"One of the last accidents of the kind occurred while the canal was nearing completion to a Durham boat, one of the best of that class of river craft, called the Butterfly. It was descending the river, then swollen, laden with flour, potash and wheat in bulk, when it became unmanageable, swung round, and struck its broadside against a pier of the Canajoharie bridge, and broke near the center. The contents of the boat literally filled the river for some distance, and three hands on the boat were drowned. The name of one was afterward ascertained to be John Clark. His body was recovered twelve miles below, and was buried on the river bank, in the present village of Fultonville. His bones having been dislodged by the spring freshet of 1845, they were taken up and buried in the village burying-ground. Nicholas Steller, who witnessed the disaster, says that the man steering the boat retained the long tiller (15 or 20 feet long), which was broken loose from the boat; and by its assistance he gained the north shore 80 rods below the bridge.

"Most of the flour on the boat was saved along the river. The owner of the craft, a Mr. Meyers, had its fragments taken to Schenectada and rebuilt, after which it entered the canal, and went into Cayuga Lake. While there engaged, his boat sunk laden with gypsum, and he was drowned. Thus ended the Butterfly and its owner."

Jeptha Simms, 1882[305]

Meyers was running his boat out of the lower end of Cayuga Lake, making a routine shipment to Schenectady. It is likely he encountered a spring freshet, given the estimated date of his journey. Boat runs during high water in the Spring had the advantage of depth on the rifts, running easily over bottoms that a few weeks later might be impassable. But the force of water and the unpredictable current, often hiding new gravel bars and eddies formed since the last season, posed a real danger.

The Canajoharie bridge that Meyers' boat broke against was a covered bridge built on three stone piers set in the river built by noted bridge builder Theodore Burr in 1808. This predated the great covered bridge he built across the Mohawk at Schenectady by one year. The Canajoharie bridge replaced an earlier single span bridge, built in 1803, that had collapsed. To the captain of a 60 foot long Durham boat, hurling along sideways in the rushing current of the swollen Mohawk, the stone piers of these new-fangled covered bridges must have loomed horribly on the horizon.

house and barn rebuilt, the pastures crowded with cattle, sheep, etc...

Capt. Charles Williamson, 1792[306]

After so many weeks of seeing little else but forest and rustic frontier architecture, this fine brick house, which apparently had just recently been completed, must have appeared as a dramatic contrast. Inside, they were to receive hospitality more reminiscent of Albany or Schenectady, than deep in the Mohawk Valley.

Two hours after, the proprietor entered, with a laborer in his employment, and after saluting us very cordially, he ordered refreshments to be prepared.

This man was Colonel Fisher, one of the principal land proprietors of the country, and a county judge. We talked about our journey until supper time. Thanks to his attentions, the table was better served than American suppers generally are, as they usually consist of only bread, butter, etc. We did honor to it with our appetite,

and one might have admired the way we disposed of the turkey, fowl, and fresh pork.

The Colonel begged our permission to eat with his hat on, as he had been scalped by the Indians in the late war, and was left for dead, on his place, with two brothers, whom they had killed after burning his buildings; but Providence saved him.

After supper he conducted us to an extremely neat chamber, furnished with two good beds, in which we rested with all the more pleasure, as for more than a month we had slept in our blankets on the ground.

The next day, the French party got a guided tour of this affluent Dutch farmstead, taking note of the unusual or innovative features of its operation.

Friday. Nov. 8th. In the morning Col. Fisher took us to see his very neat and commodious building. His barn, built after the Holland style, is a great isolated building

Col. Visscher's "Danoscarra"

Detail of 1792 engraving showing early farm, similar to the description of "Danosacrra", including two hay ricks near the barn.

The details of the events of 1780, preserved in the account that follows, might well have been shared with the French visitors that evening in 1793; their last on the river:

"About twenty of the enemy first arrived at the old Fisher place, and attempted to force an entrance by cutting in the door, but being fired upon from a window by the intrepid inmates, they retreated round the corner of the house... The brothers defended the house for some length of time after the enemy gained entrance below, and a melee followed in the stairway, on their attempting to ascend. Several balls were fired up through the floor... which the brothers avoided by standing over the large timbers which supported it. At this period the sisters escaped from the cellar-kitchen, and fled to the woods not far distant... Mrs. Fisher, about to follow her daughters from the house, was stricken down at the door by a blow on the head from the butt of a musket, and left without being scalped.

"As the enemy ascended the stairs, Col. Fisher discharged a pistol he held in his hand, and calling for quarters, threw it behind him in token of submission. An Indian, running up, struck him a blow on the head with a tomahawk, which brought him to the floor. He fell upon his face, and the Indian took two crown scalps from his head, which no doubt entitled him to a double reward, then giving him a gash in the back of the neck, he turned him and attempted to cut his throat, which was only prevented by his cravat, the knife penetrating just through the skin...

"The house was plundered, and then set on fire... After the enemy had left, his consciousness returned, and as soon as strength would allow, he ascertained that his brother John was dead. From a window he discovered that the house was on fire... Descending, he found his mother near the door, faint from the blow dealt upon her head, and too weak to render him any assistance. With no little effort the colonel succeeded in removing the body

continued next page

continued from page 140

of his brother out of the house, and then assisted his mother, who was seated in a chair, the bottom of which had already caught fire, to a place of safety; and having carried out a bed, he laid down upon it, at a little distance from the house, in a state of exhaustion.

"Tom, a black slave, belonging to Adam Zielie, was the first neighbor to arrive at Fisher's. He enquired of the colonel what he should do for him? Fisher could not speak, but signified by signs his desire for water. Tom ran down to the Dadenoscara, a brook running through a ravine a little distance east of the house, and filling his old hat, the only substitute for a vessel at hand, he soon returned with it; a drink of which restored the wounded patriot to consciousness and speech...

"Col. Fisher directed Tom to harness a span of colts, then in a pasture near, (which, as the morning was very foggy, had escaped the notice of the enemy,) before a wagon and take him to the river at David Putnam's... When the wagon arrived near the bank of the river, several tories were present, who refused to assist in carrying the Fishers down the bank to a canoe, whereupon Tom took the colts by their heads, and led them down the bank... The family were taken into a boat and carried across the river to Ephrain Wemple's, where every attention was paid them, When a person is scalped, the skin falls upon the face so as to disfigure the countenance; but on its being drawn up on the crown of the head, the face resumes its natural look; such was the case with Col. Fisher, as stated by an eye witness.

"Seeing the necessity of his having proper medical attention, Col. Fisher's friends on the south side of the river, sent him forward in the canoe by trusty persons, to Schenectada, where he arrived just at dark the same day of his misfortune...

"After he recovered, he gave the faithful negro who treated him so kindly when suffering under the wounds of the enemy, a valuable horse... Judge Fisher - a living monument of savage warfare - was an active and useful citizen of the Mohawk valley for many years, and died of a complaint in the head - caused, as was supposed, by the loss of his scalp, on the 9th day of June, 1809.

"Some years after the Revolution, Judge Fisher, or Visscher, as it is now written by several of the family, to whom the homestead reverted on the death of his brothers, erected a substantial brick dwelling over the ashes of his birth place, where he spent the evening of his days amid the associations of youthful pleasure and manly suffering. This desirable farm residence... is pleasantly situated on a rise of ground in the town of Mohawk, several miles east of Fonda, Montgomery county. It is given the Indian name of the adjoining creek, in the hope of preserving that name."

Jeptha Simms, 1845[307]

In the middle there is a large planked floor, where the wheat is beaten out by means of a roller attached at its little end to a central post, while at the large end there is a bar to which horses or oxen are fastened, and they move it around in a circle. This roller is armed with teeth like the cylinder of a music box, and these wooden pegs crushing into the straw beat out the grain. It is true the straw by this process is all broken up, but this is of little account, as the stock is all fed upon hay.

This machine is an English invention, and we thought that the bruising of the wheat and the loss of the straw, so profitable to the cultivator, would not compensate for the saving of hand labor.

The two sides of the barn were formed with stalls, or stables, for oxen, cows, horses, and sheep, which are open to the air and closed only by bars, although under the same roof as the barn itself, where the winter forage is sheltered very nicely.

The lower part has an immense floor, on which is stored the hay and the straw from the threshing floor. As for the grain, we saw, a little in front of each door, two square mows, covered with a movable roof supported by four posts, furnished with holes and pins, by means of which the roof could be lowered as the pile was reduced by threshing. The heads of the sheaves were towards the center, and the butts of the straw outside, by which means the grain was perfectly preserved and even better than the barn. It is less exposed to the depredation of insects and rats than in France, and this method proves a great economy, as well

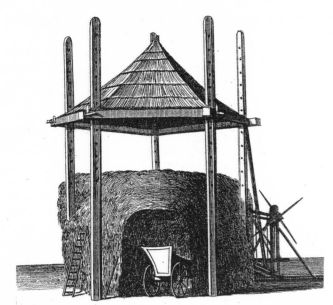

An 18th century adjustable grain rick of the type described in 1793.

in building as in the saving of grain.

This barn, with its four stacks of grain, presented a much more agreeable appearance than the confused arrangement of buildings which we notice in our own farm yards.

Fisher's impressive farm represented the vanguard of a re-occupation of the lands adjacent to the inland waterways, which would make such establishments increasingly common during the coming decades. But here also was encountered the hospitality which had been expected more frequently by the Frenchmen on their journey into the American frontier:

In order not to deviate from the customs of the country, we tendered the price of our amicable entertainment in money to the respectable master of the family, with such apologies as we thought proper, but he replied, with a smile, that although this was the custom, he would not consent to take any thing from us. We bade him adieu, and wished, for the honor of Americans, that there were more people like this good farmer and rich proprietor, whose frank hospitality we might prove.

By immediate contrast, the party stopped at mid-day at an even grander house, but with far less impressive service.

At the hour for dinner, we landed at the confiscated house formerly owned by Colonel Johnson, but now kept as a tavern, for the purpose of enquiring how we might adventurously purchase from the State. Notwithstanding the little fortune which this man has made, we found no bread in his house, and were obliged to go two miles further to the tavern where we had breakfasted in going up.

This latter tavern was apparently the house of Isaac Veeder, which stood near the mouth of the Chuctanunda Creek [Amsterdam]. It was in this house, identified as that of "Isaas Veeder", that the first town meeting of Amsterdam was held three months later. And it was to the house of "Isaac Veeder, where we

had been the fall before," that Desjardins came the following year.

The final few miles of the downriver voyage were passed without comment. Perhaps the voyagers were weary of making entries, too exhausted to be concerned with the details of their journey, or unimpressed by landscapes that they had already recorded in detail on the trip up, some weeks before. Certainly the navigation down from Fort Hunter to the safe harbor at Schenectady was far less eventful than any comparable stretch of river to the west, although the broad, shallow channel often provided some of the most difficult rapids for the upstream sailor.

At four o'clock we arrived at Schenectady, where Mr. Judson and the carpenter left us. We unloaded our goods and placed the bateau in the care of Mr. Murdock, a partner of Mr. Porteus, of whom we hired a wagon to take us to Albany in the morning. We supped at the City Tavern, with Mr. Hudson, who this time had us lodge in the chamber, and M. Brunel in a room over the stairway.

The party was once again comfortably lodged at the tavern in Schenectady, having stepped for the last time from the batteau that had carried them to the brink of the Great Lakes, and safely back.

How strange the urban scene might have been to those who had traversed the New York wilderness - lodging in the rustic log cabins of frontier settlers, the bark houses of the Oneidas, and under the canvas of their own small tents. But this impression is not recorded in the journal. Perhaps the warmth of a good fire, a rich meal, and the diversions of the tap room, too much occupied their energies to allow for the recording of their thoughts.

To others, coming downriver to see this port for the first time, Schenectady was often found worthy of note:

...at length we reached Skenectady, the end of our navigation... Skenectady is a small town, as old as Albany, and containing mostly old houses, built in the Dutch style, which give it altogether the appearance of an ancient European city. The Mohawk River, which is here closely hemmed in, takes a large sweep in the vicinity of this town,; and a cataract renders the navigation impossible. You here quit the vessel, and proceed by land to Albany...

Skenectady is the emporium as well for the provision, which comes down the Mohawk River, designed for Albany, as for the merchandize, which from the stores at Albany is transmitted to the countries, intersected by the Mohawk River and other streams, flowing into the former as far as the district of Genesee.

Duke de la Rochefoucault Liancourt, 1795[308]

"The possibility of constructing a canal, by which the falls as well as other impediments of the navigation of the Mohawk River may be avoided, is acknowledged on all hands; and plans, it is asserted, are in contemplation, to facilitate the painful passage we have just made, and to supersede the necessity of occasional land-carriage. This would be a great and useful undertaking, equally honorable and advantageous for the State of New York. Vessels of fifteen or twenty tons burden, it is said, might be employed in this navigation, which would thus become an outlet, far preferable to that of the River St. Lawrence, which admits of only boats of three or four tons burden."

Duke de la Rochefoucault Liancourt, 1795[309]

There were but sixteen miles of sand hills yet to be crossed to complete their expedition along the inland route, and this was quickly passed by wagon the next day.

Saturday. Nov. 9th. Set out from Schenectady at seven in the morning, and arrived in Albany at eleven.

Perhaps closed inside their stage wagon, with the curtains drawn down against the cold, the party did not take note of the road through the "Pine Bush" as others traveling that way a few months earlier had:

I left the town towards evening and returned to Albany. It is a very unpleasant road to pass, there being but a few settlements on it, the sand deep, and the lands covered with pitch-pine.

Gen. Benjamin Lincoln, 1793[310]

Making the dusty passage to Albany in just four hours, the French party avoided the inconvenience that often befell those attempting to surmount the final sixteen miles of their journey:

...we wished to reach Albany as soon as possible. A stable-keeper engaged to carry us the same night to Albany, though it was already late; we took accordingly our seats in his wagon, bolstered with straw.

About four miles from Skenectady, the driver informed us, that he could not proceed farther. Grumbling, we submitted, therefore, to the necessity of taking up our night's lodging in a bad inn, where, as soon as Dupetitthouars had occupied the only bed which was in the house, I entered into a conversation with the landlord and our driver, which turned upon politics, the universal topic in this country...

After a three hours' journey through a country, which is much like the woods of Anjou, sandy, covered with fern, and bearing none but sickly trees, we at length arrived in Albany.

Duke de la Rochefoucault Liancourt, 1795[311]

So it was that in the chill of an early November morning, the expedition once again gazed upon the cluster of buildings hugging the edge of the Hudson River; completing their journey to the edge of the American wilderness, and back again.

Epilogue

The harbor at Schenectady, circa 1800, drawn on the spot in 1898 by Rufus Grider from
eyewitness descriptions. The image shows the wharf, the warehouses
of the forwarding firms, and Durham boats departing for the West.

The 1790s was an era of dynamic change in the vast territories of the Northeast gradually to become known as "Upstate New York".

With the influx of settlers, new energies animated the region through which the
Mohawk/Oneida waterway network passed. Productive agricultural clearings replaced the
forest, the merchant replaced the hunter, and the forces of the cash profit market soon
gained priority over the limited perspectives of subsistence and regional trade.

Transportation provided the mechanism for moving the produce of these emerging
settlements to market, and facility of transport directly affected the profitability of the
enterprise.

New demands placed on the inland navigation corridor by these developments in the
1790s would foster an atmosphere of evolution and experimentation within which the
improvements created by the Western Inland Lock Navigation Company would emerge in
the decade following the expedition described in this narrative.

Soon a continuous navigation channel, an integration of improved natural waterways
and artificial canals, would connect Schenectady with Oswego, making it possible in
1798 for boats twice the size and able to carry seven times the cargo to replace the
humble batteaux.

These large river freighters - the Durham boats - would become increasingly common
in New York's inland waters in the opening years of the nineteenth century. They sym-
bolized a qualitative breakthrough in the development of an effective infrastructure for
international transportation in the Early Republic; hinting at the true canal boats to follow
with the opening of the Erie Canal in 1825.

Source Notes

1 Rev. Elijah Woolsey, *The Supernumerary; or, Lights and Shadows of Itinerancy,* The Christian Advocate and Journal and Zion's Herald (New York, July 1830 – December 1831), November 12, 1830, p. 44.

2 Elkanah Watson, *History of the Rise, Progress, and Existing Condition of the Western Canals* (Albany, 1820), p. 25.

3 Jacob Lindley, *Journal,* In *Friends' Miscellany,* edited by John and Isaac Comly, No. 2, Vol 2 (Philadelphia, 1832), p. 55.

4 Jeremy Belknap, *Journal of a Tour from Boston to Oneida, June, 1796* (Cambridge, 1882), p. 28-29.

5 Gen. Benjamin Lincoln, *General Lincoln's Journal,* Collections of the Massachusetts Historical Society, Vol, V of the Third Series (Boston, 1836), p.114-115.

6 George R. Howell and W.W. Munsell, *History of the County of Schenectady, NY from 1662 to 1886* (New York, 1886), p. 49.

7 Gen. Benjamin Lincoln, p.113.

8 Julian Ursyn Niemcewicz, Diary, translated by Metchie J.E. Budka, "Journey to Niagara, 1805, from the Diary of Julian Ursyn Niemcewicz", New York Historical Society Quarterly, Volume XLIV, Number 1, January 1960, (New York, 1960), p.82-83.

9 _____ , p.91.

10 John M. Duncan, *Travels Through Part of the United States and Canada in 1818 and 1819,* 2 vols (New York, 1823), Vol. II, p. 5-6.

11 Elkanah Watson, 1820, p. 29.

12 Rev. Elijah Woolsey, 1830-1831, September 24, 1830, p. 16.

13 Jeptha R. Simms, *The Frontiersmen of New York* (Albany, 1882), Vol. 1, p. 348.

14 _____ , p. 351.

15 Simon Desjardins and Pierre Pharoux, *The Castorland Journal,* translated by Franklin B, Hough, A7009, Box 84, Franklin B, Hough Papers (New York State Library, Albany), 1794, p. 243.

16 Jacob Lindley,1832 p. 57-58.

17 William W Campbell, *The Life and Writings of De Witt Clinton* (New York, 1849), p. 35.

18 Rufus Grider, *Notebooks,* Vol. 2 (New York State Library), p. 3.

19 Jeptha R. Simms, 1882, Vol. I, p.33.

20 Rufus Grider, Vol. 2 (New York State Library), p.3.

21 _____ , p.3.

22 _____ , p.3.

23 Jeremy Belknap, 1882, p. 28.

24 Jeremy Belknap, *Journal of a Tour from Boston to Oneida, June, 1796* (Cambridge, 1882), p. 13.

25 _____ , p.13.

26 Jonathan Pearson, *A History of the Schenectady Patent* (Albany, 1883), p. 423.

27 William W Campbell, 1849, p. 55.

28 Christian Schultz, *Travels on an Island Voyage...* 1810 (Reprinted, Ridgewood, NJ: The Gregg Press, 1968), p.6

29 Simon Desjardins and Pierre Pharoux, 1794, p. 242.

30 William W Campbell, 1849, p. 38.

31 Jeremy Belknap, 1882, p. 13.

32 William W Campbell, 1849, p. 38.

33 Philip Schuyler, et, al, The Report of a Committee Appointed to Explore the Western Wate (Albany, 1792), p.6.

34 Samuel W. Durant, History of St. Lawrence Co., New York, 1878, (Reprint, Interlaken: Heart of the Lakes Publishing, 1982), p.147.

35 John Cochrane, Typescript of undated manscript, 1972 (Massachusetts Historical Society)

36 Jeptha R. Simms, *The Frontiersmen of New York* (Albany, 1882), Vol. 1, p. 351.

37 Simon Desjardins and Pierre Pharoux, 1794, p. 7.

38 *The American Museum, or Repository of Ancient and Modern Fugitive Pieces, Prose and Poetical,* Vol 2 (Philadelphia, 1787), p. 352.

39 Simon Desjardins and Pierre Pharoux, 1794, p.242.

40 *Extracts From the Vanderkemp Papers,* Publications of the Buffalo Historical Society, Vol, 2 (Buffalo, 1880), p.48.

41 Jeremy Belknap, 1882, p.14.

42 E.B. O'Callaghan, editor, Documentary History of New York, 4 volumes (Albany, 1849-51), Vol. I, p.528.

43 Philip Schuyler and William Weston, *Report of the Directors of the Western and Northern Inland Lock Navigation Companies...Together with the Report of Mr. William Weston, Engineer, New York, 1796,* Reprinted in Buffalo Historical Society Publications, Vol. 2 (Buffalo, 1880), p.173-4.

44 Christian Schultz, 1968, p. 10.

45 Joshua Marsden, *The Narrative of a Mission to Nova Scotia, New Brunswick, and the Somers Islands with a Tour to Lake Ontario* (London, 1816), p.188.

46 Arthur T. Smith, *Papers of the Herkimer County Historical Society,* Vol., 2 (Herkimer and Ilion, 1902), p. 59.

47 Philip Schuyler, *Second Report of the Western Inland Lock Navigation Company - 1798.* Buffalo Historical Society Publications, Vol. 13. (Buffalo, 1909), p. 200.

48 Philip Schuyler, et, al, 1792, #206 p.7.

49 William W Campbell, 1849, p.44.

50 Jeremy Belknap, 1882, p.15.

51 William W Campbell, 1849, p.48.

52 Elkanah Watson, 1820, p. 30.

53 Philip Schuyler, et, al, The Report of a Committee Appointed to Explore the Western Waters... (Albany, 1792), p.7-8.

54 Philip Schuyler, et, al, 1792, p.13.

55 Philip Schuyler and William Weston, (1798), 1880, p.173.

56 _____ , p.173-4.

57 William W Campbell, 1849, p.48.

58 Julian Ursyn Niemcewicz, 1960, p. 90.

59 Levi Beardsley, *Reminiscences* (New York, 1852), p. 35-36.

60 William W Campbell, 1849, p. 49-50.

61 Jacob Lindley, 1832, p. 62..

62 William W Campbell, 1849, p. 39-40.

63 Elkanah Watson, 1820, p. 30-31.

64 Elkanah Watson, 1820, p. 12.

65 Elkanah Watson, 1820, p. 30.

66 Philip Schuyler and William Weston, 1796, 1880, p. 164-5.

67 Anonymous, "A Drawn Map of the County of Albany, 1756", Shelfmark K Top CXXI.9.2 (The British Library, London).

68 Isaac Weld, Travels Through the States of North America and the Provinces of Upper and Lower Canada During the Years 1795, 1796 & 1797, 2 Vols., (4th ed.) Vol. 1. (London, 1807), p. 77.

69 Elkanah Watson, 1820, p.12-13.

70 Joshua Marsden, 1816, p. 187.

71 Elkanah Watson, 1820, p.14.

72 Timothy Dwight, Travels: In New England and New York, 4 vols (London, 1823), Vol. II p.131-132.

73 Timothy Dwight, 1823, Vol. II, p.287.

74 Clinton A. Weslager, The Log Cabin in America; From Pioneer Days to the Present (New Brunswick, New Jersey, 1969), p.56.

75 Felice Harcourt, ed. *Memoirs of Madame De La Tour Du Pin* (London: Century Publishing, 1969), p.235.

76 Captain Basil Hall, *Travels in North America in the Years 1827 and 1828,* Vol, II (Philadelphia, 1829), p.69-71.

77 *Extracts From the Vanderkemp Papers,* 1880, p.58.

78 Elkanah Watson, 1820, p. 14.

79 William W Campbell, 1849, p.54-55.

80 Elkanah Watson, 1820, p.31.

81 Gen. Benjamin Lincoln, 1836, p.120-121.

82 Philip Schuyler and William Weston, 1796, 1880, p.174.

83 Elkanah Watson, 1820, p. 32.

84 William W Campbell, 1849, p. 54.

85 Christian Schultz, 1968, p. 16.

86 Jared Van Wagenen, Jr. *The Golden Age of Homespun* (Ithaca, 1953), p.166-167.

87 Philip Schuyler, 1798, 1909), p.202-203.

88 William Newham Blane, *Excursion Through the United States and Canada During the Years 1822-23,* in Roger Haydon, *Upstate Travels: British Views of Nineteenth Century New York* (Syracuse: Syracuse University Press, 1982), p. 192.

89 Levi Beardsley, 1852, p. 34.

90 William Hartshorne, *William Hartshorne's Journal of Journey to Detroit, 1793* (Archives, New York Yearly Meeting, Religious Society of Friends, New York), p. 5.

91 Elkanah Watson, 1820, p.33.

92 Philip Schuyler, 1798, 1909), p.201.

93 Jacob Lindley, 1832, p 63.

94 James Cockburn, *A Survey of a Tract of Land, the Property of John and Nicholas Roosevelt & Co.,* 1792 (New York State Archives, Albany)

95 Capt. Alexander Thompson, Journal, 1783, (Typescript provided by Oswego County Historical Society)

96 Extracts From the Vanderkemp Papers, 1880, p.59-60.

97 William W Campbell, 1849, p.58.

98 Christian Schultz, 1968, p. 17.

99 Augustus Porter, *Narrative of the Early Years in the Life of Augustus Porter*, Buffalo Historical Society (Buffalo, 1848), p. 278-280.

100 William W Campbell, 1849, p. 58.

101 William W Campbell, *The Life and Writings of De Witt Clinton* (New York, 1849), p.57.

102 James Cockburn, 1792

103 Philip Schuyler to General Williams, Stillwater, July 14, 1793, Philip Schuyler, *Papers* (New York Public Library)

104 Pomeroy Jones, *Annals and Recollections of Oneida Count,* (Rome, 1851), p. 670-671.

105 Memoir of an Emigrant: The Journal of Alexander Coventry, M,D…,1783-1831, Vol, II, (Typescript by Albany Institute of History and Art and the New York State Library, 1978), p.898.

106 Philip Schuyler, July 30 entry. Journal, 1802, The Philip Schuyler Papers (New York Public Library)

107 Philip Schuyler to George Huntington, Canada Creek, August 11, 1802. Philip Schuyler, Papers (New York Public Library)

108 George Huntington to Barent Bleecker, Rome, October 24, 1802. Philip Schuyler, Papers (New York Public Library)

109 Philip Schuyler to George Huntington, New York, May 30, 1803. Philip Schuyler, Papers (New York Public Library)

110 Gen. Benjamin Lincoln, 1836, p. 121.

111 William Hartshorne, 1793, p. 6.

112 Duke de la Rochefoucault Liancourt, *Travels Through the United States of North America, The Country of the Iroquois, and Upper Canada in the Years 1795, 1796, and 1797,* 4 vols (London, 1799), Vol. 2, p.33.

113 *Extacts From the Vanderkemp Papers,* Pubications of the Buffalo Historical Society, Vol, 2 (Buffalo, 1880), p, 68

114 Philip Schuyler and William Weston, 1796, 1880. p. 163

115 Elkanah Watson to Thomas Eddy, letter, Albany, 1800, Elkanak Watson, Papers, GB 13294, folder 2, (New York State Library)

116 Elias Kane and Jonas Platt to Major DeZeng, Whitestown, May 21, 1793, Philip Schuyler, *Papers* (New York Public Library)

117 John Richardson to John Porteous, Wood Creek, November 3, 1793, *The Porteous Papers* (Buffalo and Erie County Historical Society),

118 Elkanah Watson, 1820, p. 34-35.

119 William W Campbell, 1849, p. 59.

120 Christian Schultz, 1968, p. 18-19.

121 William W Campbell, 1849, p. 62.

122 James Cockburn, 1792

123 Christian Schultz, 1968, p. 20.

124 Pomeroy Jones, 1851, p.747-8.

125 Daniel E. Wager, Our County and Its People: A Descriptive Work on Oneida County New York, (Boston, 1896), p.56.

126 Pomeroy Jones, 1851, p.748.

127 Elkanah Watson, 1820, p. 36.

128 James Dean, Letters (Oneida County Historical Society),

129 *Extracts From the Vanderkemp Papers,* 1880, p.68.

130 William W. Campbell, 1849, p. 61-2.

131 Pomeroy Jones, 1851, p.748-749.

132 Jacob Lindley, 1832, p. 64.

133 John Lees, *Journal,* Society of Colonial Wars of the State of Michigan (Detroit, 1911), p. 20.

134 Lieut. Richard Aylmer to Sir William Johnson, March 16, 1767. Milton W. Hamilton, *The Papers of Sir William Johnson,* Vol. XII (Albany, 1953), p.278-9.

135 *Extracts From the Vanderkemp Papers,* 1880, p. 68-69.

136 Christian Schultz, 1968, p. 21-22.

137 Samuel W. Durant, History of Oneida County, New York (Philadelphia, 1878), p. 581.

138 Christian Schultz, 1968, p.22.

139 William W Campbell, 1849, p.63.

140 _____ , 1849, p. 62-63.

141 Christian Schultz, 1968, p. 22-23.

142 Elkanah Watson, 1820, p.36.

143 Elkanah Watson, 1820, p. 38.

144 *The Scriba Papers,* Vol. 29 (New York State Library),

145 William W. Campbell, 1849, p. 64.

146 James Cockburn, 1792

147 Christian Schultz, 1968, p.23-24.

148 *Extracts From the Vanderkemp Papers,* 1880, p.80-84.

149 James Cockburn, *1792*

150 William W Campbell, 1849, p. 66.

151 *Extracts From the Vanderkemp Papers,* 1880, p.79.

152 Christian Schultz, 1968, p. 24-25.

153 William W Campbell, 1849, p. 64-65.

154 *Extracts From the Vanderkemp Papers,* 1880, p.80.

155 Crisfield Johnson, *History of Oswego County* (Philadelphia, 1877), p. 44.

156 *Extracts From the Vanderkemp Papers,* 1880, p. 85.

157 Pomeroy Jones, 1851, p.721.

158 *The Scriba Papers,* Vol. 29 (New York State Library), p. 229-230.

159 Duke de la Rochefoucault Liancourt, 1799, Vol. II, p.19-20.

160 William W Campbell, 1849, p.67-68.

161 The Scriba Papers, Vol., 29 (New York State Library), p.229.

162 Elkanah Watson to Thomas Eddy, Albany, November 27, Elkanah Watson Papers, (New York State Library) GB13294 Box 53, folder 2.

163 Christian Schultz, 1968, p. 21.

164 *Extracts From the Vanderkemp Papers,* 1880, p. 97.

165 _____ , 1880, p.64.

166 _____ , p. 85.

167 John Lees, 1911, p.21.

168 *Extracts From the Vanderkemp Papers,* 1880, p. 86.

169 Elkanah Watson, 1820, p.39.

170 Joshua V.H. Clark, Onondaga; or Reminiscence of Earlier and Later Times, (Syracuse, NY, PA, 1849), p.184-5.

171 Harry Croswell, *The Balance & State Journal,* Vol. 1, No.5 Jan 29,1811

172 Christian Schultz, 1968, p. 26.

173 _____ , p.26-27.

174 Harry Croswell, No. 5. January 29, 1811

175 Duke de la Rochefoucault Liancourt, Vol. II, 1799, p.19.

176 William W Campbell, 1849, p. 70-72

177 *Extracts From the Vanderkemp Papers,* 1880, p. 86-87.

178 James Cockburn, 1792

179 Joshua V. H. Clark, *Onondaga; or Reminiscences of Earlier and Later Times.* Vol. 2 (Syracuse, 1849), p.185-6.

180 William W Campbell, 1849, p.73.

181 *Extracts From the Vanderkemp Papers,* 1880, p. 87.

182 Elkanah Watson, 1820, p. 39

183 *Extracts From the Vanderkemp Papers,* 1880, p.97.

184 William W Campbell, 1849, p. 79.

185 *Extracts From the Vanderkemp Papers,* 1880, p.87.

186 Christian Schultz, 1968, p.35-36.

187 James Cockburn, 1792

188 Harry Croswell, No. 6., February 5, 1811.

189 William W Campbell, 1849, p.74.

190 Christian Schultz, 1968, p. 38

191 John Lees, *Journal,* Society of Colonial Wars of the State of Michigan (Detroit, 1911), p. 21.

192 William W Campbell, 1849, p. 74.

193 Christian Schultz, 1968, p. 36-37.

194 Jacob Lindley, 1832, p.67.

195 William W. Campbell, 1849, p. 75

196 John Sanders, *Centennial Address Relating to the Early History of Schenectady...* (Albany, 1879), p. 247-8.

197 Christian Schultz, 1968, p.5-6.

198 _____ , p.34-35.

199 _____ , p. 37-38.

200 William W Campbell, 1849, p. 76.

201 James Cockburn, *A Survey of a Tract of Land, the Property of John and Nicholas Roosevelt & Co., 1792* (New York State Archives, Albany)

202 Philip Schuyler, *Journal, 1802,* The Philip Schuyler Papers (New York Public Library), July 27 entry.

203 Christian Schultz, 1968, p. 38-39.

204 Rev. Elijah Woolsey, 1830 – 1831, November 12, 1830, p.44.

205 Elkanah Watson, 1820, p.40.

206 Duke de la Rochefoucault Liancourt, Vol. I, p.532-537.

207 Jacob Lindley, 1832, p. 67.

208 Harry Croswell, No. 6., February 5, 1811.

209 Charles Storer to John Porteous, Fort Herkimer, May 14, 1793, *The Porteous Papers* (Buffalo and Erie County Historical Society)

210 *Extracts From the Vanderkemp Papers,* 1880, p.90.

211 Rev. Elijah Woolsey, 1830 – 1831, September 24, 1830, p.16.

212 Rev. Elijah Woolsey, 1830 – 1831, November 12, 1830, p.44.

213 Duke de la Rochefoucault Liancourt, 1799, Vol. II p.7-9.

214 _____ , p.10-11.

215 Philip Schuyler, Journal, 1802, The Philip Schuyler Papers (New York Public Library), July 27 entry.

216 Cadwallader Colden, *The Letters and Papers of Cadwallader Colden, Vol, I: 1711-1729,* Collections of the New York Historical Society for the Year 1917 (New York, 1918), p.128.

217 George Henry Loskiel, *History of the Mission of the United Brethren Among the Indians in North America, 1794,* Vol. I, Translated by Christian Ignatius La Trobe, Brethren's Society for the Furtherance of the Gospel (London, England), p.53.

218 Capt. Alexander Thompson, *Journal,* 1783, (Typescript provided by Oswego County Historical Society)

219 *Extracts From the Vanderkemp Papers,* 1880, p.97.

220 _____ , p. 72.

221 Duke de la Rochefoucault Liancourt, 1799, Vol.II, p.12-13.

222 Isaac Weld, 1800, Vol. II, p. 326.

223 John C. Campbell, ed, Landmarks of Oswego County New York (Syracuse, 1895), p. 734.

224 James Cockburn, 1792

225 *Extracts From the Vanderkemp Papers,* 1880, p. 78.

226 Duke de la Rochefoucault Liancourt, 1799, p.21.

227 *Extracts From the Vanderkemp Papers,* 1880, p.85.

228 _____ , p. 76.

229 Duke de la Rochefoucault Liancourt, Vol.I, p.24-26.

230 Lewis Beers, *Journal, 1797* (DeWitt Historical Society of Tompkins County), p. 116.

231 *Extracts From the Vanderkemp Papers,* 1880, p.78.

232 Duke de la Rochefoucault Liancourt, Vol. II, p. 21-22.

233 Duke de la Rochefoucault Liancourt, Vol. II, p.21-22.

234 The Scriba Papers, Vol. 29, p. 172, April 6, 1804.

235 William W Campbell, 1849, p. 66.

236 Colonel Gabriel Christie to John Pownall, January 11,1776 (Public Record Office) Great Britian.

237 Barent Bleecher to Philip Schuyler , Albany, March 7, 1796, The Philip Schuyler Papers (New York Public Library).

238 William Morton, *Journal, 1798,* SC11451 (New York State Library), p.73-74.

239 Franklin B. Hough, Notices of Peter Penet and of his Operations Among the Oneida Indians (Lowville, 1866), p.19.

240 The Rohde Journal, 1802, (Translation by Charles Gehring in progress, p.c.)

241 Jack Henke, Oneida Lake (Utica: North Country Books, Inc., 1989), p. 86.

242 Gen. Benjamin Lincoln, 1836, p. 127-128

243 Jeremy Belknap, 1882, p. 20-21.

244 Jacob Lindley, 1832, p. 65.

245 Jeremy Belknap, 1882, p.24.

245 _____ , p. 22-23.

246 Elkanah Watson, 1820, p.41.

247 Jeremy Belknap, 1882, p. 21-22

248 Joseph Bloomfield, Journal, in Citizen Soldier: The Revolutionary War Journal of Joseph Bloomfield, Edited by Mark E, Lender and James Kirby Martin . (Newark, New Jersey: New Jersey Historical Society, 1982), p.66.

249 Jeremy Belknap, 1882, p.22-23

250 Julian Ursyn Niemcewicz, 1960, p.96.

251 Duke de la Rochefoucault Liancourt, Vol. I, p. 281.

252 Simon Desjardins and Pierre Pharoux, 1794, p. 345.

253 Pomeroy Jones, 1851, p. 866.

254 _____ , p.867.

255 J.A. Graham, *A Descriptive Sketch of the Present State of Vermont* (London, 1797), p. 161.

256 Timothy Dwight, *Travels: In New England and New York,* 4 vols (London, 1823), Vol. 3 p. 180.

257 Elkanah Watson, 1820, p.30.

258 Moses DeWitt to Simeon DeWitt, Oneida, October 31, 1793. Simeon DeWitt, Papers (Syracuse University Library)

259 William Hartshorne, 1793, p. 4.

260 *Extracts From the Vanderkemp Papers,* 1880, p.51-52.

261 Jeremy Belknap, 1882, p. 25.

262 _____ , p. 19.

263 Pomeroy Jones, 1851, p. 498.

264 Capt. Charles Williamson, *Journal,* In Frank. E. Przybycien, *Utica: A City Worth Saving* (Utica: Dodge-Graphic Press, 1976), p. 25-26.

265 Julian Ursyn Niemcewicz, 1960, p. 93

266 Duke de la Rochefoucault Liancourt, Vol. I, p.293-295.

267 Jeremy Belknap, 1882, p. 18.

268 Timothy Dwight, Vol.II, p.118-119.

269 Pomeroy Jones, 1851, p.498.

270 Jeremy Belknap, 1882, p.14.

271 Simon Desjardins and Pierre Pharoux, 1794, p. 244 & p. 375.

272 _____ , 1794, p. 375.

273 Daniel E. Wager, 1896, p. 78.

274 Pomeroy Jones, 1851, p. 496-497.

275 Pomeroy Jones, Annals and Recollections of Oneida County, (Rome, 1851), p.498.

276 _____ , p.500-501.

277 John Sanders, Centennial Address Relating to the Early History of Schenectady... (Albany, 1879), p. 248.

278 Pomeroy Jones, 1851, p.500-501.

279 William Hartshorne, 1793, p. 4.

280 Gen. Benjamin Lincoln, 1836, p. 119.

281 Elkanah Watson, 1820, p. 34.

282 "Second Report of the Western Inland Lock Navigation Company - 1798". Buffalo Historical Society Publications. (Buffalo, 1909),Vol. 13, p. 201-202.

283 Philip Schuyler, Manuscript report, Albany, August 18, 1802, Philip Schuyler, Papers (New York Public Library)

284 Elkanah Watson, 1820, p.34.

285 DeWitt Clinton to David Thomas, Albany, December 23, 1825, David Thomas Papers, (New York State Library)

286 William W Campbell, 1849, p.58.8

287 Elkanah Watson to Thomas Eddy. Letter Report on Status of Inland Navigation. Nov. 27, 1800, Elkanah Watson, Papers, GB 13294 (New York State Library)

288 Elkanah Watson to Thomas Eddy. Letter Report on Status of Inland Navigation. Nov. 27, 1800., Elkanah Watson, Papers, GB 13294 (New York State Library)

289 The Scriba Papers, Vol., 2, 1804, p. 218-221.

290 *The Scriba Papers,* Vol., 29 (New York State Library), 1804, p.219-220.

291 _____ ,p.218.

292 Jeremy Belknap, 1882, p. 15.

293 Jeptha R. Simms, 1845, p.71.

294 Rufus Grider, Notebooks, (New York State Library), Vol. 8, p.73.

295 Duke de la Rochefoucault Liancourt, 1799, Vol. II, p.45-47.

296 Simon Desjardin and Pierre Pharoux, 1794, p.344.

297 _____ , 1794, p.376.

298 Simon Desjardin and Pierre Pharoux, *The Castorland Journal*, 1795, p.519.

299 Simon Desjardin and Pierre Pharoux, *The Castorland Journal,* 1796, p.587-8.

300 Elkanah Watson to Thomas Eddy. Letter Report on Status of Inland Navigation. Nov. 27, 1800, Elkanah Watson, *Papers*, GB 13294 (New York State Library)

301 William W Campbell, 1849, p.44-45.

302 Simon Desjardins and Pierre Pharoux, 1795, p.519.

303 William W Campbell, 1849, p.40.

304 Jeptha R. Simms, 1882, Vol. 1, p.352.

305 _____ , p.352.

306 Capt. Charles Williamson, Journal, In Frank. E. Przybycien (Utica: A City Worth Saving (Utica: Dodge-Graphic Press, 1976), p. 25.

307 Jeptha R. Simms, 1845 , p. 350-354

308 Duke de la Rochefoucault Liancourt, 1799, Vol. II, p. 49, 51.

309 _____ , p.49-50.

310 Gen. Benjamin Lincoln, 1836, p. 115.

311 Duke de la Rochefoucault Liancourt, 1799, Vol. II, p. 52-54.

Bibliography

The American Museum, or Repository of Ancient and Modern Fugitive Pieces, Prose and Poetical. Vol 2. Philadelphia, 1787.

Anonymous. "A Drawn Map of the County of Albany, 1756". Shelfmark K Top CXXI.9.2, The British Library, London.

Beardsley, Levi. *Reminiscences.* New York, 1852.

Beers, Lewis. *Journal. 1797.* Beers/Curtis Collection, DeWitt Historical Society of Tompkins County.

Belknap, Jeremy. *Journal of a Tour from Boston to Oneida, June, 1796.* Cambridge, 1882.

Blane, William Newham. *Excursion Through the United States and Canada During the Years 1822-23.* in Haydon, Roger. *Upstate Travels: British Views of Nineteenth Century New York.* Syracuse: Syracuse University Press, 1982.

Bloomfield, Joseph. *Journal.* In *Citizen Soldier: The Revolutionary War Journal of Joseph Bloomfield.* Edited by Mark E. Lender and James Kirby Martin. Newark, New Jersey: New Jersey Historical Society, 1982.

Campbell, William W. *The Life and Writings of De Witt Clinton.* New York, 1849.

Churchill, John C. ed. *Landmarks of Oswego County New York.* Syracuse. 1895

Cochrane, John. Typescript of undated manuscript, 1972. Massachusetts Historical Society.

Cockburn, James. A Survey of a Tract of Land, the Property of John and Nicholas Roosevelt & Co., 1792, New York State Archives, Albany.

Colden, Cadwallader. *The Letters and Papers of Cadwallader Colden. Vol. I: 1711-1729.* Collections of the New York Historical Society for the Year 1917. New York, 1918

Croswell, Harry. *The Balance & State Journal.* Vol. 1, Nos. 4-13. Albany, January - March, 1811.

Dean, James. *Letters.* Oneida County Historical Society.

Desjardin, Simon and Pierre Pharoux, *The Castorland Journal,* translated by Franklin B. Hough. A7009, Box 84, Franklin B. Hough Papers, New York State Library, Albany.

DeWitt, Simeon. *Papers.* Syracuse University Library.

Duncan, John M. *Travels Through Part of the United States and Canada in 1818 and 1819.* 2 vols. New York. 1823. 33.

Durant, Samuel W. *History of Oneida County, New York.* Philadelphia, 1878.

Durant, Samuel, W. *History of St. Lawrence Co., New York.* 1878. Reprint, Interlaken: Heart of the Lakes Publishing, 1982.

Dwight, Timothy. *Travels: In New England and New York.* 4 vols. London, 1823.

Emmons, Edward Neville. *The Stevens Family.* Typescript manuscript. Knoxville, PA, 1908.

Evans, Griffith. *Journal of a Trip From Philadelphia to Fort Stanwix ... 1784-1785.* Microfilm, reproduced from the copy in the Huntington Library. Not paginated in original.

Extracts From the Vanderkemp Papers, Publications of the Buffalo Historical Society, Vol. 2. Buffalo, 1880.

Graham, J.A. *A Descriptive Sketch of the Present State of Vermont.* London, 1797.

Grider, Rufus. *Notebooks,* 9 Vols., New York State Library, Albany.

Hall, Captain Basil. *Travels in North America in the Years 1827 and 1828.* Vol. II. Philadelphia. 1829.

Hamilton, Milton W. *The Papers of Sir William Johnson.* 13 vols. Albany, 1953

Harcourt, Felice.,ed. *Memoirs of Madame De La Tour Du Pin.* London: Century Publishing, 1969.

Hartshorne, William. *William Hartshorne's Journal of Journey to Detroit, 1793.* MSS 1/2016, Archives, New York Yearly Meeting, Religious Society of Friends, New York.

Henke, Jack. *Oneida Lake.* Utica: North Country Books, Inc., 1989.

Hough, Franklin B. *Notices of Peter Penet and of his Operations Among the Oneida Indians.* Lowville, 1866.

Howell, George R. and W.W. Munsell. *History of the County of Schenectady, NY from 1662 to 1886.* New York, 1886.

Johnson, Crisfield. *History of Oswego County.* Philadelphia, 1877.

Jones, Pomeroy. *Annals and Recollections of Oneida County.* Rome, 1851.

Lees, John. *Journal.* Society of Colonial Wars of the State of Michigan. Detroit, 1911.

Lindley, Jacob. Journal. In *Friends' Miscellany*, edited by John and Isaac Comly. No. 2, Vol. 2.. Philadelphia, 1832.

Lincoln, Gen. Benjamin. *General Lincoln's Journal.* Collections of the Massachusetts Historical Society. Vol. V of the Third Series. Boston, 1836.

Loskiel, George Henry. *History of the Mission of the United Brethren Among the Indians in North America. 1794.* Vol. I. Translated by Christian Ignatius La Trobe. Brethren's Society for the Furtherance of the Gospel, London, England.

Memoir of an Emigrant: The Journal of Alexander Coventry, M.D….1783-1831. Vol. II. Typescript by Albany Institute of History and Art and the New York State Library, 1978.

Marsden, Joshua. *The Narrative of a Mission to Nova Scotia, New Brunswick, and the Somers Islands with a Tour to Lake Ontario.* London, 1816.

Morton, William. *Journal. 1798.* SC11451 New York State Library.

Niemcewicz, Julian Ursyn. *Diary*, translated by Metchie J.E. Budka, "Journey to Niagara, 1805, from the Diary of Julian Ursyn Niemcewicz", New York Historical Society Quarterly, Volume XLIV, Number 1. January 1960. New York.

O'Callaghan, E.B., editor. *Documentary History of New York.* 4 volumes. Albany, 1849-51.

Pearson, Jonathan. *A History of the Schenectady Patent.* Albany, 1883.

The Porteous Papers, Buffalo and Erie County Historical Society.

Porter, Augustus. *Narrative of the Early Years in the Life of Augustus Porter.* Buffalo Historical Society. Buffalo, 1848.

Rochefoucault Liancourt, Duke de la. *Travels Through the United States of North America, The Country of the Iroquois, and Upper Canada in the Years 1795, 1796, and 1797.* 4 vols. London, 1799.

The Rohde Journal, 1802. Translation by Charles Gehring in progress.

Schultz, Christian. *Travels on an Inland Voyage…*, 1810. Reprint, Ridgewood, N.J.: The Gregg Press, 1968.

Schuyler, Philip, et. al. *The Report of a Committee Appointed to Explore the Western Waters ….* Albany, 1792.

Schuyler, Philip and William Weston. *Report of the Directors of the Western and Northern Inland Lock Navigation Companies…Together with the Report of Mr. William Weston, Engineer.* New York, 1796. Reprinted in Buffalo Historical Society Publications. Vol. 2. Buffalo, 1880. P. 157-180.

Schuyler, Philip. *Journal. 1802.* The Philip Schuyler Papers, New York Public Library.

Schuyler, Philip. *Papers.* New York Public Library.

Schuyler, Philip. *Second Report of the Western Inland Lock Navigation Company - 1798.* Buffalo Historical Society Publications, Vol. 13. Buffalo, 1909. P. 195-208.

The Scriba Papers, Vol. 29, New York State Library, Albany.

Simms, Jeptha R. *The Frontiersmen of New York.* Albany, 1882.

Simms, Jeptha. *History of Schoharie County and Border Wars of New York.* Albany, 1845.

Smith, Arthur T. *Papers of the Herkimer County Historical Society.* Vol. Two. Herkimer and Ilion, 1902.

Thomas, David. *Papers.* New York State Library.

Thompson, Capt. Alexander. *Journal. 1783.* Typescript provided by Oswego County Historical Society.

Van Wagenen, Jared, Jr. *The Golden Age of Homespun.* Ithaca, 1953.

Wager, Daniel E. *Our County and Its People: A Descriptive Work on Oneida County New York.* Boston, 1896.

Watson, Elkanah. *History of the Rise, Progress, and Existing Condition of the Western Canals.* Albany, 1820.

Watson, Elkanah. *Papers.* New York State Library.

Weld, Isaac. *Travels Through the States of North America and the Provinces of Upper and Lower Canada During the Years 1795, 1796 & 1797.* 2 Vols. 3rd edition. London, 1800.

Weslager, Clinton A. *The Log Cabin in America; From Pioneer Days to the Present.* New Brunswick, New Jersey. 1969.

Williamson, Capt. Charles. *Journal.* In Frank. E. Przybycien, *Utica: A City Worth Saving.* Utica: Dodge-Graphic Press, 1976.

Woolsey, Rev. Elijah. *The Supernumerary; or, Lights and Shadows of Itinerancy.* The Christian Advocate and Journal and Zion's Herald, New York, July 1830 – December 1831.

Illustration Sources

Locations on page are indicated as R (right), L (left), T (top) and B (bottom). Arranged in order of first appearance of source.

Unless otherwise noted, all published works were obtained from the New York State Library.
Manuscripts in the New York State Library are indicated as NYSL.
Manuscripts in the New York State Archives are indicated as NYSA.

Pictures

Schultz, "Travels on an Inland Voyage..." 1810: front cover.

Diderot, "Encyclopedia.... ", 1762-77: 2

Image Collections, Metropolitan Museum of Art: 6R

Bryant, "Picturesque America...", 1872: 10, 94, 114

Grider, "Notebooks...", c.1880 (NYSL): 13, 18, 133, 144

Barber & Howe, "Historical Collections..., 1841: 14, 111, 135

Barber, "Historical Collections...", 1851: 66, 72R

Simms, "History of Schoharie County..., 1845: 14R

Drepperd, "Pioneer America...", 1949: 16, 40, 49, 50, 63, 100B

New York Historical Society, Image files: 22R, 109B

Lossing, "Pictorial Fieldbook of the American Revolution...", 1850: 22L, 31, 70, 100T

Lossing, "Our Country...", 1885: 24, 42

Courtesy Wayne E. Morrison, private collection: 26L

Hardin, "History of Herkimer County...", 1893: 26R

New York Public Library, image collections: 30

National Archives Canada, image collections: 34, 139

Fort Stanwix National Monument, image collections: 38L, 38R

Courtesy Richard Nutt, private collection: 46R

Bucks County Historical Society, n.d.: 52, 80

Turner, "Pioneer History of the Holland Purchase...", 1850: 55, 117

American Museum of Natural History, image collections: 68

Campbell, "Travels in the Interior...", 1791-2: 76, 140

Oswego County Department of Tourism, image collections: 79

National Park Service, Image collections: 93

Vermont Division of Historic Preservation, image collections: 103

New York State Office of Parks, Recreation & Historic Preservation, image collections: 104

St. Louis Mercantile Library, image collections: 106

New York State Museum, image collections: 109T, 124

Ellis, "Upper Mohawk Country...", 1982: 123

Taylor, "Missionary Tour Through the Mohawk Valley...", 1802: 125

Evans, "The Young Millwright...", 1807: 132.

Van Wagenen, "The Golden Age of Homespun", 1953: 141

Van Berkhey, "Natuurlijke Historie...", 1810: 142

Courtesy Chris Sandford, private collection: Back cover.

Maps

Chapter head maps: Upper - Kitchin, "Communication between Albany and Oswego", 1772 (NYSL). Lower - Drawn for this publication, 2000, New York State Museum

DeWitt, "Albany...", 1794 (NYSL): 5

Rivez, "Hudson River...", 1757, Huntington Library: 6L

Wright, "Survey of the Mohawk Valley...", 1803, Oneida County Historical Society: 7L, 12, 15, 23T, 23B, 27, 69, 126, 134.

Rocque, "A Plan of Schenectady...", 1762, (NYSL): 7R

Wright, "Mohawk Valley...", 1811 (Canal Museum of New York): 16

Maps in the Scriba Papers (NYSL - by cartographer or subject)
Anon., c.1795: 45, 56
Cockburn, 1792: 39
Cockburn, 1795: 107
Roosevelt, 1792: 61, 71
Rotterdam, 1797: 102
Scriba, 1795: 72L, 77, 99
Wright, 1794: 73, 94
Wright, 1795: 76, 92
Wright, 1796: 62
Wright, 1798: 67

DeWitt, "A Drawing of the Portage...", 1792 (NYSL): 25

Anon., 1757 (The British library): 32

Randel, "A Map of Rome...", 1809 (NYSL): 41

Crown Collection (NYSL): 46L, 85, 86

Schuyler, "Late Oneida Reservation...", c.1796 (NYSA): 51

Wright, "A Map of Lands Along Fish Creek...", 1809 (NYSA): 54, 57

Sauthier, "A Chorographical Map...", 1779 (NYSL): 98

Geddes, "Map of the First Pagan Purchase...", 1809 (NYSA): 108

Schuyler, "Oneida Castle...", 1798 (NYSA): 115

Kitchin, "Communication...", 1772 (NYSL): 128